IRON HEART PUBLISHING

HISTORY OF EDUCATION
BOOK ONE

SPIRIT

A JOURNEY INTO THE
EXOTERIC AND ESOTERIC
FOUNDATIONS OF EDUCATION

S. MUSA

ISBN-13: 978-1-989450-24-6

Published by IronHeart Publishing.
www.ironheartpublishing.com

بسم الله الرحمن الرحيم

الحمد لله
وصلاة والسلام على رسول الله
وعلى آله وصحابته أجمعين

In the name of Allah, the Most Merciful, the Most Gracious.
We praise and glorify Him, Most High.
We pray for peace and blessings upon His noble Messenger, and we
send salutations upon all the righteous kin and companions of His
beloved Messenger.

I dedicate this book to my parents.
To my father (حفظه الله) who named me Salih before my birth,
and to my mother (الله يرحمها) who gave me the tools to warn
against the modern-day conspirators of Thamūd. May Allah grant
my father a good end, and my mother Jannah al-Firdaus.

Ameen

The purpose of this study is purely for the pursuit of knowledge and enlightenment.
The contents of this book do not represent a universal view. No part of this book is an attempt at predicting or discerning future events or outcomes, nor is there an intent to impose views, doctrines, or ideologies.

The author acknowledges that there may be other intellectual views more accurate and authentic than his, in which case, he encourages active participation and correspondence.

Kindly approach this book and its contents with an open mind and an open heart. If a difference of opinion arises, we encourage the reader to do an impartial and objective study so as to present an alternative view by which both the reader and the author can benefit.

Contents

Part 2: Evolution of Esoteric Education

Chapter 3: The Divine Laws

PREFACE

All praise is due to Allah, Lord of the Worlds, and may peace and blessings be upon His Messenger, Muhammad ﷺ, the Seal of the Prophets. I thank Him for the life, intellect, and health to undertake this work. Every step of this journey comes from His boundless mercy and guidance. From the moment a single question ignited my curiosity, through hours of late-night manuscript revisions, this journey has unfolded as a personal pilgrimage. It has also been a demanding scholarly expedition. My research has carried me from hospital beds to dusty library shelves and into the glow of digital screens. Over several years, I have traversed continents, explored thousands of books, listened to countless lectures, and posed hundreds of questions to seekers, scholars, and sages—all in pursuit of one goal: *uncovering the truth behind hidden realities.*

My research is grounded in a foundational concept within academic literature called **Esoteric Historiography**. This framework names a problem—how orthodox scholarship long relegated streams such as Islamic spirituality, alchemy, Hermeticism, and Kabbalah to history's 'dustbin'—and offers a solution: a method for reclaiming these traditions' own voices on their own terms.

In the chapters that follow, you will see the careful path I took, spending years cross-referencing Islamic sources, medieval manuscripts, and occult theory—to ensure that every key source speaks for itself. It insists on reading complete ancient texts with both mind and heart, suspending judgment until we have truly understood their message. Equally important, it reminds us that "esoteric" is not a separate, timeless realm but a label that Western scholarship invented to mark certain ideas as being outside of "normal" thought.

Esoteric historiography guides our journey through each chapter. We trace how currents once called "hidden" were silenced, suppressed, misrepresented and mocked by mainstream dogmas—these same streams of "ancient wisdom" prevailed in occult circles following beside, and at times against, the great streams of accepted thought. Along the way, we will encounter flashes of insight—where a concept helps bridge a connection to an idea perhaps never considered, or fact that has been long-forgotten. These are intentional moments designed to draw you, dear reader, deeper into the unfolding mystery of the past. As we trace how traditions were received and reshaped through the lenses of Enlightenment and modern critique, a richer story shall emerge—one where the 'esoteric' is not a fringe oddity, but is an essential thread in the fabric of intellectual history.

I have had a traditional career in education—teaching and leading in secondary schools and at the university level. Although born Muslim, I began consciously practicing Islam at 19. Since then, I have devoted my spare time to learning in mosque circles, overseas Arabic institutes, and online lectures. In my earlier years, I had explored conspiracy theories as a hobby, but only after three key events aligned did I turn my focus to esoteric and occult knowledge.

First Spark: Teaching Invitation (2013).

When Dr. Bilal Philips's Islamic Online University invited me to lecture on "The History of Education: An Islamic Perspective," I immersed myself in hundreds of hours of reading, distilled them into coherent scripts, and recorded thirty hours of lectures. That immersive process deepened my understanding of how cultures, governments, and philanthropists shape learning across civilizations—profoundly more illuminating than any academic course I had taken.

Second Spark: A Provocative Question.

While reviewing my course slides, a coworker paused at a slide describing Idris (إدريس ﷺ) as a "little-known Prophet" and asked, "How can you say that?" His surprise both embarrassed and intrigued me. Within days, I plunged into tafsirs, medieval manuscripts, and Hermetic writings— what began as a single slide note blossomed into a lifelong exploration of hidden teachings that have quietly influenced philosophy, science, and spirituality across the ages.

Third Spark: Cosmic Insights and Personal Trial.

During a car ride, a friend pointed out Quranic verses on cosmic order that mirror modern physics—and suggested chemical imbalances may reflect jinn activity. Those ideas lingered until five years later, when a severe flu vaccine reaction hospitalized me with blood clots in my lungs and a six-day, medically induced coma. My family suspected *sihr* (magic) or *ayn* (evil eye), while physicians diagnosed an illness of unknown origin. Emerging from that ordeal, I felt a renewed sense of purpose: *To weave Islamic sources, scientific insights, and esoteric teachings into a cohesive narrative—this very work.*

I share these experiences not just as personal narrative but to show how genuine insight grows through conversation— between teacher and student, text and lived experience, tradition and innovation. My aim is to blend rigorous scholarship with engaging narrative, so you not only grasp reality's structures but feel the awe that draws us toward its Source. This journey guides you chronologically through Allah's unfolding of history, offering an approach that is both accessible and inspiring.

My sincere hope is that, upon completing each of the three structured books, you will be spiritually and intellectually inspired, as well as equipped to see broadly, think critically, and question passionately.

These three sparks set the stage for my six-year investigation, unfolding through three distinct phases:

- **Theory:** Deep study of occult and medieval writings revealed patterns beyond ordinary perception and sparked intense internal debates as I strove to reconcile these insights with the Quranic and Prophetic guidance. I asked Allah for protection and guidance along the way, continually begging Him to keep my intentions pure.

- **Criticism:** Simply consulting these texts invited concern from peers and family. To protect myself, I confined my study strictly to theory—avoiding practical rites for fear they might take root in my heart—and continually renewed my intention that this knowledge serve only as a safeguard against its misuse.

- **Synchronicity:** A series of strange synchronicities and "hermeneutical" experiences began to unfold around me—coincidences so precise they felt like proof that the unseen truly moves among us. These trials cemented my conviction that awareness is our first line of defense. Only after we recognize the problem, and its remedy, can we then internalize the conviction to act individually and collectively towards meaningful change.

Now, grounded in traditional Islamic scholarship and enriched by disciplined esoteric study, I warmly invite you to become part of a community of learners empowered to guard themselves and their societies against unseen challenges. Consider this Preface your open invitation to step into that circle.

Roadmap for Book I: Spirit

Part 1: Foundations of Exoteric Education
Chapters 1–2

Chapter 1 – The Divine Quadrivium
1. Section 1: Metaphysics
   Confronts the questions "Where did we come from?
   Why are we here? Where are we going?" and shows why
   only divine revelation can fully answer them.

2. Section 2: Physics
   Unpacks the four forces of nature and the angels who
   sustain them.

3. Section 3: Chemistry
   Traces alchemy's evolution into chemistry, exploring
   how jinn interact through vibrational frequencies that
   shape thought and action.

4. Section 4: Biology
   Surveys life's stages, from single-celled organisms to
   human intellect, under Divine decree.

Chapter 2 – The Divine Trivium
1. Section 1: Knowledge (*'Ilm*)
   Charts reality through facts and data, illustrating how
   pride corrupts pure reasoning.

2. Section 2: Understanding (*Fahm*)
   Synthesizes information into coherent patterns, guiding
   the soul toward truth.

3. Section 3: Wisdom (*Hikmah*)
   Integrates insight into action, showing how righteous
   living grows from lessons learned.

Part 2: Evolution of Esoteric Education
Chapter 3, Sections 0—4

1. Section 0: The Father of Esoteric Wisdom
   Introduces Idris/Enoch/Thoth/Hermes as the hidden
   teacher uniting revelation, philosophy, and alchemy.

2. Section 1: Mentalism
   "The All is Mind; the Universe is Mental."

3. Section 2: Correspondence
   "As above, so below."

4. Section 3: Vibration
   "Nothing rests; everything vibrates."

5. Section 4: Polarity
   "Everything is dual."

With this 12 Section roadmap, let us embark on our
exploration, beginning with the **Introduction to Book I:**

Spirit.

INTRODUCTION

THE JOURNEY OF KNOWLEDGE

بِسْمِ اللهِ الرَّحْمٰنِ الرَّحِيْمِ

Allah is the Supreme Educator of sapient beings on all levels of reality and has taught humanity divine wisdom in each generation. Out of all living beings—plants, insects, animals, and spirits—humans alone possess the unique ability to seek, retain, and apply knowledge to shape their world. Unlike creatures who are driven by instinct, we have been entrusted with an elevated consciousness—a divine spark that grants us the drive to pursue higher aspirations beyond mere survival. We have been honored with the title and sacred duty as *khulafa* (vicegerents), chosen caretakers and guardians on earth. This trust requires us to reflect on the preserved past, plan for our collective future, and act with wisdom and justice for all in the present.

Education, in this sense, is far more than a pursuit for material enrichment; it is a form of spiritual alchemy that transmutes the soul to a level wherein it exists in a state of harmony with the natural order of the world. This process of learning to fulfill this goal becomes a type of initiation into the blessed path of the Prophets and Messengers, who were sent as educators to awaken their people from spiritual slumber, cultivate wisdom, and channel the divine currents of blessings and rewards for all existence. When guided by divine revelation, education becomes the key to unlocking inner realms, illuminating darkened paths, and empowering humanity to fulfill its true purpose—to align with the Divine Will and prepare for the life to come.

Education, from the Latin educere meaning "to lead out," is the process of moving from ignorance to understanding. It involves gaining knowledge, skills, values, beliefs, and habits—drawing out what is already within the human soul.

In Islam, education (ta'lim) is inseparable from nurturing (tarbiyyah), encompassing intellectual, moral, and spiritual development under Divine Guidance; the term tarbiyyah is closely associated with ar-Rabb (the Lord, Sustainer, and Cherisher), and emphasizes that true upbringing comes ultimately from Allah, whether through a teacher, a text, or lived experience.

This divine framework of education continues to hold relevance in the modern era. In the modern information-Age, education is solely responsible for empowering individuals to assume greater responsibilities and ascend as leaders, not only within the human race but also over animals, insects, and plants. In contrast, the absence of education can reduce individuals to a state of perpetual servitude, limiting them to efforts that fulfill the goals and visions of others. Globally, having limited education typically invites assumptions of ignorance or diminished societal value. Thus, education is seen, not only in the Islamic perspective, but in simple human rationale, as the most powerful tool for improving life conditions and fulfilling humanity's sacred trust as khulafa.

This book grew out of a course I delivered in 2013 at the Islamic Online University, called *The History of Education: An Islamic Perspective*. In that course, we explored the full arc of human history—from our origins to the prophesied end—

through the lens of how education has shaped, and been shaped by, societies across the world. I drew on the Quran, the Sunnah of the Prophet Muhammad ﷺ, and a synthesis of both well-known and lesser-known historical sources to build the course's foundation. Finding resources that abridged both Islamic and secular views on education proved challenging. Most books seemed only to adhere to one camp or the other, leaving a gap I felt needed addressing. That gap led me to start asking some deeper questions:

- How does seeing the world through an Islamic lens change the way we understand history and education?

- In what ways have those in power—both sincere and self-serving—used education as a tool, either to uplift or to control?

- And what lessons from the past—whether through knowledge, methods, or lived experiences—can help us grow in understanding and expand present awareness?

Through this book, we aim to uncover:

- Insights from both Islamic and secular traditions that can enrich how we approach education today,

- The recurring patterns in educational history that continue to influence our present and future,

- And the powerful role that Quranic teachings have played in shaping educational thought and practices.

What we aim to present here is an unapologetically Islamic perspective—one that does not shy away from challenging Eurocentric historical interpretations. We blend symbolic allegory and the correspondence method to integrate Islamic

19

metaphysics with established scientific theories. Rather than reading symbols and texts strictly at face value, we explore them metaphorically, seeking deeper spiritual truths and drawing parallels between natural phenomena and the unseen reality.

- **Allegorical correspondence** is our top-down approach. We begin with divine or cosmic principles and map their outward "signs" (*ẓahir*) onto inner realities (*baṭin*). For example, can the rhythm of the stars mirror stages in the soul's journey? And if so, how? And why?

- **Symbolic allusion** is our bottom-up method. We start with culturally resonant motifs—like the Garden of Eden, Noah's Ark, or geometric patterns—and use them as stepping stones, building toward drawing richer theological and philosophical insights.

At its core lies the belief that the macrocosm (the vast universe) and the microcosm (our individual selves) are profoundly linked. By exploring these layers of meaning, We invite you on a journey to deepen your understanding of the world and your place within it. This holistic approach honors both the spiritual and material dimensions of creation and invites us to attune ourselves to life's deeper mysteries. While not every faith-based interpretation will align with modern science, our goal is to find a synthesis, not to force alignment and agreement.

Having read other macro-level historical works, I noticed something troubling: many authors subtly insert their own biases—often dismissive or reductionist—into the narrative. Take, for example, *Sapiens: A Brief History of Humankind* by Yuval Harari, which offers an insightful overview of the broad history of humanity. However, Harari views the world through an evolutionary biological framework. His core argument is that humans began as insignificant animals, eventually evolving into beings who, through science and technology, will ultimately enable him to conquer death and live forever.

Not only is the argument baseless and foolish, but he goes further to suggest that belief in Allah or creation is simply a collective myth–something that only holds power because people arbitrarily agree to believe in it, and that such a thing will disappear once that belief fades. Likewise, in his follow-up book, *Homo Deus: A Brief History of Tomorrow*, Harari argues that religion has been on the losing side of a long battle with science—and that this trend will only continue until that loss is definitive. He states that religious scholars are obsolete, no longer able to use their scriptures to address the economic or technological realities of our time. According to Harari, religion offers meaning and order, but science offers power—and in our age, he believes we are evolving inevitably towards power, justifiable even at the cost of losing an arbitrary sense of purpose.

Another example is the *Big History Project,* an ambitious project with public access developed by Bill Gates and Professor David Christian, which explores the history of the universe from its origins to the present day. It integrates various disciplines, such as cosmology, astronomy, geology, biology, and human history, into a unified narrative. It maps out eight major "thresholds" of growing complexity, from the formation of matter to the rise of modern civilizations. Throughout, the course emphasizes purely scientific explanations and human agency—focusing solely on what we, as humans, can observe, measure, and control.

At the heart of this worldview is Humanism—an outlook that celebrates human progress and ethics, but does so without religion and with a firm denial of anything beyond what we can sensorially perceive. It suggests that our future is entirely in our hands—that we do not *need* divine guidance or a savior beyond ourselves.

Islam outright rejects the notion of absolute human agency. To deny the Unseen is to deny reality itself. At the core of our faith is *Tawhid*—the Divine Unity of Allah. We see life as a journey, not a conquest. We see death as a destination, not an adversary. This, for us, is a struggle to refine our character, purify our souls, and live by the guidance Allah has given us,

21

and His assurance of contentment in this life and the next. Where Humanism focuses on material progress and self-determination, Islam offers something more—an integrated view of both the seen and unseen, the material and the spiritual. It gives us a fuller picture of who we are and why we are here.

Humanism venerates humanity rather than the Creator, asserting that modern science will ultimately endow mankind with god-like powers. The crude logic here being that 'there is no need for God if man can become god-like by his own ability.' This worldview regards this supposed 'advancement' as the next step in humanity's evolutionary struggle to attain eternal happiness on earth. Those who subscribe to this worldview in all its varied aspects believe that religious concepts such as Divine Revelation and the afterlife are obstacles to progress—antiquated hindrances, or barriers, rather than pathways to higher truths.

Over the past five centuries, humanism has proliferated globally, propelled by European colonial expansion and the Industrial Revolution. These forces have all but obliterated traditional wisdom and cultural practices. They not only transformed economies and technologies; they systematically dismantled human-defining epistemologies and cultural frameworks, supplanting them with European social institutions and a secularized, pagan-tinged version of Christianity. This led to the fragmentation of numerous learning methods and pedagogies, as well as the marginalization of non-Western ways of knowing. Indigenous wisdom and cultural practices rooted in metaphysical dimensions such as dreams, visions, and prophecies were viewed as irrational archaic concepts that do not represent reality. The scientific method aimed to become the only dominant and 'approved' framework for validating knowledge, yet further delineated into being purely empirical, materialist, and reductionist in its assumptions.

While not negating the validity of the scientific method, we must acknowledge that science itself, for all its power and precision, does not encompass the totality of reality.

Science is not without flaws. It focuses on the observable, measurable, physical world, but cannot reach into the inner realm of consciousness—a domain not only real but universally experienced.

Consciousness is the luminous core of sentience and personhood. It is that inner dimension through which one can reflect, reason, and contemplate. It is that unspoken witness within, connecting each individual to a transcendent order beyond sensory perception.

The human desire to understand ourselves is inseparable from the deeper yearning to know our Creator. In Islam, these yearnings aren't separate or abstract; they lie at the very heart of our faith. To fulfill this purposeful connection, Allah has sent prophets and educators—individuals of elevated consciousness—to guide humanity toward spiritual enlightenment through the purification of the heart and engagement in religiously sanctioned spiritual practices. Thus, Islamic education is not merely about information; it is about transformation. It encompasses both the esoteric and the exoteric, the inward and the outward, the spiritual and the material, the heavenly and the earthly, aligning the intellect with the heart, and the heart with its Creator.

This book aims to articulate an Islamic interpretation of "Big History," a unified narrative of existence that encompasses cosmology, biology, philosophy, and spirituality. It is intended for both Muslims and non-Muslims who seek a deeper understanding of the *Maraatib al-Uluum* (interconnectedness of knowledge) as seen through an Islamic lens. For Muslims, it provides a conceptual framework to reclaim a spiritually grounded and holistic model of education rooted in Tawhid. For non-Muslims, it invites engagement with a different civilizational perspective—one that sees no contradiction between faith and reason, science and revelation, progress and transcendence.

By bridging Islamic and secular paradigms, we invite you to consider education as a transformative tool shaped by divine wisdom. The philosophical and spiritual insights embedded in the Islamic tradition offer a vision of learning that is both universally relevant and firmly grounded in heritage, capable of cultivating mutual respect across cultural and intellectual boundaries.

Traditional accounts of educational history often oscillate between narratives of liberation and domination, charting the rise and fall of institutions, empires, and ideologies. We aim to synthesize those paradigms to show a more comprehensive pattern of education throughout history and what to anticipate in the future, according to prophecy. To the best of my knowledge, no previous work has attempted this synthesis from a distinctly Islamic metaphysical perspective.

Lastly, the reader is presumed to have some cursory knowledge of Islam and its teachings. Throughout this work, I will revisit well-known Quranic narratives, interpreting them through educational and philosophical lenses in order to uncover timeless patterns relevant to the human pursuit of knowledge and meaning.

Our journey will span from the origins of human history to its prophesied conclusion. Along the way, we shall weave together threads from the physical, philosophical, and social sciences, illuminating the essential unity of all true knowledge. My purpose is to demonstrate that fragmentation of knowledge—so often treated as a sign of intellectual progress—is, in fact, deception. We assert that all knowledge, at its highest level, is spiritual. When disconnected from its metaphysical roots, knowledge risks becoming a mechanism of confusion rather than clarity.

My sincere hope is that this book will empower and inspire young Muslim students to engage deeply with the Quran—not merely as a sacred text, but as a living guide filled with inexhaustible insight.

As Allah says in the Quran,

﴾ سَنُرِيهِمْ ءَايَـٰتِنَا فِى ٱلْءَافَاقِ وَفِىٓ أَنفُسِهِمْ حَتَّىٰ يَتَبَيَّنَ لَهُمْ أَنَّهُ ٱلْحَقُّ ۗ أَوَلَمْ يَكْفِ بِرَبِّكَ أَنَّهُۥ عَلَىٰ كُلِّ شَىْءٍ شَهِيدٌ ﴿

24

"We will show them Our signs in the horizons and within themselves until it becomes clear to them that this ˹Quran˺ is the truth. Is it not enough that your Lord is a Witness over all things?" (41:53).

I offer this work in humility. Inevitably, what errors and deficiencies it contains, are mine alone. Any wisdom it offers belongs solely to Allah, the source of all truth. I am but a vessel, entrusted for a moment with the sacred task of seeking and sharing insight. I pray that this effort brings benefit and causes no harm. May it be accepted as a sincere offering on the scale of good.

PART 1:

FOUNDATIONS OF
EXOTERIC EDUCATION

CHAPTER 1
THE DIVINE QUADRIVIUM

SECTION 1
METAPHYSICS

﴿ اللَّهُ خَالِقُ كُلِّ شَيْءٍ ۖ وَهُوَ عَلَىٰ كُلِّ شَيْءٍ وَكِيلٌ ﴾

"Allah is the Creator of all things, and He is the Maintainer of everything"
(39:62).

"The day science begins to study non-physical phenomena, it will make more progress in one decade than in all the previous centuries of its existence."
~ Nikola Tesla

Before the beginning of time, there was Allah, the Creator and Sustainer, who existed beyond the limits of space and matter. In Islam, Allah is the ultimate source of all things, governing the vast cosmic order with divine wisdom. Understanding and applying this knowledge yields the greatest return on the investment of one's time in life. This is the supreme knowledge, most worthy of intense study.

The order of all things is perfect, even during moments of intense chaos. Everything has been, is being, and will be arranged according to Allah's wisdom. Some of this wisdom is found in the divine books that were revealed to Prophets and Messengers in the past, while some remains hidden, awaiting discovery through study and contemplation. Yet, certain truths will always remain beyond human comprehension due to the inherent limitations of our faculties.

Allah, the One eternal consciousness, is the creator of time, space, mass, and energy. His nature cannot be described in words or symbols. All of existence originates from Him and ultimately returns to Him. Before creation, only Allah existed—eternal, without beginning or end, complete in His essence and free of all need. Out of His divine will and wisdom, He brought creation into existence—not from solitude or desire, but as a manifestation of His power, knowledge, and mercy. Creation did not add to Him, nor was it born of necessity, but it revealed His names and attributes through the unfolding of the cosmos. From the unseen command, "Be," came all things, fashioned with precision and purpose. Thus, Allah is the source of all that exists—every idea, entity, and action flows from His will.

Allah's sovereignty spans from the grand design of the universe to the minutest sparks of life. Even microbes that cannot be seen without instrumentation—such as bacteria, viruses, and archaea—are ever-present and thrive only by His will and mercy. Their continuous cycles of growth and decay in the Arctic ice, the ocean's depths, and every living body remind us that not a speck of creation lies beyond Al-Qayyum (the Sustainer's) plan.

For those who deny the unseen, the notion of an eternal Creator might seem illogical. However, human understanding is constrained by sensory perception and empirical tools. Science, while powerful, remains bound to the material world, analyzing observable phenomena and categorizing the universe into measurable forces and processes. It cannot probe beyond these confines.

Metaphysics, on the other hand, extends beyond material reality, addressing fundamental questions about existence, purpose, and the divine. From an Islamic perspective, believing in Allah as the ultimate reality is not merely logical, it is the only conclusion that truly explains the nature of existence. He is the uncaused cause, requiring no form, sleep, or family to exist. As the Quran affirms:

$$\text{﴿ لَيْسَ كَمِثْلِهِ شَيْءٌ ﴾}$$

"There is nothing like Him." (42:11)

Even with revelation, human understanding of Allah's essence remains limited. It is known that He is veiled by light (Ibn Majah) and that from Him, all forms of matter emerged. Yet, matter itself is merely a structured form of energy, appearing solid to our senses but existing in constant motion. At its core, everything is energy, a concept that modern physics is only beginning to comprehend

Metaphysics is the highest branch of knowledge, for it seeks to explain the fundamental nature of being—beginning with the question **'what is?'** and ultimately leads one to an understanding of Divinity. Metaphysics is the 'invisible' science, which studies what is above the 'visible' natural sciences. To truly understand what is visible below, we must understand what is invisible above. Metaphysics explores the unseen realities that transcend the physical world. The esoteric realm refers to inward, spiritual truths that guide personal reflection and divine connection, while the exoteric realm encompasses outward, observable phenomena in the material world. Together, these realms form a holistic understanding of reality.

Metaphysics is more of a philosophy than a science. Unlike empirical sciences, metaphysics does not rely on direct observation and experimentation. It is developed based on a series of questions that lie beyond material analysis. Questions such as:

- **Existence and Reality:** What is real, and how do we define existence?

- **Empirical and Conceptual Objects:** Are objects we perceive with our senses different from those that exist conceptually?

- **Cosmology and Cosmogony:** Was the universe designed and what is its purpose, or is it the product of chance?

- **Free Will and Determinism:** Do humans have free will, or are we subjected to determinism?

- **Identity and Change:** What is the nature of identity and change?

- **Mind and Matter:** Is the mind separate from the body, or is there a third element?

- **Necessity and Possibility:** Is everything that happens necessary, or are there infinite possibilities?

- **Religion and Spirituality:** Does Allah exist, and what is His role in relation to us?

- **Space and Time:** How do we understand the physicality of the universe?

For Muslims, the Quran provides certainty where philosophy struggles. According to the Quran, Allah is One, and He is the Creator of all things (2:163; 6:102). We belong to Allah, and we are returning to Him (2:156). The Quran heals dead hearts and guides believers (10:57). Allah sent Messengers as proof of His existence and to clarify our purpose (4:165). This world is a test, and true life exists in the Hereafter, where people will be rewarded or punished based on their actions (11:7; 29:64; 101:6-9). The ultimate goal is to worship and serve Allah (51:56).

Many metaphysical philosophers attempt to remove a

creator from the equation, but in doing so, they fail to provide definitive answers. The same metaphysical questions asked thousands of years ago remain unresolved today. However, for Muslims, Allah is the ultimate reality and the solution to metaphysical conundrums. He is the One who consciously created the physical world.

The unseen metaphysical world is the true foundation of existence, giving rise to the physical world. It is **esoteric**, understood by only a select few, yet it sustains all **exoteric**, or outward reality. The universe operates on **electromagnetic** principles divided by two essential forces:

- **Magnetic** (spiritual, unseen) energy, corresponding to the **metaphysical realm**.

- **Electrical** (physical, visible) energy, governing the **material world**.

These two forces form a unified field wherein all things transition between these states. The tangible, electrical manifestations of the physical world emerge from the intangible, magnetic essence of the unseen. This interplay reflects the dynamic nature of existence: just as energy moves between states in the physical world, so too does consciousness, shifting between material experience and higher, transcendent realities.

The metaphysical realm parallels the physical in form but without its limitations. In the material world, existence is bound by time, space, and bodily needs, while in the unseen realm, it is unconditioned and limitless. Human existence follows a journey of transition, from life in the material world to the eventual return to the eternal metaphysical plane. This journey shows that the physical world is not an isolated reality but is rather a temporary phase of a larger, cyclical process of return and realization.

Science, too, attempts to explain the origins of the universe. Modern cosmology suggests that approximately **13.8 billion years ago, energy, matter, space**, and **time** came into existence in an instant. This moment marks the first Quadrivium in material existence. The term Quadrivium, meaning "where four roads meet," symbolizes the foundation of creation:

- **Energy** – The force driving all things.

- **Matter** – The manifestation of energy.

- **Space** – The stage where physical existence unfolds.

- **Time** – The measure of change.

Even today, the true nature of **energy** is unknown. What we do know is that matter is simply condensed energy. Einstein's famous equation, $E = mc^2$ (energy is equal to mass times the speed of light squared), confirms this—showing the deep connection between spiritual energy and physical matter. **Matter** contains energy, and energy drives matter to move and change states. For example, energy can transform an ice cube into water and, with more energy, turn that water into steam. Matter is anything that has mass and occupies space, including air, water, rocks, and people. It can be classified into four states: **solids, liquids, gases,** and **plasma**, which form another type of quadrivium.[1]

Quantum physics challenges this traditional view, suggesting that matter does not truly exist in a fixed form. Instead, all matter is composed of rapidly vibrating energetic particles, such as electrons, which combine to form molecules and, eventually, larger masses. Simply put, at its core, all matter is energy.

Space also contains a quadrivium, consisting of four fundamental dimensions which form the basis of our universe: three dimensions of space (**length, width, height**) and one of

---

1 Note: Plasma is ionized gas that has so much energy that some of the electrons are close to breaking free from their nucleus. When gas is pumped with energy, it can become plasma. Plasma is the most abundant substance in our universe. Human blood consists of approximately 55% plasma. In the universe, over 99% of matter is plasma. The sun is the greatest source of plasma for our earth. The sun provides energy to all the diverse forms of life on earth.

time. As humans subjected to these universal dimensions, we are all appointed a **specific length of years lived**; some people have a **wider impact on people** than others, few can **reach heights that enable them to be leaders over others**, and one or two individuals are captivating enough to **embody the era in which they lived**. All humans exist within the same three-dimensional framework of space and time. The difference is based on how we use our time.

Our perception of space and time changes depending on whether we view the world in exoteric or esoteric terms. In **space-time**, the physical world in which we live, space dominates, and time moves linearly. This is the dimension where energy coalesces into matter, and everything is bound by Newtonian physics.

We experience time as a sequence—past, present, and future. However, esoterically, there is another dimension known as **time-space**, where time dominates, and space is flexible. In this dimension, we move beyond linear time, interacting with the quantum field, the realm of possibilities where past, present, and future exist simultaneously. In time-space, everything is energy, and intentions, thoughts, and emotions influence matter and outcomes.

We experience the time-space realm after deep meditation, in the dream state, and after our souls leave our bodies, thereafter we enter the hidden spiritual dimension. The idea of Time being the dominant force is hence understood as the "4th-Dimension" in physics, which serves as the basis for explaining the relativity between space and matter. While this dimension cannot be physically perceived, it can be somewhat illustrated, and is often understood as an "inner-dimension".

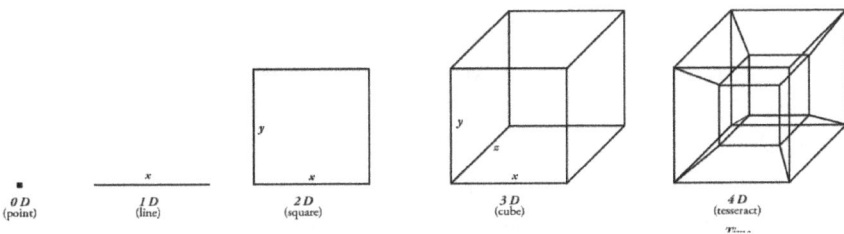

0 D
(point)

1 D
(line)

2 D
(square)

3 D
(cube)

4 D
(tesseract)

Fig. 1 - Three Spatial Dimensions and one Higher Dimension of Time

Without "time," all things would happen at once. According to the space-time realm, time measures the changing positions of objects in space. In the beginning, there were no objects in space. The most dominant argument is that we created the concept of time and made it measurable and linear. For example, a Solar year is a measure of the time it takes for the Earth to travel once around the Sun (according to modern theories). A Lunar year is a measure of the time it takes for 12 new moon phases to complete its cycle.

Examining the 'Big History' patterns of our world using the framework that argues that Allah is the metaphysical creator of the physical world requires *"**Moon-consciousness.**"* It is an Islamic paradigm based on the text of the Quran as explained through the teachings and life of Prophet Muhammad ﷺ.

"Moon-consciousness" requires an intentional shift away from the dominant secular paradigm of *"**Sun-consciousness,**"* which rejects *Shariah* (the religious laws Allah legislated). *Sun-consciousness* is based on the Gregorian calendar, which is adopted globally and has marginalized Islamic cultural and religious practices. It is the product of Western dominance and colonialism, which was imposed on non-Western societies, thereby disrupting traditional ways of timekeeping.

The moon's waxing and waning have long symbolized natural rhythms of birth, growth, decay, and renewal, symbolizing the interconnectedness of creation. This interconnectedness is mirrored in the human body, where different cells regenerate in approximately 7-year cycles.

The Ancient Sumerians organized their calendars around the moon's phases, dividing months into approximately four 7-day periods corresponding to the **new moon**, **first quarter**, **full moon**, and **last quarter**. In Babylonia, the seventh day was sacred to Sin, the moon god (deity), and was observed as a time for reflection and rest. These practices were later revived by the Jews on their Sabbath and are used in modern history's Saturday.

While ancient cultures recognized the moon's significance, Islam provides the ultimate divine framework that aligns these celestial rhythms with spiritual practices and human purpose.

Recognizing the divine harmony in celestial rhythms helps Muslims reconnect with their spiritual roots and understand their role in creation's cyclical patterns.

These celestial patterns not only regulate time but also serve as metaphors for humanity's spiritual journey from darkness to enlightenment. Those with Moon-consciousness understand that night precedes the day and that Allah is the creator of light. Symbolically, this reflects the human condition regarding education, as Allah, the ultimate source of light, elevates humanity from darkness to enlightenment, conveying significant educational patterns throughout the Quran. In essence, Moon-consciousness reorients our understanding of time and history, aligning it with divine rhythms and fostering a deeper connection to our spiritual heritage.

Those who adopt moon-consciousness as their paradigm believe that Allah is the Metaphysical Origin from which all realities spring and to which all return. For them, the visible world is only a faint reflection of a deeper order—structured by divine wisdom and sustained by His will. Celestial cycles, space-time currents, energy fields, and biological rhythms are not random events; they are ayat (signs) that lead back to their Source. This recognition lies at the heart of metaphysics and forms the root of all knowledge, guiding the seeker to contemplate the Grand Designer who fashions every outward form with an inward purpose.

Fig. 2 - The Light of the Lamp

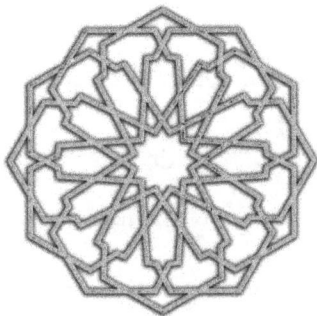

SECTION 2

PHYSICS

﴾ ... لَّا يَعْصُونَ ٱللَّهَ مَآ أَمَرَهُمْ وَيَفْعَلُونَ مَا يُؤْمَرُونَ ... ﴿

"...[they, i.e., angels] never disobey whatever Allah orders-always doing as commanded" (66:6).

"the laws of physics... are algorithms for the handling of information..." ~ Rolf Landauer

In Islamic cosmology, the term *samawat* (heavens) embraces all creation—every star we see and every hidden realm beyond our senses. The observable universe is only the first of 7 heavens, each existing beyond human comprehension and technological reach.[2] Our solar system resides within the lowest of these 7 heavens, where the earthly world is primarily known and visible, while the higher heavens are unseen and beyond human perception. Allah describes His absolute dominion over all that exists in the heavens and the earth.

---

2   Quran 2:29; 17:44; 23:86; 41:12; 65:12; 67:3; 71:15; 78:12

﴾ اللَّهُ لاَ إِلَهَ إِلاَّ هُوَ الْحَيُّ الْقَيُّومُ

لاَ تَأْخُذُهُ سِنَةٌ وَلاَ نَوْمٌ لَهُ مَا فِي السَّمَاوَاتِ وَمَا فِي الأَرْضِ

مَنْ ذَا الَّذِي يَشْفَعُ عِنْدَهُ إِلاَّ بِإِذْنِهِ يَعْلَمُ مَا بَيْنَ أَيْدِيهِمْ وَمَا

خَلْفَهُمْ وَلاَ يُحِيطُونَ بِشَيْءٍ مِنْ عِلْمِهِ إِلاَّ بِمَا شَاءَ وَسِعَ كُرْسِيُّهُ

السَّمَاوَاتِ وَالأَرْضَ

وَلاَ يَئُودُهُ حِفْظُهُمَا وَهُوَ الْعَلِيُّ الْعَظِيمُ ﴿

"Allah! There is no God [worthy of worship] except Him, the Ever-Living, All-Sustaining.
Neither drowsiness nor sleep overtakes Him. To Him belongs whatever is in the heavens and whatever is on the earth.
Who could possibly intercede with Him without His permission? He [fully] knows what is ahead of them and what is behind them, but no one can grasp any of His knowledge—except what He wills [to reveal]. His Seat encompasses the heavens and the earth, and the preservation of both does not tire Him. For He is the Most High, the Greatest."
(2:255, Ayat al-Kursi)

Authority over all creation belongs solely to Allah. No person, place, or thing within the heavens or the earth has the rightful authority to claim dominion of all except for Allah. Many have claimed this divine authority in the past, only to be proven false after history bore witness to their deaths, as the immutable laws governing existence cannot be upheld by one who no longer exists. The result of those who reject the truth contained in the signs of the verses and the universe is absolute loss.

As Allah says:

﴿ ٱللَّهُ خَٰلِقُ كُلِّ شَىْءٍ وَهُوَ عَلَىٰ كُلِّ شَىْءٍ وَكِيلٌ ﴾

﴿ لَّهُۥ مَقَالِيدُ ٱلسَّمَٰوَٰتِ وَٱلْأَرْضِ وَٱلَّذِينَ كَفَرُواْ بِـَٔايَٰتِ ٱللَّهِ أُوْلَٰٓئِكَ
هُمُ ٱلْخَٰسِرُونَ ﴾

*Allah is the Creator of all things, and He is the Maintainer
of everything.
To Him belong the keys of the heavens and the earth. Those
who disbelieve in the signs of Allah—it is they who will be
the losers. (39:62-63)*

The creation of the universe has been described in several
places within the Quran.[3] One verse explicitly describes how
the universe and the earth were once connected in the form
of nonexistence but were consciously pulled apart in all
directions, forming unique aspects of existence. Then, the verse
explains that all forms of life (humans, animals, insects, plants,
and microbes) come about from water.

﴿ أَوَلَمْ يَرَ ٱلَّذِينَ كَفَرُوٓاْ أَنَّ ٱلسَّمَٰوَٰتِ وَٱلْأَرْضَ كَانَتَا رَتْقًا فَفَتَقْنَٰهُمَا
وَجَعَلْنَا مِنَ ٱلْمَآءِ كُلَّ شَىْءٍ حَىٍّ أَفَلَا يُؤْمِنُونَ ﴾

*Do the disbelievers not see that the heavens and the earth
were [once] a single entity, then We ripped them apart?
And We created from water every living thing. Will they
not then believe? (21:30)* [4]

The Quran describes the initial separation of the heavens
and the earth as beginning with Allah's commandment of *Kun*
(Be!), which initiated the creation process and set the divine
order into motion.

---

3   7:54; 10:3; 11:7; 25:59; 32:4; 50:38; 57:4 while in other places it
says earth and the heaven 21:30; 2:29; 20:4

4   Note: *Ar-Ratq* means together in nonexistence and *Al-Fataqa* apart
in existence.

$$\text{﴾ بَدِيعُ ٱلسَّمَٰوَٰتِ وَٱلْأَرْضِ}$$

$$\text{وَإِذَا قَضَىٰٓ أَمْرًا فَإِنَّمَا يَقُولُ لَهُۥ كُن فَيَكُونُ ﴿}$$

Originator of the heavens and the earth. When He decrees a matter, He only says to it, "Be," and it is. (2:117)

$$\text{﴾ إِنَّمَآ أَمْرُهُۥٓ إِذَآ أَرَادَ شَيْئًا أَن يَقُولَ لَهُۥ كُن فَيَكُونُ ﴿}$$

His command is only, when He intends a thing, that He says to it, "Be," and it is. (36:82)[5]

This decree not only brought the physical universe into existence but also introduced the concept of time, as movement and change became measurable realities.

This command brought with it both unseen and seen laws that encompass one great universal law: one that is everlasting. All chaos materialized, and everything solid was established according to a grand pattern that encompasses all things. The harmonious rhythm of created things follows the pattern of a beginning, a middle, and an end. As creation came into being by Allah's will and command, Allah remained distinct and separate from His creation. Yet, His creation is filled with signs that point to His existence, wisdom, and power without resembling or containing Him in any way.

Heavenly and terrestrial bodies came into existence at different stages. This process of transforming the universe was conceived and created effortlessly, without preparation, practice, or struggle. This simple word and its results demonstrate Allah's Knowledge, Will, and Power. The cosmos unfolds and expands by precise, unchanging principles—what modern science calls physics. In Islamic perspective, these "algorithms" of existence are the living expressions of divine intent.

Physicists seek a grand unified theory (GUT) that would unify three of the four fundamental forces of nature—

5   Also from the Quran 6:73; 16:40; 36:82; 40:68

electromagnetism, the strong nuclear force, and the weak nuclear force—into a single framework. Gravity, while also a fundamental force, remains outside the scope of current GUT models.

- **Electromagnetism**: Governs the interactions between charged particles, enabling electricity, magnetism, and light propagation.

- **Strong nuclear force**: Binds protons and neutrons together in atomic nuclei, fueling nuclear fusion in stars and sustaining life by providing energy.

- **Weak force**: Responsible for radioactive decay, allowing elements to transform, playing a crucial role in stellar evolution.

- **Gravity**: The weakest of the four, yet it governs planetary motion, cosmic structure, and the balance of celestial bodies.

These forces manifested instantly upon the universe's creation. Even a slight imbalance in their proportions would prevent the existence of life. The sun, moon, and Earth are precisely positioned, with an ideal chemical makeup, ensuring an environment fit for human existence, which is a testament to divine precision.

[see Figure 3 on the next page]

Strong Force
binding the nucleus

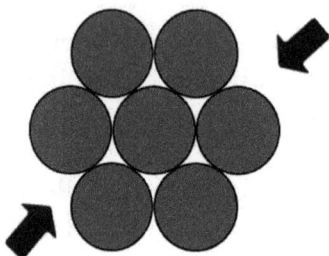

Electromagnetic Force
binding the atom

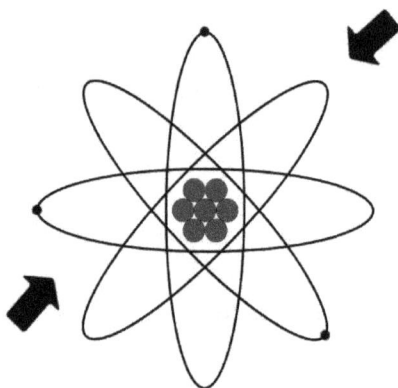

Weak Force
in radioactive decay

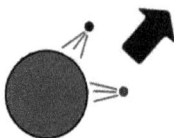

Gravitational Force
binding the Solar System

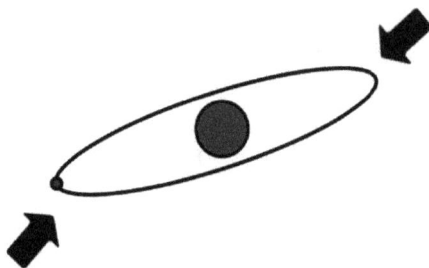

Fig. 3 - The Four Fundamental Forces

Physics is the study of matter, energy, and their interactions, expressed in mathematical terms. In essence, physics is the study of everything in the natural world, from the smallest elementary particles to the largest galaxies. Physics attempts to explain '**how**' physical things in our universe happen in mathematical form.

Mathematics, the language of physics, provides us with a structured framework to understand the natural world. Through understanding math, one can understand the numerical principles that dictate the natural rules of the world.

Natural sciences are often classified as "hard" sciences, while social sciences—focused on human behavior and societal structures—are considered "soft" sciences. Mathematics, a fundamental hard science, serves as the key to deciphering the universe's quantitative intricate order. For centuries, scholars have debated whether mathematics was invented or discovered. Are there limits shaped by human logic, or is it limitless with more to uncover? The answer is not clear, while its ability to reveal the underlying patterns of the cosmos is undeniable.

Physics branches into specialized fields, addressing fundamental questions:

- **Atomic Physics:** How do electrons arrange themselves around atomic nuclei?

- **Nuclear Physics:** What forces hold the atomic nucleus together?

- **Biophysics:** How do biological systems follow physical laws?

- **Geophysics:** What shapes the Earth's form and internal processes?

- **Mechanics:** How do objects respond to force and motion?

- **Acoustics:** How do vibrations manifest as sound?

43

- **Quantum Mechanics:** How do subatomic particles behave at microscopic scales?

In Islam, angels are luminous beings of light, who execute Allah's commands across all layers of existence. They fill all voids of space in numbers beyond human comprehension. They are genderless bodies of light that are of a low density beyond our sensory perception. Aishah reported that the Messenger of Allah ﷺ said, "Angels were created from light, jinns were created from a smokeless flame of fire, and 'Adam was created from that which you have been told (i.e., sounding clay like the clay of pottery)." They exist in a spectrum of light invisible to us—perhaps even a form of energy unknown to human understanding. Allah says that they do not tire or disobey in their duty of enforcing the laws that He establishes (66:6). These are laws by which everything must abide.

Just as plants draw life from rains sent down from above, so do angels serve as the universe's "flora," watering creation with divine mercy. In the same way that flora root themselves in soil and lift their leaves to the heavens, angels nurture and nourish every living being in every realm. Their unseen assistance is like celestial irrigation, ensuring that every created thing—from clouds to creatures—receives the sustenance ordained by the Sustainer.

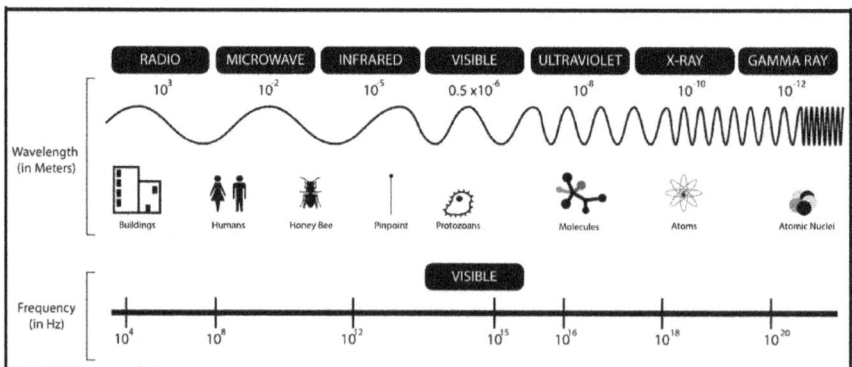

Fig. 4 - The Electromagnetic Spectrum

Allah is the creator of the universal laws of physics, and angels enforce those laws, even though He does not need any entity to enforce rules for Him. As part of His creation, they are His servants, carrying out His will in accordance with His names and attributes. Some angels bring nourishment and mercy in the form of rain or snow like *Mika'il*; some bring the light of guidance and the fire of destruction in the form of divine books and punishment, like the *Ruh al-Qudus*, "holy spirit" *Jibra'il*.

It would then appear as though each angelic function symbolically aligns with the fundamental forces:[6]

- *Jibra'il* (Gabriel): Oversees electromagnetic forces, facilitating all known physical phenomena on Earth. He delivers divine revelation as energy transmissions, akin to electromagnetic waves, illuminating the minds of the Messengers.[7]

- *Mika'il* (Michael): Regulates the strong nuclear force, sustaining life by controlling the energy released through fission and fusion in the sun.[8] This energy drives weather patterns, producing rain, storms, and climatic cycles essential for life on Earth.[9]

- *Izra'il* (Azrael): Oversees the weak nuclear force, governing radioactive decay. This decay releases radiation that, in high doses, leads to cellular deterioration and physiological failure, marking the transition between life and death.[10]

---

6   Note: This idea was first suggested by Prof. Abdul Rashid Khan in *Astrophysics & The Holy Quran* pp. 171-178.

7   Evidence for Jibrai'l being the one responsible for carrying the message of Allah: 2:97-98; 26:192-195; 40:15.

8   Evidence the sun is the source of heat and light radiations: 91: 1-2; 71: 15-16; 78: 12-13

9   Evidence that rainfall is heavenly in nature: 30:48; 2:22; 2:164; 23:18; 25:48; 50:9; 16:65; 29:63; 2:19; 13:13.

10   Evidence that Izra'il (never explicitly mentioned by name) and other angels are the cause of death: 79:1-2; 8:50; 47:27; 32:11; 16:28; 16:32.

- **Israfil** (Raphael): Governs gravitational forces, maintaining cosmic order by ensuring celestial bodies remain in balance. As the angel of both Order and Destruction, he will signal the end of time with the Trumpet Blow, unraveling the universe's stability.[11]

MIKA'IL
Strong Force
binding the nucleus

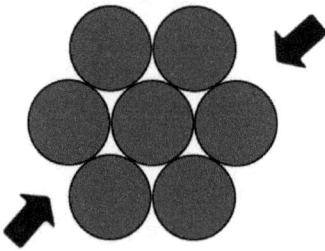

JIBRA'IL
Electromagnetic Force
binding the atom

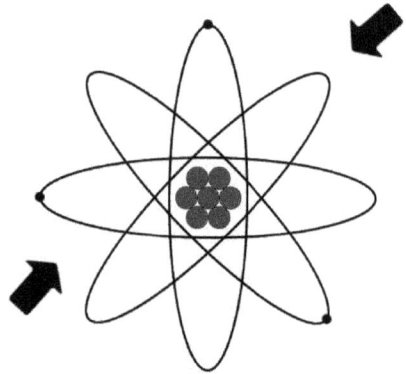

Weak Force
in radioactive decay

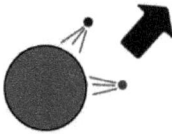

IZRA'IL

Gravitational Force
binding the Solar System

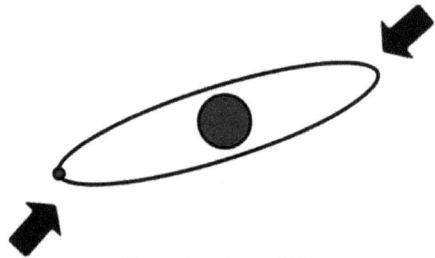

ISRAFIL

Fig. 5 - The Four Forces and the Four Angels

11 Evidence that everything is held together by gravity (77:25-26); Evidence Israfil destroys the existing order of the universe (39:68).

Angels carry out Allah's decree across both cosmic and earthly domains, enforcing divine will to bring about change for reasons known only to Him. Some events may seem sudden, events that disrupt the natural order—whether cosmic disasters in the universe or natural disasters on Earth—are set into motion by angels, executing Allah's command in alignment with the physical laws He has established. In the Quran, numerous accounts describe past nations that were collectively engulfed in sin and ultimately destroyed by divine punishment.

As stated in Surah Al-'Ankabūt (29:40):

﴿ فَكُلًّا أَخَذْنَا بِذَنۢبِهِۦ ۖ فَمِنْهُم مَّنْ أَرْسَلْنَا عَلَيْهِ حَاصِبًا وَمِنْهُم مَّنْ أَخَذَتْهُ ٱلصَّيْحَةُ وَمِنْهُم مَّنْ خَسَفْنَا بِهِ ٱلْأَرْضَ وَمِنْهُم مَّنْ أَغْرَقْنَا ۚ وَمَا كَانَ ٱللَّهُ لِيَظْلِمَهُمْ وَلَٰكِن كَانُوٓا۟ أَنفُسَهُمْ يَظْلِمُونَ ﴾

"So each We seized for his sin; and among them were those upon whom We sent a storm of stones, and among them were those who were seized by the blast [from the sky], and among them were those whom We caused the earth to swallow, and among them were those whom We drowned. And Allāh would not have wronged them, but it was they who were wronging themselves."

Allah assigns angels to oversee and regulate all elements of nature—fire, water, air, and earth. For instance, the Quran describes angels responsible for cloud formation and movement:

﴿ وَٱلصَّٰٓفَّٰتِ صَفًّا ۝ فَٱلزَّٰجِرَٰتِ زَجْرًا ﴾

By those [angels] lined up in rows.
And those who drive [the clouds].
(As-Saffat 37:1-2).

47

They facilitate natural phenomena such as earthquakes, lightning storms, rainfall, snowfall, hailstorms, wind movement, evaporation, and astrological events beyond ordinary perception.

Despite humanity's advancements in science and technology, the fundamental laws governing the universe remain immutable. Programs like the High-Frequency Active Auroral Research Program (H.A.A.R.P.) and cloud seeding demonstrate mankind's growing ability to manipulate natural processes. These innovations reveal deeper layers of physical laws, leading to groundbreaking scientific theories and applications. However, humans can only work within the framework of these laws, never altering the foundational principles that reflect the perfect design of creation.

Those who ponder the physical world through the lens of the angels remember that there are countless celestial beings, each entrusted with precise tasks across realms seen and unseen—on earth, in the heavens, and within dimensions beyond our perception. Revelation grants us only fleeting glimpses of their duties, hinting at deeper realities we cannot fathom. In truth, every law of physics is a divine command, executed by these hidden architects of creation, motion, and order. Viewed this way, science and scripture are not rival domains but twin threads of a single tapestry. The cosmic laws are no cold mechanisms of chance; they are a living symphony, animated by the will of Allah and performed by His angelic host.

SECTION 3

CHEMISTRY

﴿ وَٱلْجَآنَّ خَلَقْنَٰهُ مِن قَبْلُ مِن نَّارِ ٱلسَّمُومِ ﴾

"As for the jinn, We created them earlier from smokeless fire"
(15:27).

"You can talk about depression as a 'chemical imbalance' all you want, but it presents itself as an external antagonist—a 'demon,' a 'beast,' or a 'black dog...'"
~ Barbara Ehrenreich

According to the most dominant opinion, approximately **380,000 years[12] after the universe's initial expansion,** it cooled enough for matter and energy to form into atoms. Atoms are the basic building blocks of matter and are categorized into elements. Over time, atoms combine to form

---

12 Measured in "Earth Years."

molecules—for example, two hydrogen atoms and one oxygen atom form a water molecule. These molecular interactions define modern chemistry.

Chemistry is the study of matter—its composition, properties, and reactions to changes of state such as temperature or pressure—guided by fundamental principles governing material interactions. The science of Chemistry seeks to interpret the '**results**' of physical processes while uncovering the deeper laws that shape our material world. This field is further divided into specialized branches, each addressing its own scientific questions:

- **Physical Chemistry:** How is pure physics applied to chemical problems?

- **Inorganic Chemistry:** How do inorganic compounds synthesize and behave?

- **Organic Chemistry:** What are the structures, properties, and reactions of organic materials?

- **Analytical Chemistry:** What methods determine the compositional quality and quantity of matter?

- **Biochemistry:** What are the chemical processes that give rise to life?

- **Industrial Chemistry:** How can raw materials be transformed into beneficial products?

The jinn, like angels, constitute a distinct class of sentient beings created by Allah. Their origin, however, unfolds in two stages, each associated with a different kind of "fire."

The first is described in Arabic as *"nar al-samum,"* literally "scorching fire." This term, which comes from the root samum ("poison"), refers to a poisonous flame or desert wind so intense that it penetrates the skin. In fact, the Quran uses as-samum to describe the fires of Hell (15:27).

The second stage is called "*marij min nar,*" often translated simply as "smokeless fire." Here, marij denotes a bright, inorganic blaze—pure and carbonless, unlike the organic flame produced by wood or other earthly materials (55:15).

Though English renders both simply as "fire," the Arabic shows two distinct substances: one deadly and penetrating, the other pure and elemental. Much as a human is first formed from clay then refined into living flesh, so the jinn are forged from created, fiery elements before assuming their final, unseen form.

Just as fungi dwell in hidden, nutrient-rich layers, decomposing the old to nourish new growth, so the jinn inhabit transformative realms beyond our senses. Like mushrooms pushing through dark soil, they emerge into our plane via subtle chemical and energetic processes. Some fungi even release spores that, when ingested, release chemicals that alter perception and transport the mind into otherworldly landscapes, mirroring how a jinn's vibratory whispers can carry the soul into unseen dimensions.

In their role as cosmic decomposers and alchemists, the jinn catalyze change, breaking down barriers between the seen and the hidden and reshaping creation in wondrous and perilous ways.

Their vibratory frequency makes them undetectable in their natural state. They dwell in a parallel dimension that is outside our physical plane, but possess the ability to materialize within our plane and control various forms of matter. They have their own forms of consciousness and intellect. Like humans, jinn form tribes and nations, with diverse beliefs, hierarchies, and rites of passage. The Quran states that some are righteous and others follow evil paths (72:11). Though they live in a realm beyond our senses, their origin in elemental fire reminds us that Allah's creation extends far beyond what we see.

This invisible yet transformative aspect of the jinn finds a parallel in the early practice of alchemy, the predecessor of modern chemistry, which sought to transform base elements into noble ones, such as gold.[13]

---

13   Note: Alchemy- from "Khem" or "Out of Darkness" is an Occult Tradition taught through allegories. An Allegory is a poem, play, picture, etc, in which the apparent meaning of the characters and events is used to symbolize a deeper moral or spiritual meaning.

Alchemists believed every material substance had the potential for refinement and that alchemy was the process to help substances reach their ideal state. Their methods included preparing medicinal herbs, meditation, and mixing different elements in pursuit of transformation.

Alchemy, however, symbolically represents a broader concept of transformation—physical, mental, emotional, and spiritual. This theme is reflected in the story of Iblis's deception of Adam and Hawwah. He falsely promised them immortality, divine status like the angels, and an eternal kingdom if they ate from the forbidden tree.[14] In this context, Iblis offered a corrupted form of alchemy, an illusion of transcendence through forbidden means. To achieve this supposed enlightenment, he lured Adam and Hawwah to the *sharjarat al-khuld* (Tree of Eternity), despite Allah granting them access to countless other permissible pleasures within the garden.[15] Though warned of Iblis's intent to expel them from Paradise, they fell victim to his enticing whispers.

Upon consuming the fruit, Adam and Hawwah experienced a descent from a higher spiritual state into a lower physical state. This shift exposed them to vulnerability. They became aware of their nakedness and found themselves burdened with hunger, thirst, the heat of the sun, and shame. Allah had previously assured them, *"Here it is guaranteed that you will never go hungry or unclothed, nor will you [ever] suffer from thirst or [the sun's] heat"* (20:118-119). Their fall into the physical world is aligned with four elemental hardships: hunger, representing dependence on the earth for sustenance; exposure, tied to the harshness of air and wind; thirst, signifying reliance on water for survival; and heat, a reminder of the sun's burning intensity. This transformation was not just a physical exile but it represented an entry into a world where survival itself became a test—one that reflects humanity's enduring struggle for sustenance, protection, and spiritual growth.

---

14   Quran 7:20; 20:120

15   Note: In the Bible this Tree is referred to as the 'Tree of Life' and the 'Tree of knowledge of good and evil'. Genesis 2:9; Genesis 2:16-17; Genesis 3:22; Revelation 22.

When they disobeyed, their spiritual state descended into physical vulnerability, bringing exposure, toil, and mortality. They shifted from a state of bliss and spiritual enlightenment to one of fear and egocentrism. The devil's promise was proven to be an evil lie. Upon realizing they were tricked; they gained experience in the trade. Before that experience, they only knew about Iblis theoretically through Allah's warning. They were naive about the strategies he could use to sway them through whispers and chemical toxins. After their disobedience, Iblis (renamed Shaytan[16] due to him being "distant" and "astray" from divine mercy), Adam, and Hawwah were all banished from the garden and sent to earth. This story serves as the ultimate cautionary lesson on the consequences of disobedience and going beyond divine limits.

This story holds a deep allegorical meaning that remains relevant throughout human history. In this section, we will explore how **Shaytan's influence can be understood through the realm of chemical interactions**. By examining this perspective, we can gain insight into how chemicals affect the mind, body, and soul. Everything material consists of chemicals, which are not inherently harmful, yet chemistry has both a corrosive (aggressive) and a healing (passive) nature. Viewing this story through the lens of chemistry, particularly its corrosive aspects, allows us to draw parallels between ancient scripture and our modern understanding of chemical toxicants. Corrosive chemical reactions in the body can impair cognition, leading to lethargy, mental fog, and a weakened will. Over time, this dulling of the mind and spirit makes individuals more susceptible to external influences.

Shaytan operates through the corrosive chemical interactions within our bodies and minds in multiple ways. One example is through **drugs**, which can disrupt brain chemistry, leading to psychotic breakdowns. These episodes often follow a pattern: an initial sense of mental, physical,

---

16   Shaytan means "accuser, adversary" in Hebrew, and in Arabic it is derived from related to the root š-ṭ-n ("distant, astray"). The English rendering of "Satan" translates to "demon" from the Greek equivalent "daimōn". It can also translate to "devil" from the Greek "diábolos" which meant "slanderer" or "liar, deceiver."

and spiritual transcendence, followed by humiliation and degradation. This deception manifests through stimulants, depressants, opiates, hallucinogens, or entheogens[17]—whether prescribed, procured, legal, or illegal.

While many of these substances originate from natural compounds, they are chemically modified to enhance potency, making them highly toxic and addictive. Unlike natural herbs, which often contain balancing elements, synthetic drugs strip away these natural checks and balances, hijacking neural pathways which can lead to severe physical, mental, and spiritual consequences. Metaphorically, we can argue that every intoxicant is a branch of the original forbidden tree, they act as a divinely ordained *fitnah*, testing our obedience and self-restraint.

Drugs often induce altered mental states, commonly referred to as 'trips,' where users experience distorted perception and thought. In ancient times, such psychotic episodes were often interpreted as jinn or demonic possession.[18] Today, Western medicine dismisses the existence of jinn, attributing these experiences to chemical imbalances. However, in the Quran, intoxicants are described as *"the handwork of Shaytan"*:

$$\text{يَٰٓأَيُّهَا ٱلَّذِينَ ءَامَنُوٓاْ إِنَّمَا ٱلۡخَمۡرُ وَٱلۡمَيۡسِرُ وَٱلۡأَنصَابُ وَٱلۡأَزۡلَٰمُ رِجۡسٌ مِّنۡ عَمَلِ ٱلشَّيۡطَٰنِ فَٱجۡتَنِبُوهُ لَعَلَّكُمۡ تُفۡلِحُونَ}$$

O you who have believed, indeed, intoxicants, gambling, [sacrificing on] stone alters [to other than Allāh], and divining arrows are but defilement from the work of Satan, so avoid it that you may be successful.

---

17   Entheogens (generating the divine within) are psychoactive substances that produce incredible visionary experiences using chemicals that are found within our body.

18   Evidence for possession: Those who consume interest will stand ʿon Judgment Dayʾ like those driven to madness by Satan's touch. That is because they say, "Trade is no different than interest." But Allah has permitted trading and forbidden interest. Whoever refrains—after having received warning from their Lord—may keep their previous gains, and their case is left to Allah. As for those who persist, it is they who will be the residents of the Fire. They will be there forever. (2:275).

﴿ إِنَّمَا يُرِيدُ ٱلشَّيْطَانُ أَن يُوقِعَ بَيْنَكُمُ ٱلْعَدَاوَةَ وَٱلْبَغْضَآءَ فِى ٱلْخَمْرِ وَٱلْمَيْسِرِ وَيَصُدَّكُمْ عَن ذِكْرِ ٱللَّهِ وَعَنِ ٱلصَّلَوٰةِ ۖ فَهَلْ أَنتُم مُّنتَهُونَ ﴾

Satan only wants to cause between you animosity and hatred through intoxicants and gambling and to avert you from the remembrance of Allāh and from prayer. So will you not desist? (5:90-91)

Through these substances, Shaytan can impair judgment and open the mind to *waswas* (obsessive whispers):

﴿ فَوَسْوَسَ لَهُمَا ٱلشَّيْطَانُ لِيُبْدِيَ لَهُمَا مَا وُۥرِيَ عَنْهُمَا مِن سَوْءَٰتِهِمَا وَقَالَ مَا نَهَٰكُمَا رَبُّكُمَا عَنْ هَٰذِهِ ٱلشَّجَرَةِ إِلَّآ أَن تَكُونَا مَلَكَيْنِ أَوْ تَكُونَا مِنَ ٱلْخَٰلِدِينَ ﴾

But Satan whispered to them to make apparent to them that which was concealed from them of their private parts. He said, "Your Lord did not forbid you this tree except that you become angels or become of the immortal." (7:20)

Beyond intoxicants, this story also provides an allegorical lesson about chemically toxic **food**. Highly processed foods and sugary drinks trigger biochemical reactions that disrupt metabolic processes, leading to systemic inflammation, hormonal imbalances, and mood instability. Studies have shown that diets high in refined sugars and additives impair mitochondrial function, the energy powerhouse of cells, resulting in chronic fatigue and mental exhaustion. A person's diet mirrors their overall well-being—excessive consumption of nutrient-poor, calorie-dense foods leads to obesity, metabolic disorders, and cognitive decline. These foods not only harm the body but also weaken mental clarity and reinforce cycles of dependency on pharmaceuticals and medical interventions.

Cooking itself is a form of chemistry. When humans prepare food, they act as organic chemists, combining ingredients in ways that trigger chemical reactions, transforming raw materials into an edible dish. Heat causes molecular changes that create distinct flavors and aromas, while consuming food releases specific chemicals in the brain, influencing mood, passion, and motivation. Dietary choices significantly impact *al-mashaaeir* (feelings) and *al-eawatif* (emotions) by regulating neurotransmitter production and gut health. The gut-brain axis, a crucial link between nutrition and mental well-being, highlights the importance of mindful eating. However, poor dietary habits rich in synthetic additives and preservatives disrupt this balance, leading to emotional instability and impaired cognitive function.

Food is far more complex than many realize. What is often perceived as hunger is, in reality, chemical desire. For the well-nourished person, hunger is not necessarily a biological need but a craving for the chemicals their body has become dependent on. This chemical dependency extends beyond food, it also manifests in desires for companionship, pleasure, and indulgence.

Overcoming these urges requires discipline, prayer, and meditation to rise above subconscious impulses and assert control over the conscious mind. *Shahawaat* (desires) take many forms, with women, food, and drink being primary examples. As Ibn al-Qayyim cited, "Conquering one's passions is often more challenging than conquering a city."

Moreover, this story illustrates how *shayateen*, from among the jinn, influence humans through the chemical and electronic reactions in the brain. Especially during the acquisition of new **information, knowledge, understanding,** and perceived **wisdom.**[19] When new information is processed, synapses form, bridging neurons and creating pathways that shape thoughts, emotions, and behavior. These neural pathways, like intricate roads, enable signals to travel and govern responses.

---

19   *Shayateen* can be from both Jinn and men: it is similar to Allah's saying," And so We have appointed for every Prophet enemies – *Shayateen* (devils) among mankind and jinn, inspiring one another with adorned speech as a delusion (or by way of deception). If your Lord had so willed, they would not have done it, so leave them alone with their fabrications. (6:112).

For instance, the sensation of an insect crawling on the skin acts as sensory **input**. The nervous system **processes** this stimulus, leading to an **output**, such as brushing off the insect. Similarly, the brain processes chemical and electronic signals when forming new connections, integrating sensory input into thought or action. Jinn exploit this system by interfering with the delicate balance of neural activity, subtly altering the flow of signals to manipulate perceptions, emotions, and decision-making. This interaction demonstrates how unseen influences can penetrate the very foundation of human cognition and behavior.

Wisdom is the highest refinement of knowledge and understanding, representing mastery over both mind and body. The wise do not merely accumulate information but act with clarity and precision, integrating experience, insight, and moral discernment. True wisdom allows one to see the interconnectedness of truths and align actions with a greater purpose. However, wisdom demands humility and sincerity; when sought with ego-driven motives such as vanity or personal gain, it becomes corrupted and leads to spiritual blindness. This misuse of wisdom resembles the influence of Shaytan, who preys on the ego to distort intentions and misguide those who seek knowledge for the wrong reasons. Good and evil are not absolute but are shaped by context, perspective, and intention. They serve as a framework for distinguishing right from wrong, ensuring that wisdom remains a force for righteousness rather than self-deception.

Unlike the Biblical portrayal of the Forbidden Tree as the source of absolute knowledge of good and evil, the Quran presents it as a test. Eating from the tree was not the cause of inherent evil but rather a temporary failure—an integral step in the journey of human growth. Failure, while painful, carries the potential for transformation. It refines judgment, strengthens resolve, and converts theoretical understanding into practical wisdom. Just as Adam and Hawwah gained clarity through their mistake, every challenge or perceived evil offers an opportunity for self-improvement and spiritual elevation.

This understanding of wisdom demonstrates that

challenges, whether from within or influenced by external forces, serve a greater purpose in distinguishing truth from falsehood. Even apparent evils carry wisdom when approached with humility and reflection.

In general, there is a word of caution that all must take heed when traversing the path of knowledge. Some knowledge may lead to excessive questioning. Previous nations were destroyed through their insatiable curiosity, as we will later explore. Hypothetical questioning about the divine, such as 'Can Allah create a rock he can't lift,' or questions made by those who do not have the intention to know what is right, are particularly dangerous. Excessive questioning eventually leads to the point where one asks the ultimate question: who created Allah?[20]

It is the question that challenges the essence of Tawhid (the oneness of Allah). Knowledge can ultimately lead to an intellectual, emotional, and spiritual dead end in the form of wavering in the soul, manifested in the philosophy of Atheism. When the soul wavers between belief and disbelief, this is *shubuhat* (**doubt**).

Another way in which the jinn world uses chemicals to control humans is by way of **chemical weapons**.

This metal machinery contains unique mixtures of toxic chemical compounds that are intended to harm or destroy an enemy's vital organs. The knowledge of how to combine machinery and chemicals to destroy on a massive scale has occurred in recent history.

For example, the Industrial Revolution gave man the power to replace family and community with governments and markets. It caused the extinction of several plant, insect, and animal species on a global level. These weapons have given man power in motion (*hawl*) and ability in aptitude (*quwwa*) in aptitude to breach the boundaries of earth and as a consequence, threaten the survival of all of mankind. Ultimately, no creature possesses either ability or power over

---

20   The Messenger of Allah ﷺ said: "The Shaytan will come to one of you and say, 'Who created such and such?' until he says to him, 'Who created your Lord?' When it reaches that stage, let him seek refuge with Allah [say A'oodhu Billaahi min ash-Shaytan ir-rajeem = I seek refuge with Allah from the accursed Shaytan] and stop thinking about it." (Bukhari).

anything except by the will of Allah. Only He is the one who is able and capable. Various prophecies describe the types of powers that will appear in the future as a test for mankind.

A final form of the jinn-chemical-human connection is **transhumanism**.

Transhumanism is the ideological pursuit of what its proponents view as the pinnacle of human evolution. Backed by powerful elites seeking to defy divine order, this movement strives to merge human biology with chemicals, machinery, and artificial intelligence. In their quest to become 'intelligent designers,' they aim to usher in an age wherein natural selection will be replaced with a superhuman future. This mirrors the promises of Shaytan, offering the illusion of transcendence while ultimately diverting humanity from its divine purpose.

They are striving to do this by any means. Some aim to "hack" the DNA of life and combat aging, while others seek to genetically modify embryos to create "designer babies." Others seek to create brain-computer interfaces to merge human cognition with artificial intelligence, in hopes of restoring lost functions for individuals with disabilities. While these technologies claim to improve human life, they ultimately are an effort to "alter Allah's creation," blurring the lines between healing and an attempt to redefine the natural order.[21]

When analyzing their aims in light of the Quran's creation story, we see that transhumanists are essentially reenacting the creation story in reverse (a practice of dark occultists and magicians, as we will later explore, inshallah). The Quran tells the story of how Adam, Hawwah, and Shaytan were all sent down to earth to live together. The story explains how Shaytan offers forbidden knowledge, which is a false promise to have humans ascend to higher ranks via the unification of man, woman, animal, and jinn to become like **angels**, i.e., perfected beings.

Transhumanists believe they will achieve **immortality**

---

21   "I will mislead them, and I will entice them, and I will command them, and they will slit the ears of cattle, and I will command them, and they will alter Allah's creation." Whoever takes Satan as a guardian instead of Allah has certainly suffered a tremendous loss. (4:119)

as a human-cyborg species dwelling in a digital paradise. Allegorically, this is their **Tree of Eternity**—limitless in beauty. They envision inheriting an **everlasting kingdom**: a realm of endless pleasure and boundless power. To reach it, they cast themselves as modern alchemists, wielding **technology** as their philosopher's stone. Like their archetypal model, the Baphomet, they seek to transcend human limitations through a chemical fusion of man and woman, animal and angel, flesh and machine. In doing so, they aim to rewrite the divine narrative, replace the Creator, and claim the power of limitless creation for themselves.

Baphomet is the symbol that best captures the transhumanistic ideal: a figure born of our desire to move past ordinary limits. As an androgynous being, part masculine, part feminine, part earthly, and part divine, it shows how merging opposites can unlock a new kind of wisdom that welcomes both the sensual and the mysterious.[22]

In conclusion, Chemistry provides us with the tools to understand the material world, while the Quranic Ayat unveil the hidden realities of the unseen world, including the realm of the jinn. Together, these perspectives offer a profound understanding of the interconnectedness between the physical and spiritual planes. By exploring this interconnectedness, we uncover how chemical interactions influence not only our bodies but also our souls, shaping our emotions, thoughts, and actions.

The allegorical connections between alchemy, desires, doubts, transhumanism, and the story of creation reveal timeless truths. The pursuit of knowledge and transformation, when misaligned with divine guidance, leads to corruption

---

22 [The] chief subject is the images which are called Baphomet... found in several museums and collections of antiquities... of stone, partly hermaphrodites, having, generally, two heads or two faces, with a beard, but, in other respects, female figures, most of them accompanied by serpents, the sun and moon, and other strange emblems, and bearing many inscriptions... represented [as] half man, half woman, as the symbol of wisdom, unnatural voluptuousness and the principle of sensuality... *"Baphomet" in Encyclopedia Americana, 1851.*

We will dive deeper into this topic in Book 3

Fig. 6
An 1856 depiction of the Sabbatic Goat (Baphomet) from 'Dogme et
Rituel de la Haute Magie' by Éliphas Lévi.
The arms bear the Latin words SOLVE (dissolve) and COAGULA
(coagulate), reflecting the alchemy of Lévi's work.

61

and spiritual decay. Shaytan's age-old strategies of tempting humanity with illusions of enlightenment and power are mirrored in modern movements like transhumanism, which aim to defy the divine order in the quest for perfection and absolute control.

True transformation, whether physical, mental, or spiritual, demands humility, obedience, and alignment with the higher purpose set forth by Allah as revealed through the Quran. By rooting ourselves in divine wisdom and understanding the effects of chemical interactions—both in substances and spiritual choices—we gain insight into how they shape our morals and well-being. Just as chemistry reveals the physical laws governing the physical world, it also mirrors unseen forces, including the influence of the Jinn, that impact our spiritual state. By balancing material knowledge with faith, we can see through the deceptions of false progress and live a life that honors both the seen and unseen dimensions of creation, aligning fully with Allah's divine order.

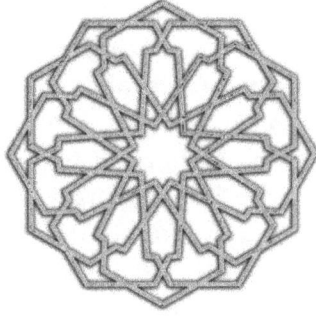

SECTION 4
BIOLOGY

﴿ وَٱللَّهُ خَلَقَ كُلَّ دَآبَّةٍ مِّن مَّآءٍ فَمِنْهُم مَّن يَمْشِى عَلَىٰ بَطْنِهِۦ
وَمِنْهُم مَّن يَمْشِى عَلَىٰ رِجْلَيْنِ وَمِنْهُم مَّن يَمْشِى عَلَىٰٓ أَرْبَعٍ ﴾

*"And Allah has created every animal from water. Of them
there are some that creep on their bellies, some that walk on
two legs, and some that walk on four..." (24:45).*

﴿ أَوَلَمْ يَرَوْاْ كَيْفَ يُبْدِئُ ٱللَّهُ ٱلْخَلْقَ ثُمَّ يُعِيدُهُۥٓ
إِنَّ ذَٰلِكَ عَلَى ٱللَّهِ يَسِيرٌ ﴾

*"See they not how Allah originates creation, then resurrects
it? Truly that is easy for Allah" (29:19).*

Nearly **3.8 billion years ago**, Earth's environment is said to have stabilized enough for simple molecules to form more complex compounds, leading to the first life forms and organisms. An organism is any individual living entity capable of reacting to stimuli, reproducing, growing, developing, and maintaining homeostasis. Living organisms on Earth are categorized into **Humans**, **Animals**, **Plants**, and **Microbes**, which include bacteria and fungi. In contrast, non-living components such as water, minerals (dust), and energy sources (sunlight/fire) support life but do not possess it. Most living organisms need air, water, nutrients (food), energy, and shelter.

While Biology classifies humans within fauna (all animal life), Islam elevates us to the highest station among them. Endowed by Allah with *aql* (intellect), *lisan* (language), *taklif* (moral responsibility), and *khilafah* (vicegerency), we stand as the most "superior" of Earth's creatures—entrusted as guardians of creation to lead with justice and compassion.

Biology is the scientific study of life and its processes, seeking to explain '**what**' life is and '**how**' exists as it does and continues to evolve. It encompasses multiple disciplines that explore the structure, function, and interactions of living organisms. Each field addresses specific questions:

- **Biochemistry:** What are the material substances that make up living things?

- **Botany:** What is the role of plants and agriculture?

- **Cellular biology:** What are the basic cellular units of living things?

- **Ecology:** How do organisms interact environmentaly?

- **Evolutionary Biology:** What are the origins and changes in the diversity of life over time?

- **Genetics:** What is heredity?

- **Molecular biology:** What are biological molecules?

- **Physiology:** What are the functions of organisms and their parts?

- **Zoology:** How do animals function and behave?

CHARACTERISTICS OF LIVING THINGS

All living things share the following characteristics:

- **Cellular Organization**: All living things are made up of cells, the smallest unit of life.

- **Reproduction**: All living things reproduce, either sexually or asexually.

- **Universal Genetic Code**: All living things share a universal genetic code (DNA).

- **Growth and Development**: All living things grow and develop.

- **Metabolism**: All living things obtain and use materials and energy.

- **Response to Environment**: All living things respond to their environment.

- **Homeostasis**: All living things maintain a stable internal environment.

- **Evolution**: All living things change over time.

STAGES OF BIOLOGICAL LIFE

The universe and all life within exhibit varying degrees of consciousness, unfolding through distinct stages of creation. Each stage reflects Allah's divine order, advancing toward specific developmental goals and transitioning from simpler to more complex forms of existence. These stages align both with the Quranic narrative and modern biological frameworks, highlighting the intricate design of life.

Cosmic Stage:
The Quran describes Allah as "originating creation" (29:19). The universe began as subatomic particles—protons, neutrons, and electrons—coalescing into clouds of matter known as nebulae (41:11). Over billions of years, gravitational collapse transformed these clouds into stars and planetary systems, including the sun and moon, which settled into precise orbits (36:40).

Through stellar processes, essential elements like hydrogen, helium, and carbon were synthesized, laying the foundation for the celestial bodies and, eventually, all forms of life.

Mineral Stage:
As the Earth solidified, Allah established physical laws that shaped its form and ensured balance in creation. The formation of the North and South poles stabilized the planet's axis, enabling the alternation of day and night and the cyclical nature of the four seasons. These poles also defined the four cardinal directions, creating a natural framework for navigation. The Quran reflects this divine precision in 41:10: "He placed firm mountains upon it, blessed it, and measured its sustenance in four days."

Features such as mountains, rivers, and valleys emerged, forming interconnected systems that would sustain life and prepare for subsequent stages of creation.

Vegetable Stage:

In this stage, vegetation marked the emergence of semi-conscious life, including flowers, plants, trees, leaves, fruits, and their juices. As plants took root, they introduced oxygen into the atmosphere, transforming the planet into a hospitable environment for higher life forms. Plants operate instinctively, following a natural life cycle of growth, reproduction, and adaptation in harmony with the changing seasons, reflecting the balance, order, and wisdom of creation. For example, trees that shed their leaves in autumn enter a period of energy conservation during winter and blossom again in spring, illustrating the Quranic verse, "We bring forth fruits of various colors" (35:27).

These cycles of birth, life, death, and rebirth are intricately tied to the four seasons, demonstrating the interconnected design that sustains all forms of life on Earth. This stage prepared the planet for the arrival of conscious beings, highlighting Allah's deliberate and harmonious creation.

Animal Stage:

Conscious life began with the animal kingdom, marked by diverse species with varying forms and functions. Animals possess five senses to navigate their environments, consume resources, and reproduce. This stage highlights Allah's ability to create life in countless forms from the same source, as reflected in 24:45: "And Allah has created every animal from water."

Self-Conscious Stage (Human Stage):

The emergence of humans marks the final stage of biological life, distinguished by self-awareness and the ability to reflect on creation. Humans possess the unique capability to explore the external laws of the world and the laws within their internal universe, leading to the development of fields like **psychology**, which delve into the complexities of thought, emotion, and behavior. This self-awareness is a direct reflection of Allah's design, as emphasized in the Quran: "We created man from sounding clay, from mud molded into shape" (15:26).

Humans are composed of elements, temperaments, humors, and genealogy, all of which shape physical traits like race and ethnicity, as well as emotional and spiritual tendencies. For example, the study of temperaments and humors has historically been used to understand individual behaviors and health. This deep awareness allows humans to recognize the intricate design of the universe, uncover their divine purpose, and align their actions with Allah's will.

Each stage represents a pivotal milestone in Allah's creation, from cosmic genesis to human self-realization. This journey reflects an evolving complexity and consciousness in the universe's grand design. Each of these components will be further explored in the context of the medicine wheel.

MEDICINE WHEEL

The medicine wheel, rooted in indigenous traditions, symbolizes the interconnectedness of life's physical, emotional, mental, and spiritual aspects. This circular model represents balance and harmony in all areas of existence. Found in ancient stone circles across North America, it acknowledges the cyclical nature of life and the unity of its components.

Each quadrant of the wheel corresponds to an element: earth, water, air, and fire, and a dimension of human existence. Good health and well-being depend on maintaining balance among these interconnected parts, as an imbalance in any one area can disrupt the whole. The following version of the model is divided into 11 components, representing the various facets of human experience, with the 12th being the center that unites the whole. This central point serves as the anchor, much like the Ka'aba unites Muslims as the focal point of worship, reminding us of the oneness that ties all elements together.

The medicine wheel teaches us to view life as an integrated system, where each aspect supports and influences the others. It reflects Allah's harmony and balance in creation, encouraging us to seek equilibrium in our own lives while aligning with the divine purpose.

1. Divine Origin:
Beyond the medicine wheel lies the singular source of all creation—Allah. In Islam He is proclaimed in four words:

$$\text{قُلْ هُوَ اللَّهُ أَحَدٌ}$$

("Say, 'He is Allah, One'")

In the Tanakh (Hebrew Bible) the same Creator is named by the four-letter Name **YHWH** (יהוה), and modern scholars call it the **Tetragrammaton**, which Kabbalists map onto fire, water, air, and earth.

- **י (Yod):** The airy principle that relates to His wisdom, holiness, and clarity, which establishes His universal laws.

- **ה (He):** The fiery principle that involves His infinite power and might.

- **ו (Vav):** The watery principle attributed to love and eternal life.

- **ה (He):** The earthly principle that belongs to His immortality and entirety.

2. Zodiac Signs:

Moving into the inside of the circle, the next component consists of the 12 zodiac signs, symbolizing humanity's connection to the elements and the cosmos. This concept is rooted in the Hermetic principle "As above, so below," which posits that events in the greater cosmos (heavens) are mirrored in the smaller cosmos (earth). Ancient civilizations observed that planets moved in regular patterns against the backdrop of the "fixed" stars. This backdrop was divided into 12 "houses," each named after its "ruling" constellation. Collectively, these houses form the Zodiac, a term derived from the Greek word for animal.

Astrology is a branch of *sihr* (magic) that links celestial movements to earthly events. The more one understands astrology, the deeper one's knowledge of sihr.[23] Horoscopes, based on the time of a person's birth, offer insights into a person's character or destiny. However, such beliefs are considered a form of *shirk* (associating partners with Allah) because they attribute knowledge of the unseen and control over one's fate to celestial bodies rather than to Allah alone. Only Allah has ultimate knowledge of the future and governs the destiny of all creation, making reliance on astrology contradictory to the principle of Tawhid. The twelve zodiac signs and their dates are presented below, not for belief, but to illustrate their

---

23   Narrated Abdullah ibn Abbas: The Prophet ﷺ said: If anyone acquires any knowledge of astrology, he acquires a branch of magic of which he gets more as long as he continues to do so (Sunan Abi Dawud).

correspondence to the elements and their foundational role in various branches of esoteric knowledge.

Aquarius: Jan-20 to Feb-19	Pisces: Feb-19 to March-20	Aries: March-21 to April-19	Taurus: April-20 to May-20
Gemini: May-21 to June-20	Cancer: June-21 to July-22	Leo: July-23 to Aug-22	Virgo: Aug-23 to Sept-22
Libra: Sept-23 to Oct-22	Scorpio: Oct-23 to Nov-21	Sagittarius: Nov-22 to Dec-21	Capricorn: Dec-22 to Jan-19

3. Elements:

The next component in the wheel is the elements that were created during the Cosmic Stage:

Fire
Water
Air
Earth

~ **Fire (nar)**: Fire serves as a force of creation that influences everything within the universe, embodying the qualities of passion, heat, speed, and expansion. Spiritually, fire symbolizes transformation and willpower, as it is both a destructive and creative force. In sacred texts, the significance of fire is evident. In the Quran, Allah is described as "the Light of the Heavens and the Earth," highlighting a divine association with light, an extension of fire (24:35). Similarly, the Bible's proclamation, "Let there be light," marks the beginning of creation, emphasizing the transformative power of light and fire (Genesis 1:3). Fire infuses movement and vitality into the world by representing the active masculine life force. As the 'father' of the elements, fire is foundational, giving rise to subsequent elements. The polarities within fire—active and passive, creative and destructive—reflect the contrasts, allowing deeper contemplation of higher realities.

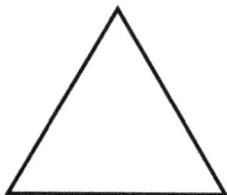

Fig. 7 - The fire element

~ **Water** *(ma')*: In contrast to fire, water represents a more passive, nurturing force. Spiritually, water reflects emotion and intuition. Before the universe's creation, Allah and His throne existed above water, emphasizing its primordial nature (11:7). Covering nearly three-quarters of the Earth's surface, water is not a product of the earth but rather a divine gift sent down by Allah, as mentioned in the Quran (23:18). This sent-down water can be seen as an extension of the primordial water from above. Water embodies the qualities of the moon and represents the passive feminine element. It is often regarded as the 'Mother' of the elements. Water's qualities of coldness and contraction complement the expansiveness of fire, making it the perfect balance to fire's heat and speed. Its polarities—nourishing and depriving, life-giving and life-taking—highlight the delicate balance of existence. The interdependence of fire and water is essential, as all life originates from water (21:30-31). Yet, it may have been the fire element that ignited the initial separation of the heavens and earth, possibly through a process akin to the "Big Bang" or possibly through the influence of air and wind.

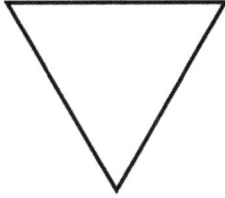

Fig. 8 - The water element

~ **Air (Hawa):** Though not traditionally considered an element, air is an essential force. Spiritually, air epitomizes intellect and communication. It is the dynamic intermediary facilitating interaction between the active (fire) and the passive (water). Air can be seen as a material manifestation of fire, as fire requires air to exist. This constant movement imparts motion to all living things, making air spiritually superior to the more material elements of water and earth. Symbolizing wind, air is perceived as feminine and active, often referred to as the 'daughter' of the elements. Air occupies the space between Earth and the Heavens, manifesting in the form of clouds that bring rain, essential for life. The Quran invites believers to reflect on the winds and clouds, emphasizing their significance in sustaining life (2:164). The wind is air in motion, and life would perish without clouds that carry the rain. Even in the human body, our lungs require air to provide oxygen to the heart to sustain life.

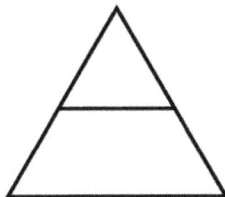

Fig. 9 - The Air element

~ **Earth (Ard)**: Earth is the fourth and final core element in the classical system. Unlike fire and water, earth is not considered a proper element in the same sense but is instead a material version of water, requiring it to sustain life. Earth solidifies the three created elements—fire, water, and air— and is the realm where all biological life forms exist. It has the unique quality of giving shape to the other three elements, allowing them to be comprehended in terms of space, measure, weight, and time. When fire, water, and air combine with earth, they form two opposing polarities, creating a four-pole magnet: north, south, east, and west.

Often seen as masculine and passive, earth symbolizes the physical world and is considered the 'Son' of the elements. Spiritually, it implies stability and grounding, serving as the foundation for all life and existence. The 99th surah in the Quran, *Al-Zalzalah* (The Earthquake), describes the day when the earth will experience a cataclysmic event, revealing the deeds of humanity, both good and evil. This emphasizes the profound and active nature of earth, encapsulating all elements within itself and playing a crucial role in the manifestation of life.

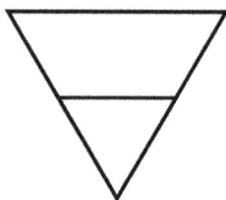

Fig. 10 - The Earth element.

In Summary: The **Earth** supports life, **Water** and **Air** animate life, and Solar **Fire** moves life. These physiochemical forces explain the principles in nature that immediately surround us, each element contributing uniquely to the grand tapestry of existence.

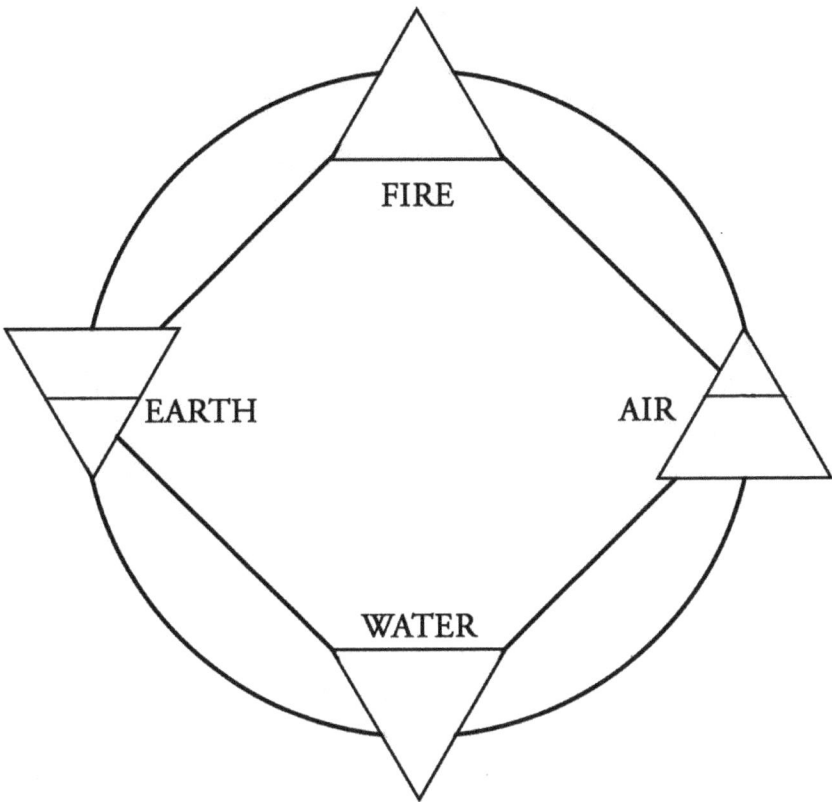

Fig. 11 - The Four Elements

4. Direction: North | South | East | West

Once the various forms of cosmic energies were arranged, harmonized, and cooled, they were channeled into the elemental shells that serve as the building blocks of the universe. This process completed the **cosmic stage**, allowing the second higher conscious plan to unfold on Earth. The planet and its **mineral kingdom** were shaped by physical laws, with these elements acting as the foundational tools of creation.

Initially, Earth existed as a gaseous body, separated from the sun yet revolving around it. Over time, it began to solidify, developing its identity by creating two poles of attraction: the North and South. Over hundreds of millions of years, physical laws continually transformed various compounds and mixtures, sculpting the planet's topography. The mountains, hills, valleys, streams, rivers, seas, clouds, rain, and seasons were all formed according to these laws, which operate in a unified system of causes and effects, actions and reactions. They are so precise that they can be expressed mathematically.

On a spiritual level, these physical laws reflect Allah's fundamental attributes that guided the formation of the Earth. This illustrates that matter is not real but merely a manifestation of consciousness; when the material universe is stripped away, only the laws of mathematics remain. The 'mind' of the Creator is both conscious and mathematical. In any direction we turn, whether east or west, we encounter the face of Allah (2:115).

5. Seasons: The next stage in creation is the **vegetable realm**, where the plant kingdom was formed. Plants digest minerals and purify the atmospheric air. Through the cyclical changes of the seasons, plants experience an annual cycle of birth, growth, and death, mirroring the patterns of human life. This cyclical nature is why the four seasons are often seen as representing the stages of human existence:

- **Spring (Childhood)**: Birth to age 20, characterized by eagerness and erratic energy.

- **Summer (Youth)**: Ages 20 – 40, marked by adventure and exploration.

- **Fall (adulthood)**: Ages 40 to 60, a period of reflection and conservatism.

- **Winter (old age)**: From age 60 to death, when one experiences physical and mental lethargy.

This alignment of seasons with life stages emphasizes the interconnectedness of nature and humanity, highlighting how the cycles of the natural world resonate with our own life experiences.

6. Temperaments: This section explores the psychological makeup of humanity as defined by temperaments. The purified air, enriched by the plant kingdom, sustains the **animal realm**, where each species possesses its own unique *meezaj* (temperament or personality type). Within the biological classification of animals, humans have the most balanced temperament. Within humanity, the most balanced temperament belongs to the believers, and among believers, it is the Prophets who exemplify the highest balance. Among all prophets, Muhammad ﷺ exemplifies perfect balance.

When individuals consciously strive to elevate their intellect and develop a temperament similar to that of the Prophets, rather than behaving instinctively like animals, they enter the **Self-Conscious Stage**. This stage is marked by the ability to recognize and correct any imbalances within one's temperament.

The four core temperaments are **choleric**, **phlegmatic**, **sanguine**, and **melancholic**. Each person has a dominant and recessive temperament.

- **Choleric**: An extroverted type characterized by independence, decisiveness, focus, and ambition. Choleric individuals are natural leaders but can also be prone to anger and impulsiveness.

- **Phlegmatic**: Often introverted, these individuals are "people pleasers." They are calm, peaceful, easy-going, and care deeply about others, though they may conceal their emotions. They excel at generalizing ideas and making compromises.

- **Sanguine**: Another extroverted type, sanguine individuals are talkative, energetic, enthusiastic, and sociable. They embrace risk and seek to avoid boredom at all costs.

- **Melancholic**: Is typically introverted; melancholic individuals are analytical and detail-oriented, thinking and feeling deeply. They tend to be self-reliant, thoughtful, and reserved and they often experience anxiety. They strive for perfection in themselves and their surroundings.

While an individual may lean more often toward one temperament than the others, each of us experiences a range of emotional states, from mild to stormy, heavy to uplifting, throughout our lives.

7. Humour: Human physiology is governed by the Four Humours, which are bodily fluids present in the bloodstream.[24]

- **Blood**: is hot and wet, and blood is the most vital of the humours, circulating through the organs and nourishing the entire body. Normal blood is sweet and odorless, playing a crucial role in maintaining health.

- **Phlegm**: is cold and wet; phlegm is produced when the body is deprived of food. It serves to keep the organs moist and prevent dryness due to movement. Normal phlegm is on the verge of transforming into blood, while abnormal phlegm may be salty, slightly warm, or sour, often appearing ripe and insipid. It is characterized by its unmixed coldness.

- **Yellow Bile**: is hot and dry; it is generated by the liver and stored in the gallbladder. It plays an essential role in digestion by breaking down fats and cholesterol, stimulating intestinal contractions, and promoting bowel movements. Additionally, it imparts a brown color to the stool.

---

24   Note: The four humor theory is no longer considered to be accurate because it does not take into account other factors that affect health such as infection and injury, and for other illnesses, although it is insightful, it did not produce effective treatments.

- **Black Bile**: is cold and dry, and it is associated with melancholy and physical ailments such as stomach issues. An excess of black bile can lead to depression, nausea, arthritis, and other heavy bodily conditions.

Treatments for the imbalance of a humour include *hijamah* (cupping), dietary adjustments, and other interventions aimed at restoring equilibrium.

8. Body Parts: The four organs associated with the previously mentioned humours are the following:

- The **HEART** pumps blood throughout the entire body, serving as the central organ of circulation.

- The **LIVER**, which processes and detoxifies the blood that flows from the stomach and intestines, producing bile to aid digestion.

- The **SPLEEN** acts as a defense mechanism, fighting off invading germs and filtering the blood.

- The **LUNGS** rhythmically inhale and exhale air, which is vital for providing oxygen and sustaining life.

According to Islam, each organ houses specific spiritual components, as indicated in the following hadith narrated by Iyad ibn Khalifa, who heard 'Ali say at Siffin:

AL-AQL **(intellect) is located in the heart.**
AL-RAHMAH **(mercy) is located in the liver,**
AL-RAFAH **(compassion) is located in the spleen.**
AL-NAFS **(the self/psyche) is located in the lungs.**[25]

This connection highlights the integral relationship between physical health and spiritual well-being.

---

25   Al-Adab Al-Mufrad.

9. Race: Allah mentions in the Quran:

﴿ أَلَمْ تَرَ أَنَّ اللَّهَ أَنزَلَ مِنَ السَّمَاءِ مَاءً فَأَخْرَجْنَا بِهِۦ ثَمَرَٰتٍ مُّخْتَلِفًا أَلْوَٰنُهَا ۚ وَمِنَ الْجِبَالِ جُدَدٌ بِيضٌ وَحُمْرٌ مُّخْتَلِفٌ أَلْوَٰنُهَا وَغَرَابِيبُ سُودٌ ﴾

﴿ وَمِنَ النَّاسِ وَالدَّوَابِّ وَالْأَنْعَامِ مُخْتَلِفٌ أَلْوَٰنُهُۥ كَذَٰلِكَ ۗ إِنَّمَا يَخْشَى اللَّهَ مِنْ عِبَادِهِ الْعُلَمَٰؤُا۟ ۗ إِنَّ اللَّهَ عَزِيزٌ غَفُورٌ ﴾

Do you not see that Allāh sends down rain from the sky, and We produce thereby fruits of varying colors? And in the mountains are tracts, white and red of varying shades and [some] extremely black.

And among people and moving creatures and grazing livestock are various colors similarly. Only those fear Allāh, from among His servants, who have knowledge. Indeed, Allāh is Exalted in Might and Forgiving.
(Fatir: 27-28).

Likewise, the Messenger of Allah said: *"Allah created Adam from a handful that He gathered from the earth, so the sons of Adam come like the earth. Some of them are* **red***, some are* **black***, some are* **white***, and some are in between (***yellow***)*
(Ibn Hibban).

These signs show that Allah has designed people with various colors, highlighting the richness of human diversity. All humans were created with a "hue," symbolizing that skin complexion is a unique attribute shaping both individual and collective identities. The historical medical theory of Geohumoralism integrates the concept of environmental influence with humoral theory, suggesting that climate and natural surroundings shape the physical and mental traits of various human populations. Originating in ancient Greece and later adopted by medieval and Renaissance scholars, this concept was later used to justify centuries of European colonialism. However, Geohumoralism is no longer accepted as a legitimate science due to its lack of empirical evidence and inherent cultural and historical biases.

Historically, the four corners of the earth were dominated by one of the four primary races: **Africans**, **Native Americans**, **Asians**, and **Europeans**.

South – Black Race (Africans)
- *Characteristics:* Historically linked to a choleric temperament (hot, dry climates).
- *Temperament:* Restless, aggressive, excitable, impulsive, optimistic, and active.
- *Blood Type:* Commonly type O.
- *Contributions:* Known for their imagination and artistic expressions, particularly through ornaments.
- *Symbolism:* Represent "Beauty" because it is the direction of the sun at its highest point, representing the peak of the day and the beauty of creation.
- *Historical Context:* Considered the oldest of the ethnicities, dominating early human history.
- *Lineage:* Descendants of Nuh's (Noah's) second son Khem/Ham.
- *Season:* Summer (heat, vitality, and the peak of the natural cycle).

East – Yellow Race (Asians)
- *Characteristics:* Associated with a sanguine temperament due to their hot and wet environment.
- *Temperament:* Sociable, responsible, outgoing, carefree, docile, and submissive to leaders.
- *Blood Types:* Predominantly type B and type O.
- *Contributions:* Renowned for their ideas, particularly through ideographic writing systems.
- *Symbolism:* Represent "Wisdom" due to the rising sun, symbolizing enlightenment, knowledge, and the beginning of a new day.

- *Historical Context:* Populated the vast and diverse regions of Asia.
- *Lineage:* Traditionally linked to Nuh's youngest son, Japheth.
- *Season:* Spring (renewal, rebirth, growth, and new beginnings)

West – Red Race (Native Americans)

- *Characteristics:* Associated with a phlegmatic temperament due to their cold and wet environment.[26]
- *Temperament:* Passive, peaceful, thoughtful, controlled, calm, and patient.
- *Blood Type:* Often type O.
- *Contributions:* Mathematics and geometry.
- *Symbolism:* Represent "Strength" due to the direction where the sun sets, marking the end of the day's labors.
- *Historical Context:* Indigenous to the Americas, with strong cultural ties to the land.
- *Lineage:* Linked to Japheth.
- *Season:* Autumn (maturity, harvest, and the cycle of life coming to fruition).

North – White Race (Europeans)

- *Characteristics:* Associated with a melancholic temperament (cold, wet environments).
- *Temperament:* Anxious, moody, rigid, reserved, quiet, and unsociable.
- *Blood Type:* Predominantly type A.
- *Contributions:* Advancements in science and technology.
- *Symbolism:* Represent "Intelligence" and "Weakness" due to harsh climates.
- *Historical Context:* Populated Europe and dominated

---

26 Note: Native American tribes lived in a vast geographic range and diverse climates, therefore it's inaccurate to broadly categorize their environment as cold and wet.

recent history through colonial expansion.

- *Lineage:* Descendants of Nuh's son Japheth.
- *Season:* Winter (cold climates and the characteristics needed for such environments).

10. Children of Nuh: Nuh had three surviving sons, HAM, SHEM, AND JAPHETH.

Narrated Samurah bin Jundab: that the Messenger of Allah (ﷺ) said: "Sam (Shem) was the father of Arabs, Yafith (Japheth) was the father of Romans, and Ham was the father of Ethiopians."[27]

Today, the descendants of Japheth are traditionally associated with populations in **Europe, Central Asia, and the Americas**—often grouped under broad ethnic labels such as Caucasian or various Asian groups. The descendants of Ham are historically linked to populations across **Africa**, typically referred to as Black or African ethnicities. The descendants of Shem, or the Semitic peoples—including Arabs, Hebrews, and their kin—are centered in the **Middle East**, a sacred zone that, in Islamic geography, occupies the spiritual and historical heart of the world. It is from this central nexus that the world's civilizations radiate outward.

11. Dimensions of the Human Experience: Going into a deeper layer, we examine the four key dimensions that make up a human being:

- **Mental**: The mental-conscious mind governs the entire human, controlling his senses, thoughts, and **will**. The center of activity of the mind is the head. The mind can contemplate its internal being through senses, emotions, and intellectual impulses. Through the spinal cord, it spreads communication between the three vital centers in the human being: the abdomen, chest, and head.

---

27   Grade: Da'if (Darussalam): Jami` at-Tirmidhi 3931."

- **Emotional**: The emotional-astral body regulates the respiratory and circulatory organs and all their auxiliaries. The center of the astral body is the heart. The astral body is directed by feelings, morality, and reasoning, which manifest itself to the conscious mind via the expression of emotion.

- **Physical**: The physical body supports the mind with the senses of touch and taste. The material body is renewed through food, which is digested in the abdomen. The physical body is made up of the skeleton, the muscles, digestive organs, and all their auxiliaries.

- **Spiritual**: The spiritual-psychic heart moves all the elements that make up the human organism. The physical organs attached to the psychic being are the nervous system and all its auxiliaries (cerebellum). The center of activity for the spiritual psychic being is the heart, which functions as the vital energy carried by the blood, which is transformed by the cerebellum into nervous energy. The nervous system spreads movement throughout the organism and supplies the conscious mind with the necessary elements for developing thoughts and imagination.

12. Center: Finally, the innermost circle reveals the Ka'aba, the physical symbol of Tawhid that unites all Muslims throughout the earth towards a central place of worship (both *salat* and *hajj* rituals). *In essence*, the Ka'aba is a location that unites the world of the physical bodies (*alam-i-jisam*) and the world of the spirits (*alam-i-arwah*). The sacred geometry found in its physical design and the rituals required are intended to link the body and the spirit with the Creator of the heavens and the earth.

The Ka'aba is the earthly house of Allah; directly above it lies the *Baitul Ma'mur*, the heavenly home of Allah. It is believed that Adam was the first to erect the foundation for the Ka'aba in that exact location. Later, Ibrahim and his son Isma'il built an ancient version of the Ka'aba, which was built in the desert valley then known as *Bakka*. For the last 1447 years, there has been a constant flow of Muslims making *Tawaf* (going around) the Ka'aba in Mecca. This is an Islamic ritual wherein visitors must run three units around the Ka'aba, followed by walking four times at a leisurely pace, totaling 7 units. The Ka'aba is the holiest location in the world for Muslims and is the direction that all Muslims must face to pray five times each day, totaling 17 *rakats* (prayer units).

It represents **UNITY, BEAUTY, BALANCE** *and* **HARMONY.**

The model of the medicine wheel depicted on the next page (fig. 12) represents the Spiritual (outer ring), into the Physical World (middle ring), then the Spiritual in the Physical World (inner ring). The outer ring represents the Unifying and Transcendent source of all creation. The inner ring represents the created four classical elements, along with the four seasons, four humours, four primary organs, and four categorical races as manifested in the Physical world. The innermost ring represents the four dimensions of human experience—mental, emotional, physical, spiritual, with the Ka'aba at the center being the physical location from where we journey back toward Divine Unity. The figure below does not depict the Semetic peoples, but their presence is implied in this center space, embodying the spiritual and historical center from which the world's communities radiate.

This model links man's internal state with his environment. Traditionally, Biology is an Exoteric science that studies the observable, factual details of the living world. Esoteric science, on the other hand, reveals the divine structure of the universe, emphasizing the interconnected balance inherent in creation. While modern biology examines physical life, true knowledge lies in synthesizing both perspectives—recognizing that the material world reflects a deeper spiritual reality. This modified version of the Medicine Wheel attempts to synthesize the basic principles of human existence, balancing the physical, emotional, mental, and spiritual dimensions of life.

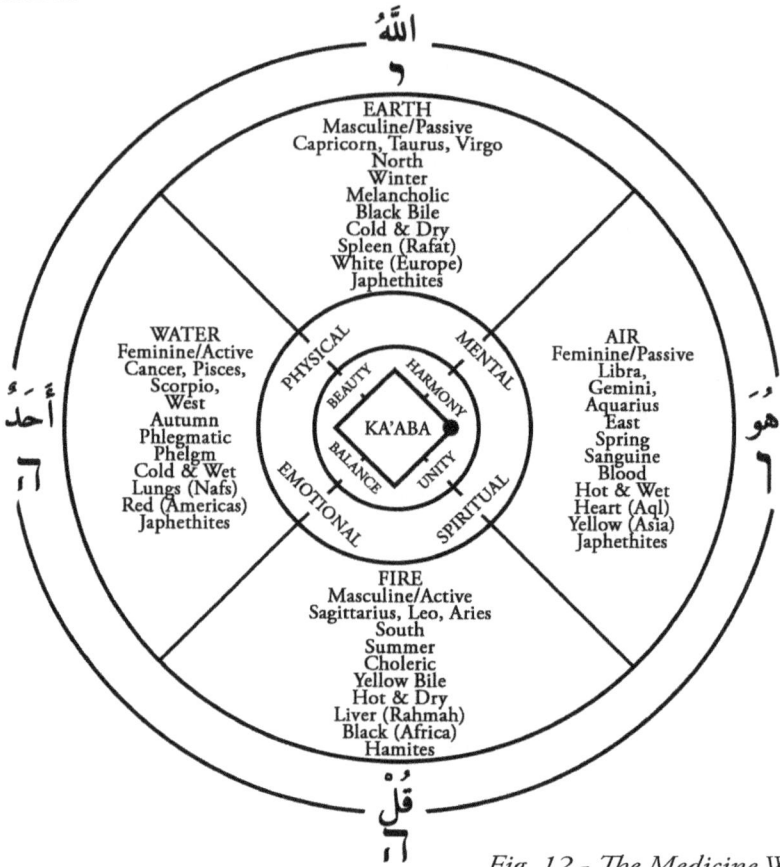

اللّهُ

أَحَد

هُوَ

قُلْ

EARTH
Masculine/Passive
Capricorn, Taurus, Virgo
North
Winter
Melancholic
Black Bile
Cold & Dry
Spleen (Rafat)
White (Europe)
Japhethites

WATER
Feminine/Active
Cancer, Pisces,
Scorpio,
West
Autumn
Phlegmatic
Phelgm
Cold & Wet
Lungs (Nafs)
Red (Americas)
Japhethites

AIR
Feminine/Passive
Libra,
Gemini,
Aquarius
East
Spring
Sanguine
Blood
Hot & Wet
Heart (Aql)
Yellow (Asia)
Japhethites

FIRE
Masculine/Active
Sagittarius, Leo, Aries
South
Summer
Choleric
Yellow Bile
Hot & Dry
Liver (Rahmah)
Black (Africa)
Hamites

PHYSICAL · MENTAL · EMOTIONAL · SPIRITUAL
BEAUTY · HARMONY · BALANCE · UNITY
KA'ABA

Fig. 12 - The Medicine Wheel

Humanity is united at the Ka'aba, located at the earth's center. Much like the celestial bodies revolve in precise orbits, humanity orbits around a divine focal point, reinforcing the idea that existence is not random but governed by cosmic and spiritual order. The genetic variations among humanity are part of Allah's design, reflecting the diversity and balance present throughout creation. The active fluids and organs inside of us impact our temperaments, which correspond to our natural environment, seasons, and directional energies. Our temperaments have been categorized into four distinct types, paralleling the four primary elements—earth, water, air, and fire—that govern both human nature and the material world. Just as elements combine to form life, the human being is a fusion of body, mind, and spirit, reflecting the unity of creation.

86

This spiritual and material synthesis is what ancient people conceptualized as **astrobiology**—the recognition that humanity is not separate from the cosmos but a microcosm of it. The universe and earth are living, dynamic entities, operating under divine laws that govern both the seen and unseen worlds. The spiritual essence of man descended from the higher realms into physical form, illustrating the Quranic principle that humanity was created from clay but infused with a divine soul (38:71-72). This dual existence—material and spiritual—demands that humans seek balance, aligning their earthly actions with their celestial origins.

Understanding the microcosm of bodily humors and the macrocosm of climates, celestial movements, and energy flows deepens our awareness of our role in Allah's grand design. The interconnectedness of all things, from the smallest atom to the vastest galaxy, reinforces the truth that all knowledge, whether biological or metaphysical, ultimately leads back to Allah. This chart bridges matter and spirit, allowing us to decode the elements that shape both our physical and spiritual realities. By merging scientific observation with divine wisdom, we gain a deeper understanding of life's purpose to serve as khulafa of creation while striving toward spiritual ascension.

LIFE BALANCE

When examining human biology and psychology with *Moon Consciousness*, we understand that negative elemental forces within humans are manifestations of our lower *nafs* (self) and our *qareen* (a companion from the jinn). The lower nafs is where our base passions and desires reside, attaching us to the material phenomena of the world. In Islamic teachings, we are commanded to strive against the inclinations of our lower nafs and our qareen to align ourselves with the positive spiritual polarity. For many, their lower nafs and qareen have overpowered their spiritual core (*ruh*), diminishing their connection to the divine and obscuring their *fitrah* (the spirit's original intellect; an inner compass aligned with Divine truth).

This spiritual hardening is often due to a disconnection from the ultimate heart softener, **the Quran**.

The Quran, the final revelation from the Creator, teaches us that life was created for a profound purpose. It provides a comprehensive framework for understanding the role and function of all knowledge. According to Islamic belief, the creation of angels and the physics they uphold, the jinn and their means of interacting with us, and all biological entities— humans, animals, insects, plants, and microbes—exist to know Allah and manifest His divine will on Earth.

Historically, humans—the dominant species of the biological realm—understood their greater purpose. But through strategic efforts over time, much of that awareness has been lost. Ancient societies recognized that the 'mind' of the Creator was the source of all matter in the universe. Since the Industrial Revolution, societies around the world have become more materialistic and less conscious of our spirit, which is the force that governs our material bodies. This has resulted in a "matter before mind" perspective of the world.

However, humanity is presently on the cusp of the greatest awakening the world has ever witnessed. This awakening was prophesied by all the Prophets and Messengers that Allah had sent to the world. Today, irreligious humans have gained dominance over the earth and are doing with it what they deem to be best, but they are mistaken. Those who are the rightful inheritors of this authority will lead this world towards the aim in which it was created. First, to do so, we must rediscover what this purpose is.

UNDERSTANDING THE DIVINE QUADRIVIUM

We conclude Chapter 1 by presenting the *Divine Quadrivium* as a fundamental framework of education that encapsulates the core principles evident in all of Allah's creation. It serves as a guide for understanding the universe as a unified whole, integrating physical, spiritual, and intellectual dimensions.

The number four symbolizes stability and completeness, appearing repeatedly in nature, mathematics, and philosophy. This chapter explores various tetrads reflecting Allah's wisdom, including the constructs of the universe, states of matter, dimensions of space, phases of the moon, and the forces of nature, as well as the angels that oversee them. Additionally, it examines the foundations of knowledge and draws lessons from the allegorical story of Adam, Hawwah, and Shaytan.

The concept of tetrads extends into spiritual and cosmological symbolism, encompassing the Tetragrammaton, zodiac groupings, elements, directions, seasons, and the cyclical stages of life. These tetrads also connect to core temperaments, humors, spiritual and physical components, and the races historically found in the four corners of the earth. By exploring these patterns, we uncover the universe's intricate design and humanity's role within it.

This chapter identifies the hierarchy of sapient beings and the four patterns shaping their world. To thrive in the material world, we must understand the branches of science, universal forces, life's diversity, and the four elements. This foundation bridges the physical and spiritual realms, guiding us toward harmony with the natural order and our higher purpose.

Allah: At the pinnacle of this hierarchy is Allah, the Creator of all energy, matter, and forms. Allah's supremacy is absolute, governing all spiritual and physical laws of the universe.

Angels: Created from a form of luminous light, angels are powerful beings tasked with executing Allah's commands without deviation. Their existence and actions are solely to fulfill divine will, making them unparalleled in their obedience and purity.

Jinnkind: Created from a smokeless, fiery substance, jinn have the ability to take physical forms and interact with the biological realm via chemical processes. They possess free will and, like humans, are accountable for their actions.

Mankind: Humans—and, by extension, all living creatures composed of solid matter (plants and animals)—inhabit the material realm. While flora and fauna represent sentient beings without free will and are bound to earthly existence, humans alone possess a unique spiritual capacity to channel their bodies and souls toward actions that please Allah. This capacity elevates humanity above all other creatures, opening the door to eternal spiritual growth and a destiny beyond the physical world.

The Divine Quadrivium is a conceptual framework that includes four essential categories, each providing a deeper understanding of the universe and its intricate design:

1. Branches of Knowledge:

To understand the essence of sapient beings, we explore four key branches of knowledge:

- *Metaphysics:* The study of existence and the nature of reality.

- *Physics:* The science of matter, energy, and their interactions.

- *Chemistry:* The study of substances and their transformations.

- *Biology:* The science of life and living organisms.

2. Forces of the Universe:

Four fundamental forces hold the universe together:

- *Electromagnetic Force:* Governs the interactions between charged particles.

- *Strong Force:* Binds protons and neutrons in the atomic nucleus.

- *Weak Force:* Responsible for radioactive decay and nuclear reactions.

- *Gravity:* The force of attraction between masses.

3. Essential Physical Life Forms:

Four physical life forms are essential to the survival of humanity:

- *Microbes (bacteria, viruses, archaea):* foundational cycles sustained by Divine will.

- *Flora (plants):* sustained by angelic decree; convert sunlight and soil into oxygen and nourishment.

- *Fungi (mushrooms, decomposers):* echo the jinn's transformative spark as they recycle matter and renew creation.

- *Fauna (animals through humans):* culminating in Allah's vicegerents endowed with intellect and moral duty.

4. Core Elements:

Four core elements sustain the heavens and the earth:

- *Fire:* Represents energy and transformation.

- *Water:* Symbolizes life and purification.

- *Air:* Essential for respiration and sustenance of life.

- *Earth:* Provides the foundation for all biological existence.

In conclusion, the Divine Quadrivium enables us to have a holistic view of the outer universe and our role within it. This framework deepens our grasp of the material and external spiritual worlds and motivates us to align our actions with divine purpose. Through this integrated approach, we can explore the mysteries of the external world with a greater appreciation for the interconnectedness of all creation, guiding us toward a more harmonious and enlightened existence.

ALLAH

Metaphysics
Electromagnetic
Microbes
FIRE

HUMANS

Biology
Gravity
Fauna
EARTH

ANGELS

Physics
Strong Force
Flora
WATER

JINN

Chemistry
Weak Force
Fungi
AIR

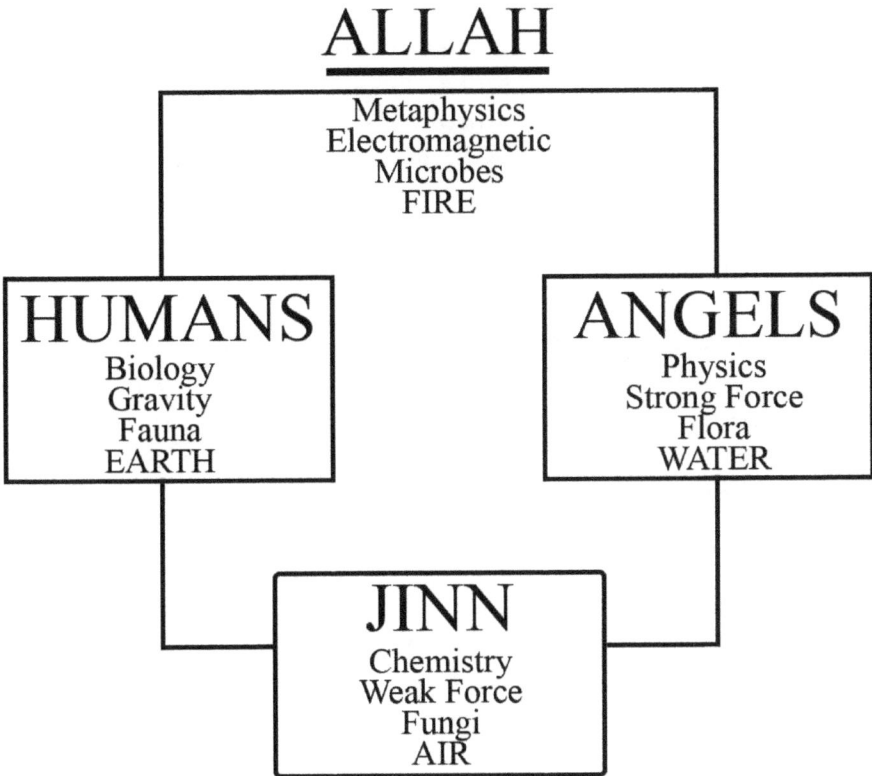

Fig. 13 - Summary of the Quadrivium.
Note: All pairings above are symbolic and meant to illustrate reflections of divine order in the cosmos. They do not represent equivalences, and nothing in creation resembles or encompasses Allah, who is beyond all categories

Understanding the Matrix in Fig. 13

In the previous sections, we examined how Allah, as the ultimate source of all existence, created four distinct realms—Metaphysics, Physics, Chemistry, and Biology—each reflecting a different aspect of His will. Rather than diving into every intricate sub-category, the heart of the matter is this: each of these "quadrants" represents a unique pathway through which Divine wisdom unfolds.

1. ***Metaphysics (Allah).*** At the very center stands Allah, the One who transcends all categories. All laws—both spiritual and physical—flow from His absolute command. In essence, every other corner of creation finds its origin, sustenance, and ultimate purpose in Him.

2. ***Physics (Angels).*** Just below the center, we find the realm of the angels—beings of pure light tasked with executing Divine decrees. Their role is to maintain cosmic order, channeling unseen forces in perfect obedience. They are not driven by desire or hesitation; their sole purpose is to carry out Allah's commands in every corner of creation.

3. ***Chemistry (Jinn).*** Next comes the realm of the jinn, created from a smokeless, fiery substance. Unlike angels, jinn possess free will and can interact with the material world—sometimes weaving invisible "chemical" influences into human affairs. This fiery domain bridges the unseen and the seen, reminding us that there are forces at work beyond our immediate perception.

4. ***Biology (Humans).*** At the material frontier sits humanity, formed from clay and sustained by earthly elements. Though composed of solid matter like plants and animals, humans occupy a special place in the

94

HISTORY OF EDUCATION BOOK ONE

Divine plan. We alone have the capacity to choose, to seek knowledge, and to align our actions with Allah's will. In doing so, we unlock the potential for true spiritual growth—rising above the purely physical plane.

Taken together, these four domains—central Divine Reality (Allah), angelic obedience (Physics), jinn's intermediate "chemical" influence (Chemistry), and human agency (Biology)—form a complete picture of creation's order. Rather than memorizing every technical detail, we can hold this simple framework in our minds and hearts:

- Allah at the core,

- Angels as the arms of divine order,

- Jinn as the hidden bridge,

- Humans as the conscious stewards of the visible world.

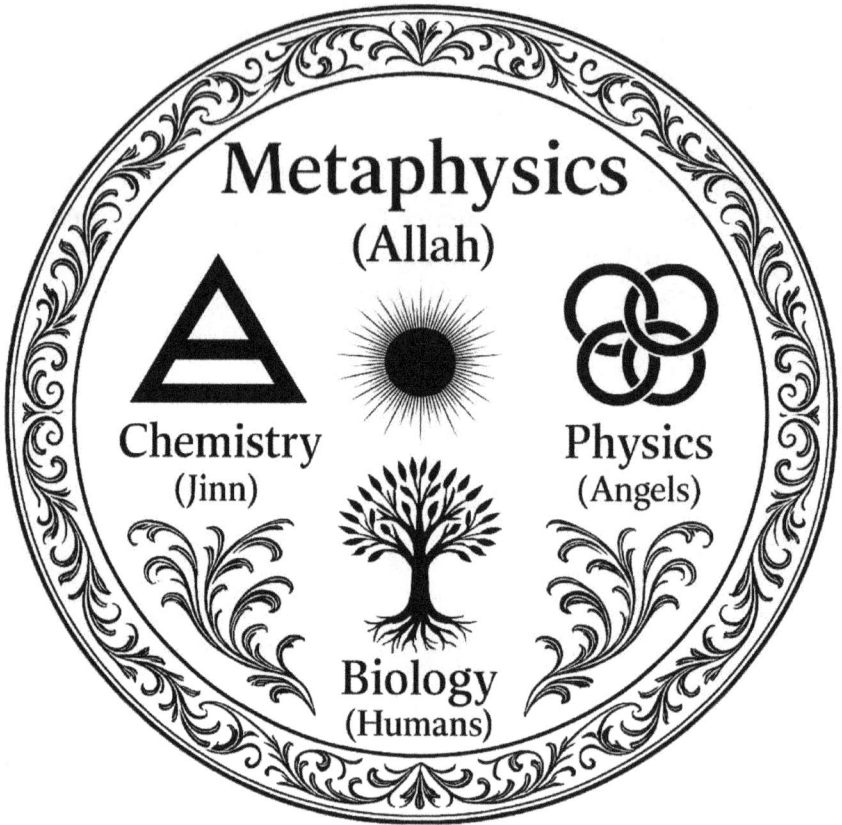

Fig. 14 - *The Divine Quadrivium: Metaphysics (Allah) at the center, with Chemistry (Jinn), Physics (Angels), and Biology (Humans) forming the outer quadrants.*

CHAPTER 2
THE DIVINE TRIVIUM

SECTION 1
IBLIS'S KNOWLEDGE

Ibn 'Umar said that Prophet Muhammad ﷺ said, "Allah created four things with His hand: the Throne, the Pen, Eden, and Adam. Then He said to the rest of creation... "Be" and it was."

Fifty thousand years before the creation of the Heavens and the earth, Allah, while His **Throne** stood over water, created the Pen with His own hands. He commanded it to record all events for eternity, capturing every detail of the past, present, and future (Tirmidhi).[28] This divine plan, known as **Qadr** (fate or predestination), represents the sixth pillar of faith in Islam, aligning all cosmic events and life forms with Allah's ultimate purpose. This knowledge is contained in a text called the Lawhul-Mahfoodh, the Preserved Tablet.

---

28 Note: The 50,000 years mentioned should not be interpreted as being equivalent to the conventional measure of time with which we are familiar.

The **Pen** symbolizes knowledge, wisdom, and education— preserving writing, symbols, and drawings for future reference while transmitting knowledge across generations.

After creating the heavens and the earth in six days, Allah created **Adam** with His own hands on the seventh day.[29] Each stage of creation on each preceding day was in preparation for Adam and his offspring.

- On the First Day, Allah created dust.

- On the Second Day, He created the mountains.

- On the Third Day, He created the trees.

- On the Fourth Day, He created the *makruhat*, disliked actions.

- On the Fifth Day, He created Nur/Nun and Angels.

- On the Sixth Day, 2000 years before the creation of Adam, He created beasts (animals) and Jinn.[30]

- On the Seventh Day, in the later period of the day, Adam was created and all that came before was readied to serve him.

The macrocosm of the universe was thus created to accommodate the microcosm of man. Allah began creation with the Pen, the tool of enlightenment, and finalized it with **Adam**, the enlightened being. Adam was shaped from clay extracted from various parts of the earth, possibly containing a mixture of fossils and elements from all previous earthly life such as Denisovans, Neanderthals and other proto-humans. His children were born with diverse colors, hair textures, and

---

29   Note: These "days" are not the "24-hour" day and night cycles of the earth. The word "day", in Arabic "Yaum" also carries the meaning of "Age" or "Epoch" in Islam.

30   Narrated by Abu Huraira in Sahih Muslim 2789; Quran: 41:9-10.

facial features, reflecting the different regions of the earth from which his elements were taken. Scientists today confirm that the human body is composed of the same elements found in the earth, including oxygen, calcium, sulfur, and magnesium—with geographic regions sharing elemental similarities with their native populations.

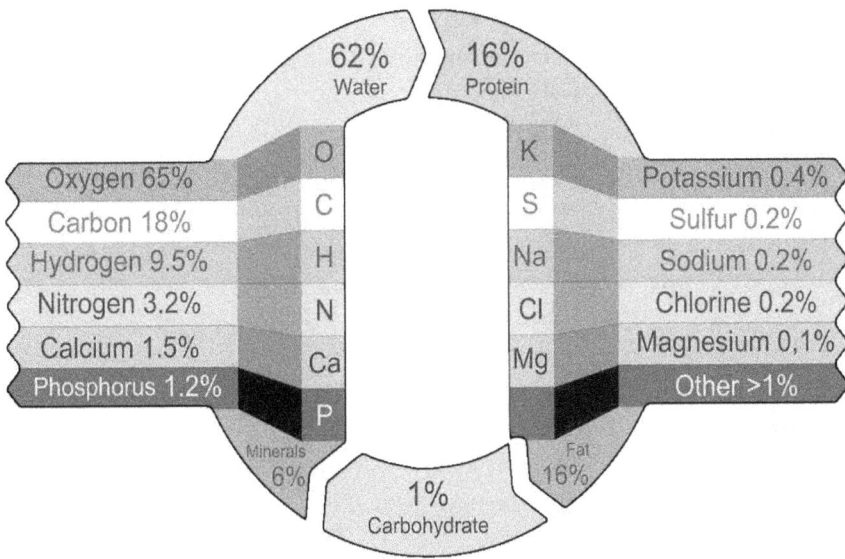

Fig. 15 - Elemental Composition of the Human Body

Adam's creation unfolded in stages: first as dust (turab, 3:59), then as sticky clay (tin, 37:11), then black mud (hama'im masnun, 15:26), and finally as hardened clay (salsalin kal-fakhkhar, 55:14), into which Allah breathed life. Scientifically, this suggests that atoms and matter preceded the formation of Adam, as all material things are composed of these fundamental building blocks.

Eden, the garden, was the **third creation Allah made with His own hands**. Adam was created within its lush surroundings, filled with countless plants and trees. His transition from lifelessness to life is described in the Quran as a process similar to the growth of plants from the earth (18:37; 71:17).

99

Before Adam was granted life, Allah informed the angels that He would create a *bashar* (mortal human) and appoint him as a vicegerent (*khalifah*) on earth. However, before his soul was breathed into him, Adam remained a lifeless body outside the gates of Eden for 40 years, which is a reminder that man was once nothing (76:1) and should never be arrogant about his existence. For he is not capable of granting life to himself.

The angels and Iblis would pass by Adam's lifeless body in awe and fear. While the angels did not probe further, as it was not their directive, Iblis, drawn by a sense of curiosity, lingered to study Adam more deeply. Unlike the angels, Iblis was not directly informed about the purpose of Adam's creation. He did, however, deduce that Adam was created for a significant reason. Observing the external features of Adam's body, Iblis gained a general understanding of his structure. He struck Adam's lifeless body, producing a loud, echoing sound like pottery. From this, Iblis inferred that Adam, and by extension, all humans, are hollow, demonstrating **deductive reasoning**.

Afterward, Iblis entered Adam's mouth to study his internal composition. He examined the smallest parts of Adam's body and observed how they interacted. Discovering the fragility of Adam's internal organs, Iblis concluded that humans are inherently vulnerable. This process reflects **inductive reasoning**. By combining deductive and inductive analyses, Iblis formed a comprehensive understanding of Adam and identified potential ways to influence him.

This method of inquiry mirrors what academic researchers do today: studying phenomena and events in the world to develop knowledge. Research is typically conducted for one of two reasons. The first is to fill a gap in the existing body of knowledge. Researchers with this goal are often positivists who study natural phenomena and believe in a single, objective reality governed by general laws. For positivists, objective matter takes precedence over the subjective mind. They often use a **quantitative approach**, employing statistical analyses of numerical data or information that can be converted into numbers. This reflects an inductive approach to research.

The second motivation for research is to solve a specific problem. Scholars who adopt this perspective are often interpretivists. They study human experiences and believe in multiple subjective realities that must be interpreted. For interpretivists, the subjective mind (ideas) takes precedence over objective matter. They typically employ a **qualitative method**, deeply analyzing verbal data and identifying themes that describe phenomena. This approach reflects deductive reasoning.

Finally, the **mixed-methods approach** combines elements of both perspectives. It seeks to provide a comprehensive understanding of phenomena by integrating qualitative and quantitative methods. Mixed-methods research involves qualitative exploration to describe unique circumstances and generate new insights while also employing quantitative techniques to provide statistically useful information that can be generalized to other situations.

Like a researcher, Iblis explored Adam's body in hopes of discovering ways to "crack the code" of the elements from which he was composed. After the code was deciphered, Iblis found ways to merge the inorganic compounds from which he was created with the organic elements from which Adam was created. Scientifically, this is the branch of knowledge where two fields are merged: Biology and Chemistry.

Biochemistry explains the processes of life and the ways in which chemical interactions sustain living organisms. Jinn are a necessary component in the lives of the children of Adam. Their elements flow through our bodies. As Prophet Muhammad ﷺ taught us, "The shaytan flows through man like blood" (Bukhari and Muslim).

Science, particularly biochemistry, does not directly explain how the shayateen bond with and interact with us. To comprehend these interactions, we must examine chemical reactions and compare them with insights from the Quran and the Sunnah. Often, there isn't a direct link between these disciplines because science is ever-evolving, while Islam offers fixed spiritual truths with multiple layers of meaning. However, by integrating the revealed signs of:

1. *Ayat Allah fi'l-Quran:* The Signs of Allah in the Quran.

2. *Ayat Allah fi'l-kawn*: The Signs of Allah in the world.

From this, we can draw analogies to arrive at a balanced interpretation of how the metaphysical world of the jinn interacts chemically with us in the biological realm.

Using analogy, we surmise that Iblis discovered all of Adam's bones and organs and compared them to that which he was already familiar within the heavenly and earthly realms. Iblis entered Adam through the mouth. Islamically, we are taught to close our mouths when yawning because that is the primary gateway for jinn possession.[31] From the mouth, Iblis likely went up to the head, which is the central location from which jinn possess humans and control their bodies. In the head, Iblis likely compared Adam's skull to a dark and mysterious cave. Upon deeper exploration, Iblis likely explored the brain, finding its core—the pineal gland.

Also known as the "third eye," the **pineal gland** processes light and regulates circadian rhythms by producing melatonin. It functions electrically by receiving and transmitting energy and is often linked to spiritual awareness and consciousness. This energy is processed through the **thalamus**, the brain's relay station, which serves a neutral/balancing role by mediating both electric (masculine) and magnetic (feminine) energies between the pineal and pituitary glands.

The **hypothalamus**, functioning as the regulator, ensures harmony between these energies by maintaining homeostasis and regulating bodily functions such as temperature, hunger, and mood. The **pineal gland's electric nature** symbolizes **masculine**, outward-projecting energy, while the **pituitary gland**, known as the "master gland," is **magnetic** and associated with **feminine energy**, attracting and regulating bodily

---

31   The son of Abu Said al-Khudri reported on the authority of his father that Allah's Messenger ﷺ said: *When one of you yawns, he should keep his mouth shut with the help of his hand, for it is the devil that enters therein* (Muslim).

responses such as growth, metabolism, and reproduction. Together, these systems demonstrate the sophisticated communication network within the brain, where the **thalamus balances** and the **hypothalamus integrates** the electric and magnetic forces, coordinating both neural and endocrine functions to maintain overall homeostasis.

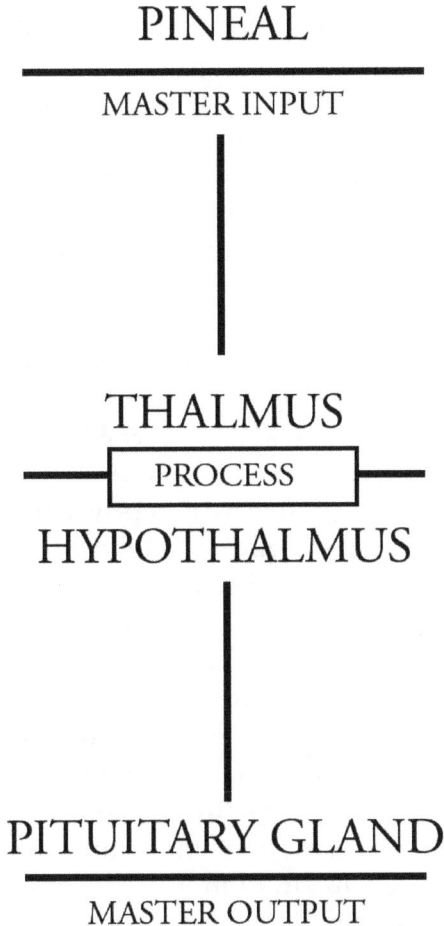

PINEAL

MASTER INPUT

THALMUS

PROCESS

HYPOTHALMUS

PITUITARY GLAND

MASTER OUTPUT

Fig. 16 - The Master Gland

Iblis may have likened the pineal gland to the moon after discovering its strong connection to the light of the sun and it being activated at night.[32] In the daytime, the pinecone-shaped gland produces and secretes serotonin, which is the chemical responsible for regulating our mood, and at night, it secretes melatonin into the bloodstream, which makes us feel sleepy. During sleep, the pineal gland acts like an antenna and allows energy, signals, and frequencies to enter from the astral dimensions (the heavens) and produce visual imagery. These are dreams.

In Islam, dreams are considered authentic sources of knowledge, as they are considered 1/46th of prophecy (Muslim). As Ibn al-Qayyium explains in his *Kitab al-Ruh*, the nefs, (soul) travels out of the nostrils during sleep and comes into the presence of Allah, prostrating before Him only if it is pure. Afterward, it can experience the *Alam al-Arwah* (the world of spirits) or meet with the *Anfas* (souls) that have died or are still alive. If the nefs is good, it will convey the truth of what was seen to the ruh (spirit), and this is called a 'truthful dream.' However, some of what is learned in the dream is true, and some may be false. If the nefs comes from a person who is a liar who desires that which is deceptive, then that nefs will meet with Shaytan mid-air and mix the truth with the false. He will wake up confused about what he/she saw. These dreams are facilitated by the pineal gland.

The pineal gland has long been recognized for its role in spiritual experiences. French philosopher René Descartes (1596-1650) referred to it as the "seat of the soul." Modern studies confirm its production of melatonin, which regulates sleep-wake cycles and may influence spiritual awareness. Esoteric teachings argue that the third eye vibrates with intuition. Prayer or meditation can prolong the vibrations and open the third eye. After the third eye is open, a person can achieve altered states of consciousness and have improved intuition, inspiration, imagination, psychic ability, ability to remember dreams, astral projection, and remote viewing

---

32   Bible: "The light of the body is the eye: if therefore thine eye be single, thy whole body shall be full of light."- Matthew 6:22

ability (sensing with the mind). The gland also releases dimethyltryptamine (DMT), a powerful psychedelic linked to near-death and out-of-body experiences. Essentially, the pineal gland and the chemicals it produces allow a person to tap into the vibratory universe around us and to perceive higher spiritual realms and time-space dimensions.

However, the pineal gland's functions can be impaired by environmental factors. Research shows that fluoride calcifies the pineal gland, preventing it from functioning effectively. When fluoride accumulates in the body, it results in calcification, which reduces melatonin levels, leading to disturbed sleep cycles and weaker spiritual sensitivity. Likewise, other environmental toxins, such as chlorine, pharmaceutical drugs, and genetically modified foods, can calcify the pineal gland. When calcification occurs, it suppresses a person's spiritual and physical health, leading to conditions like schizophrenia, where individuals see, hear, and think about non-existent realities. These symptoms appear to arise because shayateen exploit the weakened state of the calcified pineal gland, causing the victim to be confused about truth and falsehood.

A 2023 systematic review found that 61.65% of the global population have calcified pineal glands, suggesting that this phenomenon is widespread and growing. Additionally, pineal calcification is twice as common in American whites as in American blacks. Rates of calcification are slightly higher in American blacks than in indigenous Africans, possibly due to the racial mixture of American blacks.

Being that Eurocentric thought has shaped global affairs for the past 500 years. This prompts the question: what entity or power fuels this dominance?

Meanwhile, Black and Aboriginal peoples—believed to have especially large, well-preserved pineal glands—have endured the harshest subjugation. That history prompts a further question: what, exactly, is this power trying to suppress?

In the next chapter, we will attempt to answer these questions.

Mid-Brain

Corpus Callosum

Thalmus

Hypothalmus

Pituitary Gland

Cerebellum

Pons

Mammillary Bond

Medulla Oblangata

Spinal Chord

Corpus Callosum

Thalmus

Medulla Oblangata

Hypothalmus

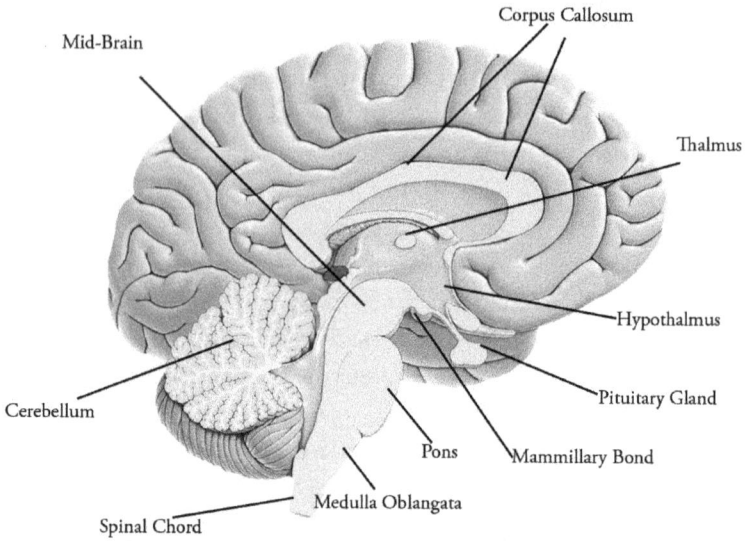

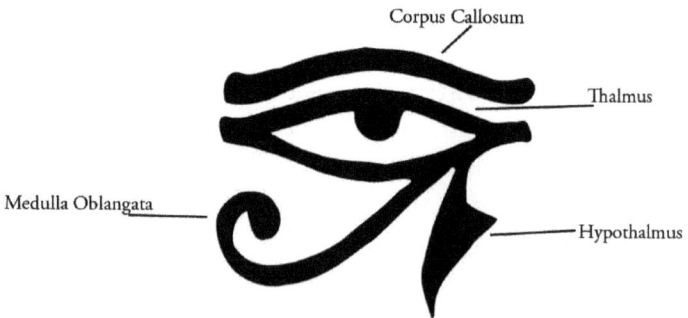

Fig. 17 - Anatomy of the Pineal Gland, depicted symbolically in Egyptian Hieroglyphics, known also as 'The Eye of Horus,' historically regarded as the 'Inner Eye.'

Iblis might have realized that he would have to exert much effort to control this gland because from there, he could influence Adam's thoughts. In later generations, scientists discovered that we all have higher levels of the chemicals in this gland until adolescence, wherein, for many, it becomes calcified and rigid, no longer able to take in sunlight or exchange energy. Calcification of the gland occurs through chemicals such as fluoride, chlorine, pharmaceutical drugs, genetically modified foods, exposure to toxins in the environment, and poor health.

In Islam, we know that both jinn and humans can affect a person with *ayn* (evil eye). Ayn begins with a deep jealousy from the core of one's lower emotions. This infatuation grows into sihr, which becomes or attracts shayateen from the Jinn. Iblis was the first to commit the spiritual crime of evil eye after seeing Adam's creation and envying him. We are taught that most of those who die from the Prophet's *ummah*, community, will die from Allah's decree first, then evil eye second.[33]

It is believed that the pineal gland may be the "eye" where this evil is manifested. While our external eyes capture the image of a person, the hidden intentions of discontent, resentment, and hatred arise from the *qalb* (the heart), for that is the source where good and bad intentions are formed, and the qalb is powered by the ruh (spirit). The spirit is linked to the pineal gland. For it is in that gland where imagined good or bad visions can be created and manifested in the real world. First, the envying person must use their imagination to construct a vivid mental picture of harm towards an enemy. Then, that emotional force encompasses his whole being. Finally, the envier controls that force by his will and hurls it against his victim.

From the head, Iblis likely went further down Adam's body. He may have observed that the lungs are shaped like birds and enable humans to roam freely through space. He may have also discovered the heart and likened it to the sun due to its central location and it being the power source for all within the body. From the heart, he likely saw the intricate network of

33   Hadith: Nayl al-Awtar 3:278.

veins and arteries and compared them to two trees intersecting, both containing many branches stretching in many different directions. Moving to the intestines, Iblis may have seen that they resemble worms, both in shape and function, as they process and break down material for sustenance. In short, he may have concluded that all biology is astrobiology.

IBLIS'S STUDY OF THE ELEMENTS

Going deeper into Adam's intricate design, Iblis's knowledge of chemistry and biology may have led him to discover one of the key elements that makes a human: carbon.[34] Carbon is the 6th element on the periodic table and is the second most abundant element in the human body after oxygen. Carbon is essential for the functioning of the body's metabolism and is a critical component of DNA. Without Carbon, humans would not exist. Moreover, Carbon is fundamental for all organic compounds and life on Earth. The atomic structure of Carbon includes 6 protons, 6 neutrons, and 6 electrons—numerically represented as **6-6-6**, a number that would later be associated with materialism and deception. When the 4 outer electrons of carbon bond with 4 outer electrons of hydrogen, Methane (CH_4) is produced.[35] Methane is a colorless, odorless, highly flammable gas naturally produced during digestion.

This is one example of shayateen bonding with the 666 Carbon element in man. Examining this scientific fact, considering an authentic narration of Prophet Muhammad ﷺ we can understand the deeper wisdom contained.

Narrated Abu Huraira: Allah's Apostle said, "When the Adhan is pronounced Shaytan takes to his heels and passes wind with noise (darat) during his flight in order not to hear the Adhan. When the Adhan is completed, he comes back and again takes to his heels when the Iqama is pronounced, and after its completion, he returns again till he whispers into the heart of the person (to divert his attention from his prayer) and makes him remember things

---

34 Note: Chemicals consist of elements and Elements are the ingredients of chemicals.

35 Note: Atoms are composed of negatively charged electrons and a nucleus in the center that is home to positively charged protons and neutral neurons.

which he does not recall to his mind before the prayer and that causes him to forget how much he has prayed." (Bukhari)

Moreover, passing gas is one of the ways the state of *wudu* (ritualistic ablution) is broken. When a person is not in the state of wudu for a prolonged period, they are more susceptible to possession by the shayateen. Finally, Iblis entered the mouth of Adam's lifeless body and exited from the anus like gas.

Phosphorus, derived from the Greek term *Phōsphoros* ("bearer of light"), plays a unique role in understanding the bond between jinn and humans. Known in Latin as "Lucifer," phosphorus emits light in various forms. White phosphorus is highly reactive, igniting spontaneously above 86°F. It is used in fireworks and weaponry but can burn tissue and cause fatal damage if inhaled or ingested.

In contrast, red phosphorus is more stable and widely used, such as on match striker pads. When a match is struck, red phosphorus transforms into white phosphorus, creating fire. While safer at room temperature, red phosphorus can become highly dangerous when combined with compounds like chlorine or ammonium nitrate, often exploited in illegal production of methamphetamines.

During World War II, the Nazis distributed methamphetamine (*Pervitin*) to soldiers to enhance stamina, aggression, and wakefulness, allowing them to march for days without rest. This chemically induced state resembles the insatiable drive of Iblis—restless, relentless, and fueled by an unnatural fire that consumes rather than sustains.

Though often overlooked, red phosphorus was a key ingredient in the production of this drug. Thus, red phosphorus served not only to ignite fire, but to ignite war and distort the human soul—turning light into darkness.

Despite these hazardous properties, phosphorus is vital for life. It is abundant in feces, urine, and fertilizers, supporting crop growth. Within the body, it is a key component of bones, teeth, DNA, RNA, and ATP, underscoring its essential role in sustaining life.

After calcium, phosphorus is the second most abundant element in the body. When Carbon is mixed with oxygen, hydrogen, nitrogen, calcium, and phosphorus, we get 99% of the essential elements needed for human life. Analyzing this scientific fact in conjunction with the following authentic narrations of Prophet Muhammad ﷺ we can better understand the deeper wisdom contained.

Narrated Zayd ibn Arqam: The Apostle of Allah ﷺ *said: These privies are frequented by the jinns and devils. So when anyone amongst you goes there, he should say: «I seek refuge in Allah from male and female devils." (Abu-Dawud)*

Narrated Anas: Whenever the Prophet went to answer the call of nature, he would say, **Allahumma inni a'udhu bika minal khubuthi wal khaba'ith,** *O Allah, I seek refuge with You from all offensive and wicked things (evil deeds and evil spirits). (Bukhari)*

Shayateen prefer to frequent toilets and gather around human waste because, essentially, that is when they are in their element. Shayateen exist in a universe parallel to viruses, impurities, and the waste products of the human body.

After examining the available evidence, it appears as though **shayateen** flow through humans and exit as the chemical elements methane and phosphorus. These are the elements that cause a human to pass gas, urinate, or defecate. The exact details regarding how spiritual possession takes place are unknown, but we can pinpoint their physical manifestations as these elements that exit our bodies. In the external world, Iblis may have realized that he could help humans use phosphorus to kill and disfigure other humans by way of chemical weapons. However, as what applies to all elements, there is a positive to every negative. Phosphorus is a necessary evil because it necessitates life.

Iblis concluded his study with the **knowledge** that Adam was hollow and weak. He said to Adam's body, "If I am granted

111

power over you, I will destroy you, but if you are granted power over me, I will disobey you." From that moment, the eternal struggle between humanity and Iblis began. Many humans have forgotten the nature of their enemy, but Iblis and his followers have never forgotten their knowledge of us. Today, the war is waged not just on the spiritual battlefield, but also through scientific advancements, psychological manipulation, and material distractions.

Iblis's initial study of Adam corresponds to the way knowledge is pursued today, through a process of observation, analysis, and deduction. The difference is that true knowledge leads to enlightenment and submission to Allah, while corrupted knowledge leads to arrogance and defiance. This battle between divine wisdom and deceptive intelligence continues to shape the world, influencing the choices we make every day.

Understanding the forces at play allows us to navigate this struggle with clarity, ensuring that knowledge is preserved as a tool for truth rather than deception.

SECTION 2

THE ANGELS'
UNDERSTANDING

﴿ ... ثُمَّ عَرَضَهُمْ عَلَى ٱلْمَلَٰئِكَةِ فَقَالَ أَنۢبِـُٔونِى بِأَسْمَآءِ هَٰٓؤُلَآءِ إِن
كُنتُمْ صَٰدِقِينَ ﴾

﴿ قَالُواْ سُبْحَٰنَكَ لَا عِلْمَ لَنَآ إِلَّا مَا عَلَّمْتَنَآ إِنَّكَ أَنتَ ٱلْعَلِيمُ ٱلْحَكِيمُ ﴾

*...then He presented them to the angels and said, "Tell Me
the names of these, if what you say is true."*
*They replied, "Glory be to You! We have no knowledge
except what You have taught us. You are truly the All-
Knowing, All-Wise."*
(2:31-32).

When we examine how Allah communicates with His
creation, we find that each interaction is educational, offering
both explicit and symbolic truths that carry apparent and
hidden meanings for those with the understanding to grasp
them. Allah engages the humble in dialogue, unveiling truths
while simultaneously veiling deeper wisdom for those who

113

seek it with sincerity. Those who approach Allah with sincere intention find the doors to guidance open, while those who question with arrogance or with the intention of disobedience, like Iblis, are left in darkness, their access to true understanding becoming closed indefinitely (45:23).

This dynamic is illustrated in the conversation between Allah, the angels, and Iblis regarding Adam's status. Before creating Adam, Allah informed the angels of His intention to create humans and place them on earth to live for many generations. The angels were surprised by this and questioned Allah, asking why He would create a being that would cause corruption and bloodshed while they constantly praised Allah and gave thanks to Him. Their question was rooted in logic, as they had witnessed the actions of the jinn and other creatures, possibly including extinct species such as dinosaurs, mastodons, mammoths, and soulless proto-humans like Neanderthals, who acted without higher intellect or divine guidance.[36] These creatures caused various types of destruction in the natural environment and killed one another. The angels were commissioned to descend to the earth and fight them until they were driven into the depths of the sea. Allah responded to the angels, "I know that which you do not know" (2:30), indicating a deeper wisdom behind His creation of humanity.

After creating Adam through each of his stages, Allah created the nafs (soul) within him and then breathed the ruh (spirit) into him, igniting his faculties of hearing, sight, and consciousness (32:9; 38:72).[37] These three faculties—**hearing, seeing, and understanding**—form the basis of knowledge acquisition. First, one must hear things from others; then, one must see and attain them for oneself; finally, one must grasp their essence to understand their true nature. Although Adam was created as a fully-grown man, we can see evidence of these

36   Ibn Kathir states that many Mufassirun say that before Adam and Jinn, there were inhabitants called the 'Binn'. When Allah Ta'ala created the Jinn, they killed the 'Binn' and removed them from the surface of the earth. (Al Bidayah Wan Nihayah, vol. 1 pg. 90 and 112).

37   Note: The *Ruh* is from the realm of *Amr* (divine command) and the Nafs is from the realm of *Khalq* where Allah creates something.

developmental stages within children. For example, when memorizing prose, a child must first listen intently to how every word, phrase, and line is pronounced. Then, they must read the text for themselves numerous times. Finally, they learn the lines by heart and understand the overall meaning of the message.

When the Spirit was blown into Adam, his body began to transform from a clay figure into biological life. Bones, flesh, and muscles formed, and the heart began pumping blood. When the soul reached the head and nose, he sneezed and said, *"Al-hamdu li-llāhi rabbi l-'alamin"* (praise to Allah, Lord of the worlds). These were the first words uttered by a human. Allah said in response, *"YarhamukALLAH"* (May Allah show you Mercy).

The soul slowly began to descend to the abdomen. Adam bent down, marveling at his form, acknowledging the divine craftsmanship of his creation. He tried to raise himself up but was unable to do so because the spirit had not yet reached his legs. This occurred during the last hour of a Friday afternoon. Adam grew impatient and said, "Oh Allah, hasten it to completion before sunset." After it reached his legs, he asked if he could walk to greet the angels sitting in the distance. When he approached them, he said, "Assalamu alaikum" (Peace be upon you). They replied with, *"Wa alaykumu as-salam wa rahmatullahi wa barakatuh"* (May the peace, mercy, and blessings of Allah be with you too). Allah said, "Oh, Adam! This is your greeting and that of your offspring" (Bukhari).

Adam was created in a sequence mirroring the creation of the universe. Allah created the heavens before the earth, and Adam received his **body** before his **soul**, and finally, he was granted **intelligence**. In this way, the universe may be seen as composed of **intelligence, a soul, and a body**. Man, as we have said, is a microcosm of the universe.

This threefold nature of man can also be understood in another form. The **body** (al-jism) consists of **flesh, blood, and bones,** representing the physical structure and sensory experiences. The **soul** (al-nafs) comprises **energy, desires, and emotions,** and it manifests in three states: the **vegetal** state for basic life processes, the **animal** state for emotions and instincts, and the **rational** state for higher reasoning and intellect. The **intelligence** (al-'aql) consists of **rational thought, intuition, and consciousness**, linking the individual to higher spiritual insights and understanding.

Afterward, Allah taught Adam the names of all things. Then Allah commanded the angels to name these things, and they humbly admitted their lack of knowledge, affirming that Allah alone is *Al-Alim* (the All-Knowing) and *Al-Hakim* (the All-Wise) (2:31-32). These names illustrate Allah's comprehensive understanding of all that is beyond human perception. He knows the past, present, and future, and everything that has and will occur only happens in accordance with his perfect wisdom. He is the only one capable of truly judging the worth and reality of things.

Adam's first experience in creation was an educational encounter, emphasizing the foundational role of knowledge in human purpose. When Allah taught Adam the names of all things, He was teaching Adam what things are according to their essence or nature. A name summarizes the key characteristics of a thing and becomes part of its identity. Adam came out of that educational experience knowing both the names and qualities of all things, no matter how great or small they were. Everything in creation has a *batin* (interior) and a *dhahir* (exterior) reality. The inner reality of a thing is its true nature, while the outer reality is its physical form. For instance, the inner reality of a tree is the four elements, and the inner reality of the four elements is atoms. Likewise, the inner reality of a person is not their physical appearance, but rather it is the personality, traits, charisma, and soul that make up the essence of who they are. This knowledge equipped Adam not only to understand the essence of things but also to fulfill his greater role in Allah's creation.

Knowledge of nature as creation also necessitated knowledge of Allah as the Creator, emphasizing the interconnectedness between understanding the world and acknowledging divine wisdom. Adam's ability to comprehend and articulate the names and characteristics of all things in the universe served as the fundamental skill that equipped him for his divinely ordained role as Allah's khalifah (successor) or ruling representative on earth. Out of all names in existence, the Names of Allah are the most supreme (7:180). Since Allah is the most majestic and noble being, the names He uses to describe Himself are the most honorable. Before the final revelation to Prophet Muhammad ﷺ, humanity possessed only partial knowledge of divine qualities. It was through the Quran and the sayings and actions of Prophet Muhammad ﷺ that the full scope of Allah's Names was revealed. Each of Allah's names carries a divine presence and quality that can inspire specific virtues in a person or cure spiritual ailments within the soul.

A prominent scholar from Saudi Arabia, Muhammad Ibn Salih al-Uthaymin (1929-2001), categorized the Names and Attributes of Allah into three categories:

- *Sifat Dhatiyyah:* Attributes ascribed to His Self.

- *Sifat Fi'liyyah:* Attributes ascribed to His Actions.

- *Sifat Dhatiyyah Fi'liyyah:* Attributes ascribed to both His Self and His Actions.

The attributes ascribed to His Self are those that intrinsically connect to the Self of Allah, and He will always be described with them. For instance, *al-Hayat* (Life), *al-'Ilm* (Knowledge), *al-Qudrah* (Ability), *al-'Izzah* (Might and Power), *al-Hikmah* (Wisdom), *al-Jalal* (Majesty), *al-'Uluw* (Highness), and more.

Regarding the attributes ascribed to His Actions, those relate to *al-Mashee'ah* (His Will), and they are not intrinsically bound to His Self and manifest at specific times. For example:

- The Ascending (*al-Istiwa*) of Allah over the Throne after He created it.

117

- The Descending (**an-Nuzool**) of Allah to the nearest Heaven of this world in the last third of the night.

- The Coming (**al-Majee'u**) of Allah on the Day of Resurrection to judge between the people.

These Attributes are part of His Actions and connect to His Will. He performs these actions when He wills.

Finally, the Attributes ascribed to both His Self and His Actions are Names and Attributes that Allah will always be described with, but they are also connected to His Will and are not intrinsically bound to the Self. Shaykh Ibn 'Uthaymeen uses the example of the *Kalām* (Speech) of Allāh. Allah's speech is part of His Self because He will always be described with speaking. However, He speaks whenever and to whomever He wills.

Other scholars have classified the Names and Attributes of Allah in varying ways, demonstrating that this area remains an active field of theological exploration and scholarly discourse. Through reflection on these names, Muslims continuously uncover deeper meanings that fortify their spiritual connection to Allah.

Muslims who follow the Sunnah (way) of Prophet Muhammad ﷺ recognize that Allah's attributes transcend human comprehension, reaffirming His absolute uniqueness. Some attributes of Allah surpass human understanding, which reflects the infinite nature of His knowledge and being.

Religious traditions preceding Islam diverged in their depiction of divine attributes, often ascribing anthropomorphic qualities to Allah. The Bible and Torah refer to Allah in human terms such as "father" and "son," or depict Him as physically "resting" on the seventh day after creating the universe (Gen 2:2). Elsewhere, they describe Him as having changed His mind about destroying a people (Exodus 32:14). However, in the Quran, Allah is described as transcendent and without comparison, for He states, "There is nothing like Him" (42:11).

As noted in Chapter 1, Section 4, the Hebrew name for God is Yahweh (YHWH; יהוה). In the Middle Ages, Jewish rabbis treated this name as so sacred that they refused to pronounce it, fearing its misuse. They believed that speaking God's true name aloud could endanger creation itself (see Exodus 20:7). To avoid this, they substituted His name with titles such as HaShem ("The Name") or Adonai ("Lord"). Consequently, many Jewish and Christian worshippers never learned the Creator's actual name, limiting their opportunity for a direct, personal connection with Him.

In contrast, Islam emphasizes invoking Allah by His Names as a means of seeking knowledge, guidance, and divine connection. As the source of all life, Allah provides the foundational elements from which humanity advances in understanding. Learning to call upon Him through His Names is essential for receiving wisdom and guidance. Leaders, for example, should strive to embody divine attributes such as justice, mercy, and wisdom, qualities integral to governance.[38] However, certain names, like *al-Mutakabbir* (The Proud), belong solely to Allah. When humans attempt to claim such attributes, it serves as a reminder to remain humble, as only Allah is above all need for humility.

It is a noble goal for Muslims to study and understand Allah's Names and Attributes, striving to align their character with these divine qualities. Calling on Allah by His names in Arabic resonates with a unique vibrational frequency, transcending the physical realm and inviting the presence of angels.[39]

Just as Adam learned the essence of all things through their names, humans have historically used symbols and signs to convey deeper meanings that transcend literal words. While words are the language of logic, symbols serve as the language

---

38   1) Note: The Names of Allah are not limited to 99. There are many more names which we do not have knowledge of. 2) Abu Hurairah reported that Allah has ninety-nine Names, i.e., one hundred minus one, and whoever believes in their meanings and acts accordingly, will enter Paradise; and Allah is *witr* (one) and loves 'the *witr*' (i.e., odd numbers). (Bukhari).

39   Abu Hurairah (May Allah be pleased with him) reported: The Messenger of Allah (ﷺ) said, "Allah, the Exalted, has teams of angels who go about on the roads seeking those who remember Allah... (Bukhari and Muslim).

of the subconscious mind. Symbolism can reveal and conceal meaning through metaphor, imagery, and signs, offering hidden significance to those with the wisdom to decode it. Ancient civilizations such as the Egyptians and Sumerians safeguarded profound truths through symbolic language, preventing the ignorant or malicious from corrupting sacred knowledge. These societies understood that knowledge, when wielded by unworthy hands, could become a tool of destruction, a lesson still relevant today.

Modern society is inundated with symbols that influence perception and behavior. Many corporate logos and advertisements employ sigils, which are symbols that historically held mystical significance. In antiquity, sigils represented divine names, cosmic forces, or desires, activated through focused intent and repetition. Those who understood their meanings could harness their power, while others were influenced unknowingly. These symbols bypass rational thought, embedding themselves into the subconscious and shaping human behavior on a deep psychological level. Today, corporate logos function similarly, subtly guiding consumer choices and emotional responses. This duality of symbols, their ability to serve as tools of empowerment for the knowledgeable while manipulating the unaware, demonstrates their lasting influence in art, spirituality, and business marketing.

In language, the batin (inner meaning) and dhahir (outer meaning) of words mirror their etymology and definition. Etymology traces a word's historical roots, revealing layers of hidden meaning, while its definition provides a precise contemporary interpretation. Understanding both aspects allows for a holistic grasp of language and thought.

Most profound ideas can be understood on two levels: literal and symbolic. This is the essence of **symbolic language**, where meaning is conveyed indirectly, requiring deeper contemplation. This is what is intended when a person uses the expression "read between the lines." To interpret symbols correctly, one must trace them back to their original intent. In Arabic, this process is called *ta'wil*, a term meaning to return a word to its *awwal*, or primordial essence.

Just as words carry both apparent and hidden meanings, so too do material objects. In today's world, many products appear beneficial yet contain hidden harm, particularly in food and medicine. At its core, food is meant to nourish the body and sustain life. However, today's industrial food production has flooded the market with chemically modified ingredients that do the opposite. Many of these substances disrupt neurological function, triggering toxic biochemical reactions that weaken both cognitive and physical health. What was once a source of healing has, ironically, become a cause of illness. As Hippocrates famously stated, *"Let food be thy medicine and medicine be thy food."* Yet in our age, people often need medicine to repair the very damage inflicted by unhealthy food.

Unfortunately, medicine itself may not always be the remedy, but it may be part of the problem. Many people place their trust in pharmaceuticals, only to find that their prescribed treatments create new problems. In Western medical schools, students are not well-trained regarding nutrition, vitamins, or herbs. When they begin to practice medicine, they often lack knowledge about the dangers of the medications they prescribe. This ignorance stems from the fact that the pharmaceutical industry has a near-monopoly on research funding, medical journal publications, and disseminating information at medical conferences. Many medications never cure the ailments patients have; at best, prescription drugs treat the symptoms of the illness. At worst, they lead to additional complications. Prescription drugs can cause side effects that require new medications, and the combination of new drugs with old drugs often results in further complications. This can become a vicious cycle, ultimately leaving the person dependent on a daily supply of medication to function.

This raises a deeper question:

What is the true nature of Western medicine?

The batin (hidden meaning) of the word "pharmacy" traces back to the Greek *pharmakeia*, a term with multiple meanings, ranging from medicine to poison to sorcery. This layered definition suggests a duality in medicine: it can be used to cure, but it can also deceive. The Bible even warns:

"...because all the nations were deceived by your pharmakeia." (Revelations 18:23)

This verse hints at a powerful force capable of manipulation through chemical means. It demonstrates that like symbolic language, medicine is a tool that can be used for healing or harm.

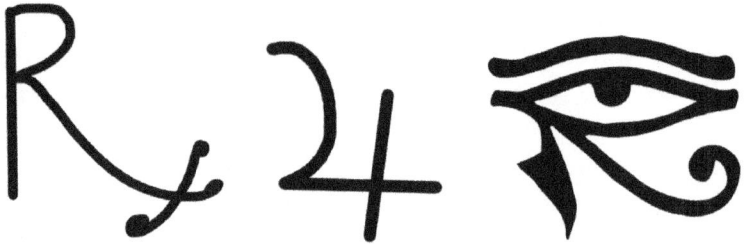

Fig. 18 -
Right: Eye of Horus (c. 2100 BC Egypt) — marked fractional doses on medicine jars and invoked Horus's protection over remedies.
Center: ♃ (Jupiter's sign) — Hellenistic–Roman pharmacists borrowed Egyptian dosing methods and added ♃ to recipes to call down Jupiter's (Zeus's) divine safeguard.
Left: ℞ — medieval ℞ (Latin recipere, "take this") gained a slanted stroke from ♃; scribes merged the cursive "R" with that Jupiter-style stroke, yielding the modern prescription mark that both instructs and subtly echoes divine protection.

Names and symbols are both components of the broader system of language, which was another aspect of Adam's educational experience. **Language** is the branch of knowledge that contains all other knowledge. Language is based on the triad of **words, letters,** and **numbers**. When combined, they can be used to describe all practical realities. Abstract reality (**mathematics**) is described with the triad of **symbols, numbers,** and **names**.

Every time the children of Adam use language, they apply the same principles that were used when the original spoken Logos *"Kun"* was expressed. When words are spoken out loud, they turn into **sound, frequency,** and **vibration**, which are the fundamental building blocks of matter. The material world was brought into existence using the power of "spoken words." This means that each spoken word has the power to manifest itself into some physical form. Like the act of sex, words are a means of creation but instead of a child, they produce emotions and ideas.

Language is a system of communication that can be spoken, signed, or written. Humans can think in images, but without language, we would never be able to bring those thoughts into our conscious awareness. In other words, language enables us to think about our thinking. Moreover, to invent new languages, you must combine the faculties of logic and intuition. It is not clear what the original language was, but all languages of the earth contain roots that extend back to the original language. As of 2025, there are 7,159 living languages in the world. Each of the world's languages is a means of formulating, reflecting on, and expressing knowledge within the various tribes and nations. The ancient languages of Hebrew, Arabic, and the Egyptian language *Medu Nejter* are closer to the original tongue and are preferred means of prayer and invocation.

Not only did Adam learn the names of things as taught to him by Allah, but he also could name new things. To name an abstract concept or a physical object, you must know the complete nature of that thing and be able to summarize it concisely. Neither the angels, jinn, nor animals had this innate ability to use their intellect to understand themselves and the world and explain that understanding through language. Adam's power over angels, jinn, and animals lies in the fact that Adam could name them, and they could not name themselves.

Adam's combination of knowledge, reason, and free will made him the most honored sentient being out of all creation. In addition, the children of Adam do not have to rely on their own individual efforts because they can pass down knowledge from generation to generation. When humans inherit knowledge, they can better adapt to their environment. This is why modern societies are more creative and complex than any in human history.

Mastery of a particular language requires one to learn what

classical scholars called the Trivium: **Grammar**, **Logic**, and **Rhetoric**. Trivium comes from Latin, meaning "place where three roads meet."

- **Grammar** involves understanding the complex system of rules and symbols governing a language's composition of clauses, phrases, and words. It ensures that language is well-structured and coherent. Grammar includes understanding the use of subjects, verbs, and objects, the inflection of adjectives into forms like good, better, and best, and the conjugation of verbs into tenses like run, ran, and have run. When students become proficient in Grammar, they become skilled in reading and comprehension, enabling them to receive knowledge accurately.

- **Logic** deals with the principles that differentiate valid arguments from invalid ones. It is essential for discerning truth. When students become proficient in logic, they develop strong reasoning skills, allowing them to analyze and understand information critically.

- **Rhetoric** is the culmination of the two previous skills; it is the art of informing, persuading, or motivating audiences in specific situations. Rhetoric enables one to express truth beautifully and effectively. When students master Rhetoric, they learn to apply their knowledge wisely and compellingly.

Each pillar builds upon the next. Grammar provides the knowledge to ascertain if a piece of information is correct by addressing the questions of 'who,' 'what,' 'when,' and 'where.' Logic provides the understanding to determine 'why' a piece of information is true or false. Rhetoric provides the wisdom to know 'how' to express the correct information to others. Without mastery of the Trivium, it is difficult to distinguish truth from falsehood.

When the methodology of the Trivium is in the hands of those who follow the path of truth, they can influence large numbers of people toward a noble aim. Powerfully expressed words or phrases generate thoughts in a recipient's mind. Pondering these thoughts stir emotions, emotions drive action, and collective action changes the world. However, when the Trivium is in the hands of someone with bad intentions, it can mobilize people to pursue a path leading to their destruction. As Prophet Muhammad ﷺ taught, "Some speech is magic."[40] Islamically, there is no good in magic at all, which we will elaborate on in the second and third books. All people with Moon-consciousness must be able to master the Trivium in their mother tongue for them to think critically about the information they consume and produce.

After the angels acknowledged that Adam possessed knowledge that they did not have, they submitted to the command of Allah and bowed to Adam out of respect and honor. The angels **understood** that Adam was a being that surpassed their expectations and was created for a higher purpose. All the angels bowed except for Iblis who was from the jinn (18:50). Allah questioned his refusal by asking Iblis if he was, in essence, a more noble creation than the creation of Adam. Iblis responded with the logical argument that he was more dignified than Adam because he was created from fire, and Adam was created from black mud (earth). Iblis's argument was false because Adam possessed an inner reality superior to the element of fire (15:26-33; 7:11-12; 38:76). Iblis's jealousy and racism caused him to be blind to Adam's inner reality.

In today's time, so-called intellectuals, among scholars, scientists, and experts, are part of a culture that promotes rational empiricism and rejects the sacred truths found in religion. Often, these thinkers pride themselves on ignoring the spiritual evidence that relates to our ultimate purpose, deeming empirical knowledge as the only real knowledge possible. Like

---

40   Narrated by Ibn Umar: "Two men came from the east and delivered speeches, and the Prophet ﷺ said, "Some eloquent speech has the influence of magic." (e.g., some people refuse to do something and then a good eloquent speaker addresses them and then they agree to do that very thing after his speech). (Bukhari).

Iblis, they are arrogant and ignorant. Allah says about them, "They know what is apparent of the worldly life, but of the Hereafter, they are unaware" (30:7).

Iblis's argument was a logical fallacy. He used analogical reasoning, comparing Adam's internal organs to what he knew from the external world. On one hand, fire is quick, radiant, and powerful, but it is also fickle, wild, and destructive. When the negative aspect of the fire element dominates a person, they may become condescending, prideful, and arrogant. By contrast, the earth element (clay) is stable, fertile, and enduring. Those with the earth element dominant in their personalities exhibit positive qualities like tolerance and humility. These traits caused Adam to receive forgiveness from Allah after his disobedience. Had Iblis used his analogical reasoning to question Allah out of humble curiosity, he might have been taught the error of his thinking, similar to how the angels were taught after questioning Allah about the purpose of Adam's creation. Allah is not to be questioned with arrogance, for He alone has the right to do whatever He desires (21:23).

Allah then banished Iblis, making him a cursed outcast. Iblis requested respite from Allah so that he would neither die nor receive punishment for his disobedience until the Day of Resurrection and Judgment. Allah granted this to Iblis but made the exception that Iblis would not have any authority over His believing true and sincere servants. Therefore, the only ones who respond to the calls of Iblis are those who are insincere, for whom hell was already written (38:71-85). From that point forward, Iblis was given the title "Shaytan," and hatred and enmity were established between him and Adam. Shaytan vowed to make it his life's mission to tempt humans and prove that we are unworthy of earning Allah's love and veneration (7:17 & 35:6).

SECTION 3
ADAM'S WISDOM

﴾ وَعَلَّمَ ءَادَمَ ٱلْأَسْمَآءَ كُلَّهَا... ﴿

He taught Adam the names of all things (2:31).

ADAM & OUR BRAINS

Adam's education began the moment his soul was breathed into his body. From that instant, he was endowed with the unique capacity to process and respond to information in three distinct ways. The first system governing Adam's awareness is the **reptilian brain** (primal instinct). When he sneezed and instinctively praised Allah, this was a reflexive response, much like the automatic reactions that sustain human survival. This instinctual control center originates at the base of the spine and extends to the pineal gland. In neuroscience, this is called the reptilian brain, the most ancient part of the human brain and the region most directly connected to the nervous system's survival functions. It is responsible for regulating breathing, heart rate, hunger, and survival-driven behaviors like the fight-

or-flight response. This region of the brain is shared with cold-blooded creatures like crocodiles, snakes, and lizards. It is purely reactive and does not engage in higher reasoning or moral decision-making. When an individual operates solely from this instinctual state, they are in 'survival mode', functioning on autopilot, driven by fear, desire, or basic necessity.

Although Adam was created as an adult, the earliest stage of his intellectual and emotional development mirrored the first 7 years of childhood. During this formative period, children are in **elementary school**, where they are introduced to foundational learning. At this stage, their minds are like sponges, absorbing experiences through their senses. Education at this level should focus on moral development, structured activities, and play-based learning, helping children build a broad understanding of core subjects and their connections to one another.

Children are connected to their fitrah (Tirmidhi), in this part of the brain. We were all born with a fitrah, and this can flourish over time, or become corrupted, until we can no longer recognize who we are in our natural state. Corruption occurs when our minds begin to tighten up, and we become defensive when the beliefs and viewpoints we acquired of the world are attacked. This closed-minded thinking opposes the creative, open, and flexible original mind (i.e., the fitrah). The fitrah allows us to innately distinguish right from wrong and acknowledge that there is a creator who is deserving of our worship. Scientifically, the pineal gland is best preserved in most people before puberty. This shows a correlation between the uncalcified pineal gland and our fitrah.

Adam eventually grew impatient and asked Allah to speed up the soul's descent. His sentiment reveals that man was created with a disposition that desires things in a hurry. However, we must work to suppress that nature because haste is from Shaytan, and patience is the key to self-mastery, discipline, and focus.[41] This desire and request is made from the middle portion of the brain, and it is responsible for

41   Deliberateness is from Allah, and haste is from the Ash-shaitan."
(Tirmidhi).

emotions, forming memories, habits, and arousal. It is known as the **limbic system**. The limbic system is our 'old mammalian' brain and is shared with other warm-blooded mammals like monkeys, horses, or cows.

This stage of Adam's existence corresponds to the period when the child is beginning to develop their moods, emotions, and memories. When an individual is in this mind-frame, they are making decisions based on their feelings. This stage lasts between the ages of 7 and 14. These are the years that children are in **middle/intermediate** school. During these years, students are more sensitive and self-conscious than at any other stage in life. They desire to express themselves creatively, think critically, use their imaginations, and have lessons related to their personal lives. Students should graduate with an in-depth understanding of the core subjects to prepare them to move toward mastery and independent thinking.

Finally, Adam desired intellectual dialogue with the angels. This desire stems from the **neocortex** portion of the brain and controls all our higher cognitive functions, such as abstract thought, imagination, consciousness, and language. This is the outermost and developmentally most recent layer of the brain and is where all the electrochemical activity in human thought occurs. This is the portion of our brain that distinguishes us from animals. When an individual is in this mind-frame, they are reasoning or rationalizing.

This stage of Adam's existence corresponds to the final phase of childhood when the child is strong in mind and body and is aware of their natural inclinations and talents. This stage is between the years of 14 to 21. These are the **high school** years, a stage where students should learn to create, invent, think critically, and approach ideas abstractly. Both parents and teachers should become more of a friend or a mentor to students. Students should practice applying the knowledge they learned at the breadth and depth levels to invent or create something new. When knowledge, understanding, and experience are integrated, this is wisdom.

This same tripartite model of breadth, depth, and application is repeated at the **Bachelor's**, **Master's**, and

Doctorate levels in higher education. Breadth is designed to help one grasp the big picture of knowledge. Depth allows them to explore and focus on specific topics for research. Application allows them to do something with that knowledge in the real world. Breadth is rapidly recalling facts and information, and this is called 'thinking fast.' Depth consciously controls our behavior, like staying calm when angry; this is 'thinking slow.' Application is the combination of both.

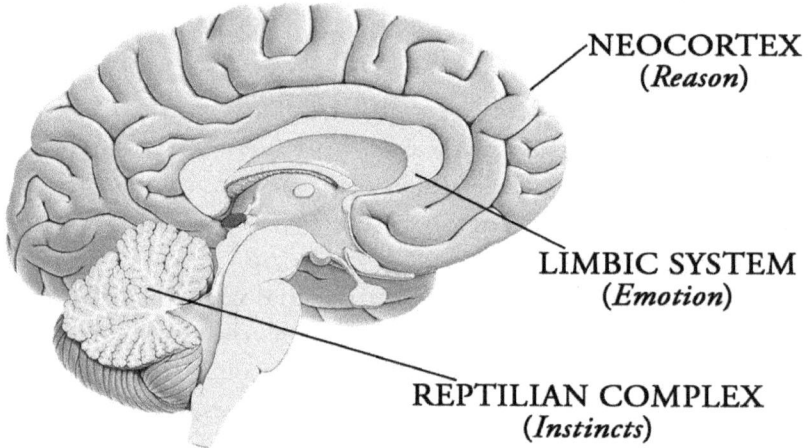

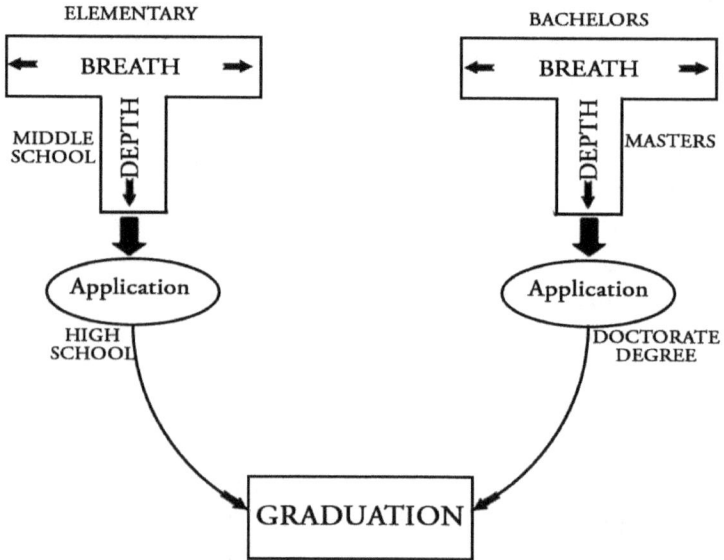

Fig. 19 - The Tripartite Model

ADAM & HAWWAH

One day, Adam awoke to find a mysterious presence beside him, a woman, gazing at him with awe. Curious, he asked, "Who are you?"

She replied simply, "A woman."

Intrigued, he questioned further, "Why were you created?"

With a voice full of meaning, she answered, "So that you may find tranquility in me."

The angels, observing this exchange, realized that Adam had been gifted not only with knowledge but also with wisdom, the ability to perceive deeper truths. Seeking to learn from him, they asked, "What is her name?"

Adam responded, "Hawwah (Life)," explaining, "She was created from me, and I am a living being."

The name Hawwah (حواء) in Arabic and Ḥawwāh (חַוָּה) in early Hebrew shares its root with the verb "to live" or "to breathe." In ancient tradition, this root: HWH (hey-vav-hey), is also linked to the Divine Name, emphasizing the connection between life, breath, and the sacred. In Latin, these letters transliterate to form E-V-E, giving us the English name Eve. This mirroring is more than a linguistic coincidence; it reveals a deeper truth, that a woman's nature is intrinsically tied to existence and life.

Each of these names forms a palindrome, a word or phrase that reads the same forward and backward. This symmetry reflects an ancient esoteric principle of time, balance, creation, and return. Just as a palindrome reflects itself, so too does reality, showing that what is above mirrors what is below, and what was in the beginning will be in the end. The Woman embodies this cycle as both the source and the vessel, and the bridge between the immaterial and the material. She brings forth life and nurtures it until its return, manifesting the rhythm of generation, dissolution, and rebirth.

In esoteric traditions, gender is understood through function: the active is masculine, and the receptive is feminine. The name Hawwah is embedded within the sacred Tetragrammaton (YHWH), revealing that the feminine is both an extension and the hidden counterpart of the masculine. She represents the concealed mystery from which all life emerges and to which all life must return.

While Adam was sleeping, Allah extracted the cartilage needed to create Hawwah from Adam's shortest left rib.[42] Before eating from sharjarat al-khuld, Adam and Hawwah did not have an animal-like nature, so reproduction did not come through sex. As mentioned in Chapter 2, Section 1, Adam's existence began as dust/minerals, then transitioned into a plant-like nature; finally, his body was like an animal.

The creation of Hawwah from Adam's ribs is likened to the plant's method of reproduction called parthenogenesis. This happens when a seed breaks away from a plant to form a new plant. Likewise, one of Adam's seeds broke off to form Hawwah. After descending to earth, Adam and Hawwah transitioned to another stage wherein they reproduced through sexual intercourse. Although sexual intercourse is animalistic, it has some similarities to the vegetable stage. Adam's semen is likened to a plant's seed, and the womb of Hawwah is likened to fertile soil from which seeds germinate and grow into babies. From the physical union of Adam and Hawwah came all the humans that have and will ever live.

Although research regarding this topic is scarce, medical researchers have discovered that out of the 206 bones within the human body, the ribs are unique in their ability to regenerate to near-normal conditions within six months after removal. However, the rib regeneration is slower and of poorer quality when the rib is not supported with gel foam. Suffice it to say that no other set of bones in our body shares this ability to regenerate.

Both Adam and Hawwah were created for the sole purpose

---

42   Note: The story of Hawwah's creation from Adam's rib is referenced in a Hadith, but the Quran does not explicitly mention how Hawwah was created. Islamic commentators likely relied heavily off of the Biblical tradition in Genesis 2:21-23.

of worshipping Allah (51:56). Also, they both contain the same spiritual nature (4:1). In Islam, both man and woman are subject to the same physical obligations, rational beliefs, and spiritual practices, such as the outward submission to Allah (**Islam**), the inward faith in Allah (**Iman**), and the perfection of worship to Allah (**Ihsan**). Islam is based on the five pillars: testifying that none is worthy of worship except Allah and that Muhammadﷺ is Allah's Messenger; praying five times a day; observing the fast of Ramadan; giving charity to the needy; and making a pilgrimage to the house of Allah in Mecca for whoever has the means. Iman is the belief in Allah, His angels, His revealed Books, His messengers, the Last Day, and to believe in Allah's decree (that both the good and evil consequences are from Allah). Ihsan is to worship Allah as if you see Him or to at least realize that whatever you do in public or private is seen by Him (Bukhari).

Although Adam and Hawwah were obligated to uphold the same religious duties, they had separate roles to fill under the umbrella of worship. Adam was created to be Allah's Khalifah (vicegerent) on earth, overseeing the administration of worldly affairs according to the divine laws of Allah (2:30). Positions of prophethood or communal leadership are reserved for men because "Men are in charge of women by [right of] what Allah has given over the other..." (4:34). Authority was given to man because he is more physically capable than the woman, which enables him to be more apt to handle tasks that require physical labor.

Conversely, Hawwah was Adam's help, comfort, and companion. Hawwah is the one responsible for femininity, sensuality, support, friendship, procreation, and mercy. The rib protects the heart from external forces. Likewise, women were created from the rib, and a man should protect his woman's heart and keep her close to his side. Allah is the initial creator and the one that continuously creates through the vessels of his creations. The woman's womb is from those vessels where the creation of humans continuously happens.

Neither Adam nor Hawwah is superior to the other. Allah created all things in pairs; men and women have separate minds and bodies, but they were created from the same soul. Men and women are essentially the same, in that regard. As Prophet Muhammad ﷺ taught us, women are the twin halves of men (Tirmidhi and Ahmad). This equality is reflected in their complementary roles and characteristics.

Their differences can be likened to the right hand versus the left hand, heaven and earth, body and soul, sun and moon, electricity and magnetism, electrons and protons, plus (positive) and minus (negative); both complement each other. Likewise, the earthly elements are linked with the components of the cosmos. The masculine and active air and fire elements complement the feminine and passive earth and water elements.

The attraction that men and women share for one another is part of our natural inclination to desire completeness. The man and the woman are deficient without each other. The sensitive, tender, and delicate qualities most women share balance the dominant, vigilant, ambitious qualities that most men share.

The union of man and woman is not two individuals forming a "couple" or "dual" but two halves uniting to form a singular whole. One complements the other, sharing their strengths and weakness to become a fortified unit. This applies within their interpersonal attraction, as well as on the family level, and further into the social and communal level. And the same is reflected in nature and in the cosmos.

When both men and women are spiritually in love, they foster a harmonious physical union wherein new life can come into being. The mathematical formula for life changes when viewed from that perspective. In that case, 1 man + 1 woman = a child (3). The child is the intermediary that could only come about from the merger of two opposite genders.

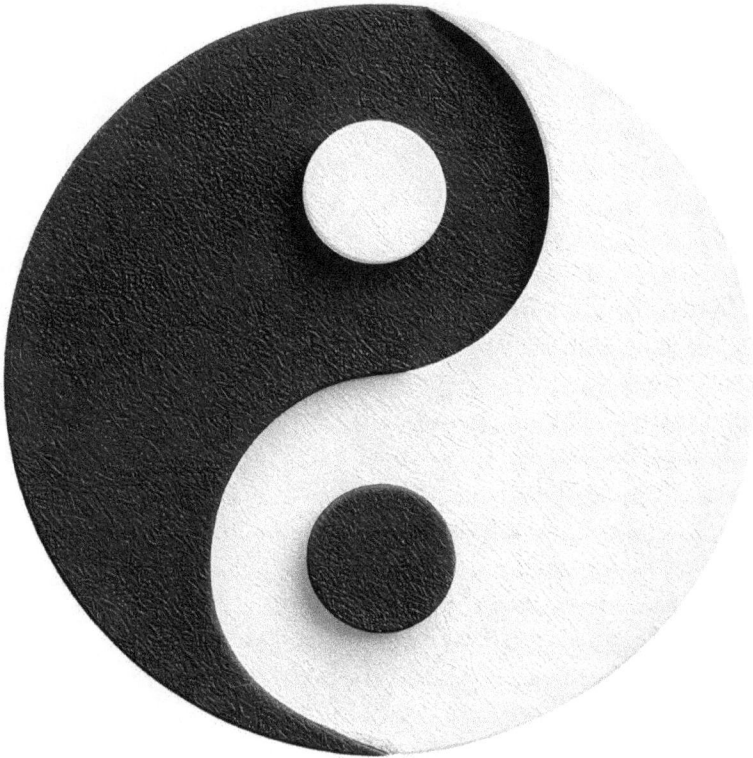

Fig. 20 - Yin Yang [43]

43   Note: All things exist in opposites. Yin (passive, cold, feminine) is the influence of softness in nature. Yang (active, hot, masculine) is represented as force in nature.

After the creation of Hawwah, Allah allowed them to live in Paradise and enjoy all its blessings except for one forbidden tree (as mentioned in Chapter 1, Section 3). Iblis devised a plan to lead Adam and Hawwah into disobedience by enticing them to approach the tree. Both Adam and Hawwah were fully aware of Iblis's nature and his intent to cause their downfall. Adam had witnessed Iblis's envy, hatred, and racism. He reflected on Iblis's deluded perception of his greatness. He thought about how Iblis argued with Allah and justified why he would not prostrate after being commanded to do so, hence exemplifying his ingratitude.

From that observation, Adam better understood the extent of Allah's tolerance. Allah would have been justified if He chose to destroy Iblis for his defiance and arrogance, but He, in His infinite wisdom, allowed the Shaytan to continue living until the Day of Judgment.

Despite the warning that Iblis would attempt to mislead them, Adam and Hawwah ate from the tree. They believed Iblis because he swore by Allah that eating from the tree would enable them to become immortal or like angels (7:20-21). Adam and Hawwah were too innocent to fathom that Iblis could take a false oath by Allah. Swearing by Allah to support a lie is a major sin and is one of the chief character traits of hypocrites. Adam and Hawwah had not yet been exposed to evil, nor had they experienced the bitterness of treachery and betrayal. Like children, in their innocence, the idea of a lie had not as yet entered their minds. And so, believing Iblis's words to be true, the thought of eating from the tree to be like angels and live forever festered in their minds for some years. Ultimately, they forgot the pact that they made with Allah to not eat from the tree, as well as the command to not trust Iblis and to take him as an enemy. Forgetting is part of the nature of *Insan* (humans). In Arabic, Insan is derived from the word *nasiya* (to forget). Education, in that sense, is less a matter of learning something new and more a reminder of what was forgotten.

Finally, one day, they decided to eat the fruit of the tree. Adam reached out his hand, picked one of the fruits, and offered it to Hawwah, and they both ate.[44] Before Adam could finish eating, he felt his heart contract as it filled with grief, guilt, and shame. The world around them changed forms, and the light concealing their nakedness was removed. Adam and Hawwah were devolving into humans. Feeling embarrassed, they broke off leaves from trees to cover themselves.

Allah addressed Adam and Hawwah, reminding them that the tree was forbidden for them and that Iblis was a clear enemy to them.

They responded, "Our Lord! We have wronged ourselves, and if You do not forgive us and have mercy upon us, we will surely be among the losers."

Allah said, "Descend, being to one another enemies. And for you, on the earth is a place of settlement and enjoyment for a time." He said, "Therein you will live, and therein you will die, and from it, you will be brought forth (resurrected)." (2:22-25).

Adam and Hawwah left the divine world of the Garden of Eden, passing through the spiritual realms of the 7 heavens, and descended into the physical realm of the earth. In Eden, they existed in a subtle, spirit-dominated state; upon entry to our denser plane, their essences "hardened" into matter and became subject to gravity—the curvature of spacetime that compels all bodies toward the earth's center and prevents us from freely exploring the higher spiritual realms.

Though gravity anchors us below, it is our five senses that truly veil the higher realms. On earth, Adam and Hawwah could still glimpse the first heaven—the visible cosmos— but the deeper spiritual layers lay concealed behind sensory boundaries of sight, sound, touch, taste, and smell. Only in dreams, visions, or deep meditation does the "Sensory Veil" lift enough for fleeting glimpses of the realms they once inhabited. Until one transcends both the pull of gravity and the bonds of the senses, the higher heavens remain beyond reach.

Adam was sad and remorseful, and Hawwah was crying. They both begged Allah for forgiveness (7:23). Allah accepted

---

44   Note: The Quran does not place the blame on the woman for the fall of man unlike the Biblical story (Genesis 3).

their repentance because it was sincere. Allah knew that Iblis would sway Adam and Hawwah, and they would eventually fall prey to the deception. Allah created Adam to dwell on the earth. Before Adam's creation, Allah did not say to the angels, "I shall make a vicegerent in Paradise." The clay used to create Adam was from the earth, and the earth was prepared for Adam, Hawwah, and their progeny to inhabit.

Shaytan, Adam, and Hawwah's descent to earth was meant to teach them and all their future offspring a lesson. Jinn and Humans have free will, an amazing and burdensome responsibility. We can choose the path of virtue or the path of vice. If we choose the path of vice, at some point, we must deal with the consequences of that decision. After we've sinned, we can follow the path of Shaytan and blame Allah for creating us with the nature that we have (7:16; 15:39). Or we can respond like Adam and blame ourselves for the state of humiliation we've incurred as a result of the spiritual crime of the sin. Either repent and return to your Lord or persist in sin.

Adam and Hawwah had faced challenges throughout their entire lives on Earth. From the very beginning, Adam and Hawwah descended to different locations and struggled to find each other. Some argue that Adam descended on the mountains of modern-day Sri Lanka, while Hawwah landed in modern-day Jeddah, Saudi Arabia. After traversing through the earth, they found each other in Muzdalifah in Saudi Arabia, the same location where millions of pilgrims gather during Hajj each year.

Reunited, they established for themselves a home and bore children. Hawwah gave birth to two sets of twins. The first set was Qabil (Cain) and his sister, and the second set was Habil (Abel) and his sister. Habil was a shepherd, and Qabil was a farmer. When the two sets of twins reached adulthood, Allah revealed to Adam that each son should be married to the twin sister of the other brother. Allah intended for the children of Adam to populate the earth with different cultures and colors, and each sister had a different color. Qabil was displeased with the sister he had to marry because she was not as beautiful as his twin.

Adam sought a solution to this problem, so he called on Allah asking for help. Allah commanded each son to make a sacrifice, and whoever's offer was accepted would be on the right side. Habil offered his best lamb, and Qabil offered his worst crop. That action revealed Qabil's internal state of insincerity, resulting in his sacrifice not being accepted. This enraged Qabil even more, and the animosity grew to the point of murderous intent. Qabil simply could not contend with seeing his brother happy, while he, from his perspective, was both rejected in his offering and lost his heart's desire for the one he wanted to marry.

Habil advised Qabil to purify his heart from its vices to obtain the psychological and emotional happiness he sought. Unfortunately, the advice was ignored. Qabil struck Habil with a stone, killing him instantly.

This incident was the first human death and the first criminal act committed by a man on earth (5:27-30).

This murder confirmed the angels' apprehension regarding the creation of man on earth. They had questioned why Allah would bring forth a being prone to bloodshed and chaos—a concern rooted in their prior experiences with destructive creatures (2:30). Qabil's killing of his brother reflected precisely what they feared. Yet, as Allah stated, "I know what you do not know," there was deeper wisdom behind the creation of humankind. Chaos, though destructive, is also necessary for renewal. It drives human survival, spurs the creation of new systems, and clears the way for the regeneration of those that have decayed. In this way, even disorder plays a role in the Creator's great design.

Secondly, humans uniquely possess free will and the capacity for moral growth—something the angels could not grasp. Adam's descendants can choose virtue even when faced with tempting desires or false ideologies. Each act of obedience, repentance, and renewed commitment to Allah deepens our spiritual maturity and brings forth mercy and grace in ways angels cannot experience. In fact, the very possibility of doing wrong becomes the spark that strengthens our compassion, humility, and true devotion. Therefore, human failures amid

139

disorder are necessary for renewal, and through these trials our redemption unfolds, showcasing Allah's attributes of forgiveness and guidance throughout our collective journey.

Adam inquired about Habil's whereabouts but Qabil responded, "I am not my brother's keeper."

Qabil hid the body for some time by carrying it on his back, looking for a place to dispose of it. After some time, his anger turned to guilt, and he began to feel the burden of his deed. Allah intended to relieve him of this burden by sending Qabil a sign as to what to do.

Two ravens began fighting in front of Qabil, causing the death of one. The surviving bird used his beak to dig a hole in the ground, rolled the victim into it, and covered it with sand. Qabil then followed the same example of hiding the body of his brother (5:31). This was the first burial of man. Adam and Hawwah grieved for their sons; one, they later discovered, was murdered, and the other was completely under the sway of Shaytan. Qabil's legacy of jealousy and murder lives on to this day.

Before Adam's death, he prophesied that a flood would come to a people from the lineage of Qabil, and they would reject a future Messenger. Adam taught his children that Allah would never leave a man alone on this earth except that He would send His Prophets and Messengers to show them how to live a righteous life for them to return to Paradise. These Prophets and Messengers are divinely inspired educators whose goal is to guide their people towards every good and warn them against every evil. Adam foretold that the Prophets and Messengers will have different names, traits, and miracles, but they will all share the same call to worship Allah alone.

A *Nabi* (Prophet) is someone chosen by Allah to convey divine guidance and news about Allah, the Hereafter, the grave, the Day of Judgment, and other matters related to the unseen world. They are tasked with reminding people of their purpose in life and guiding them toward worshiping Allah alone. Prophets also make prophecies, sharing insights into events that are yet to come, which is the origin of the English word "prophet." According to a hadith, Allah sent 124,000 Prophets

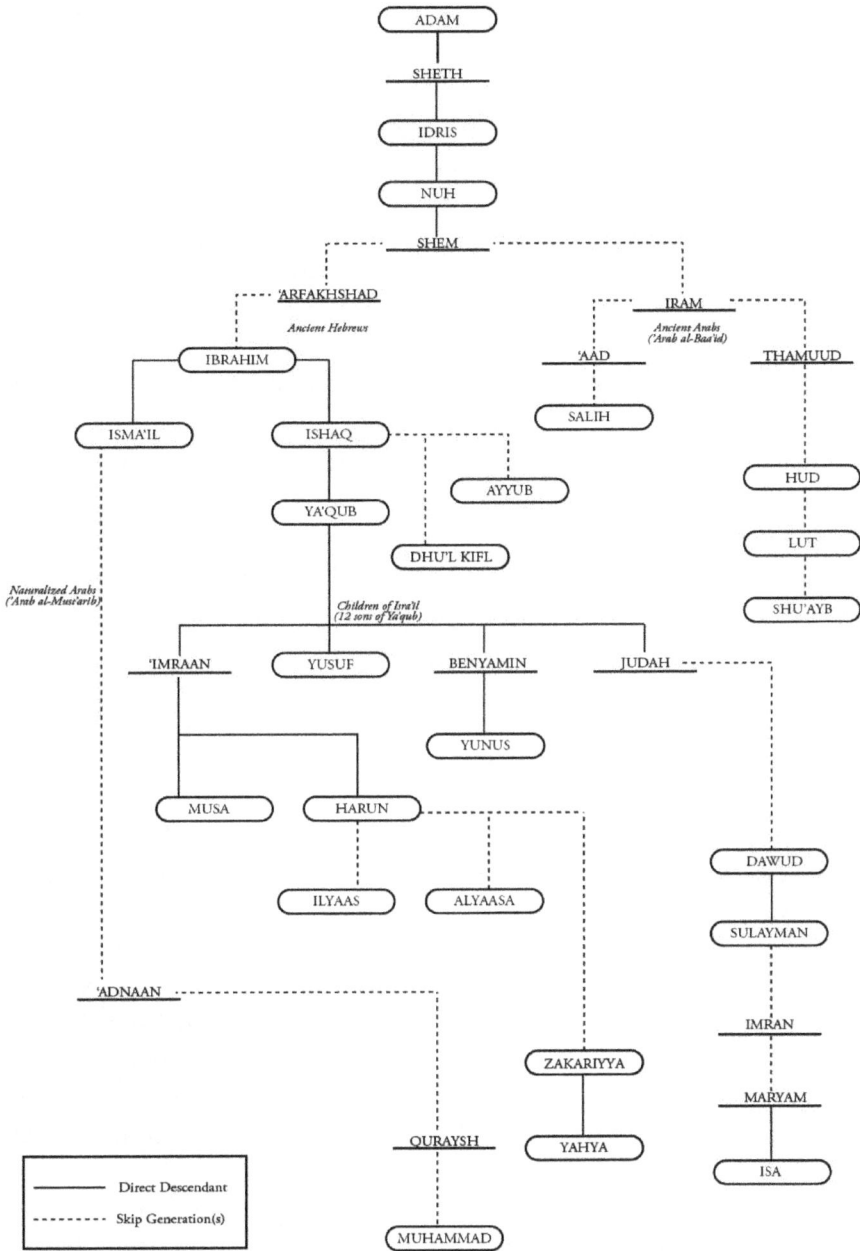

Fig. 21 - The Prophetic Line, depicting the First Generation between Adam and Nuh, the Second Generation highlighting the Semitic Origins of both ancient Arab and Hebrew peoples, and the Third Generation culminating in 'Isa as the Messiah, and Muhammad ﷺ as the seal of all prophets and messengers.

141

in human history, beginning with Adam, the first human and the first Prophet.

A *Rasul* (Messenger) is a specific type of Prophet who is entrusted with divine Revelations and brings a new *Shariah* (sacred law) or a distinct message to their community. While all Messengers are Prophets, not all Prophets are Messengers. Messengers play a critical role in shaping humanity's spiritual and moral frameworks. Allah sent 313 or 315 *Rusul* (Messengers) in human history, culminating with the Messenger of Allah, Muhammad bin Abdullah ﷺ, who delivered the final and universal message of Islam to all of humanity.

When Adam had finished advising his children and grandchildren, he peacefully closed his eyes and departed from this world. Having lived for 960 years, he returned to the eternal home from which he was initially removed, content with fulfilling his role as the first Prophet and father of humankind.

For Adam, Hawwah, and their offspring, life on Earth consisted of both tests and punishments. The creation of the tree and the command not to approach it was a test. Their descent to Earth was a direct consequence of their act of disobedience. Every event afterward, whether joyful or painful, served either as a trial to strengthen them or as a result of their choices.

The murder of their son, Habil, at the hands of their other son, Qabil, is a trial that was meant to test their patience. When they experienced ease and comfort, that test determined if they would be grateful. Likewise, all their progeny will be punished and tried in similar ways. Trials and punishments occur in three dimensions: physical, moral/spiritual, and intellectual. These challenges made Adam and Hawwah wiser.

As children of Adam, all humans have the seeds of wisdom embedded within. Each person can search within their heart to find all that we want or need. The seas below, on the surface of the Earth, and the stars above are filled with useful resources that humans can learn to use for our survival and advancement. These resources have been pivotal in advancing human civilization, enabling the development of societies and economies. Wisdom is the ability to know what good is worthy of being sought.

Wisdom can only be obtained after acquiring broad knowledge, deep understanding, and application. Iblis had broad knowledge but lacked understanding because he had corruption in his character. The angels had a deep understanding but lacked wisdom because they did not have the free will to make bad choices, nor did they have the ability to bring forth beings out of nothingness through birth or describe abstract reality through naming. Iblis and the angels only possessed fragments of Allah's knowledge, Adam and Hawwah had within them the character and the cognitive faculties to acquire experiences that would enable them to capture much more of the whole. They could see the bigger picture behind the reasons why Allah created and willed what occurred in the past, the present, and the future. Through their acquisition of mental knowledge (new index neurons) and physical experience (old index neurons), they could reform and perfect their personalities, purify their intentions, and mature. Ultimately, they developed the capacity to make decisions based on intuition and inspiration.

Wisdom is to use one's free will to follow divine guidance and to act in a way that is most correct and responsible. Humans are commanded to embark on a path of learning from the cradle to the grave so that they can continually open their minds to the wisdom of that which is true and real.

Man's ability to make mistakes, choose to follow misguidance or reject higher truths, enables him to embody honorable characteristics such as creativity, bravery, and mercy. Man can believe what he wants to believe. Man's perceptive ability can make what is good-bad and that which is bad-good. Man can believe he is a deity and oppress others if he chooses. Or he can remember the power and might of his Lord, which will humble him and enable him to realize his true status. As the popular saying goes, "Man is the master of his own destiny."

When we possess the traits of envy, racism, and hatred,

we follow the fiery path of Shaytan and Qabil. On that path, choosing to be good can become almost impossible. Our desires and the whims of our lower nefs and our Qareen become the dominant force in our lives; then we degenerate towards a nature that is worse than animals.

When we discipline ourselves to acquire the traits of honesty, humility, and patience, we are following the path toward wisdom, the path that Adam and the Prophets who succeeded him followed. On that path, it can become almost impossible to choose to be evil. Our aql (intelligence) guides us to do what is right with the knowledge and understanding that we've acquired, and we can elevate to become more honorable than angels.

UNDERSTANDING THE
DIVINE TRIVIUM

In this chapter on the Divine Trivium, we explored the core intellectual capacities imbued in Allah's creation. This framework aids in understanding both ourselves and the unseen entities that influence our inner realms.

Through an in-depth examination of each component of the Divine Trivium, we are guided toward a more holistic comprehension of our very essence.

Various triads were examined to grasp Allah's wisdom regarding the hierarchy of His creation and intellectual beings. The number three, symbolizing creation, is prevalent in nature, politics, and religion, reflecting a progression from beginning, to middle, and end, as well as from good to better to best.

These triads include the stages of knowledge acquisition (quantitative, qualitative, and mixed methods approaches), the brain's structure and functions (pineal gland, thalamus, and hypothalamus), and the creation order (Adam's body before his soul and the heavens before the earth).

The trinity of body, soul, and intelligence further reflects Allah's design in creation, emphasizing the interconnectedness of these elements.

We also explored how symbolism is conveyed through metaphor, imagery, and signs, while sigils represent divine names, cosmic forces, or personal desires. Language dynamics were also considered, with words, letters, and numbers in practical reality and symbols, names, and numbers in abstract reality. The Trivium of education: Grammar, Logic, and Rhetoric, emerged as an essential tool for mastering language, critical thinking, and effective communication. These align with the broader stages of learning: breadth, depth, and application, as seen in educational progressions from elementary to higher education (Bachelor's, Master's, and Doctorate).

Additionally, we delved into the attributes of Allah (*Sifat Dhatiyyah*, *Sifat Fi'liyyah*, and *Sifat Dhatiyyah Fi'liyyah*), emphasizing how these categories reflect Allah's infinite wisdom and creative power. Finally, we examined the spiritual dimensions of Islam: Islam (submission), Iman (faith), and Ihsan (excellence in worship), further demonstrating the divine structure of spiritual growth and the pathway to moral and intellectual perfection.

From these explorations, we have identified three core patterns essential for understanding the stages of knowledge, effective communication, and spiritual living. The model we have chosen to illustrate this divine trivium is the Philosopher's Stone, a legendary alchemical symbol representing the culmination of spiritual enlightenment and the attainment of wisdom necessary for right action. It teaches one to live truthfully and morally by aligning with the Higher Will. The Philosopher's Stone is based on the alchemical attempt to reconcile the four elements (earth, water, air, fire), represented by a square, with the three principles of matter (mercury, sulfur, and salt), represented by a triangle, and the duality of opposites (such as day and night), represented by a yin and yang circle, ultimately transforming them into one (the Stone), symbolized by a larger circle. We have adapted this model to fit the key concepts discussed in this chapter.

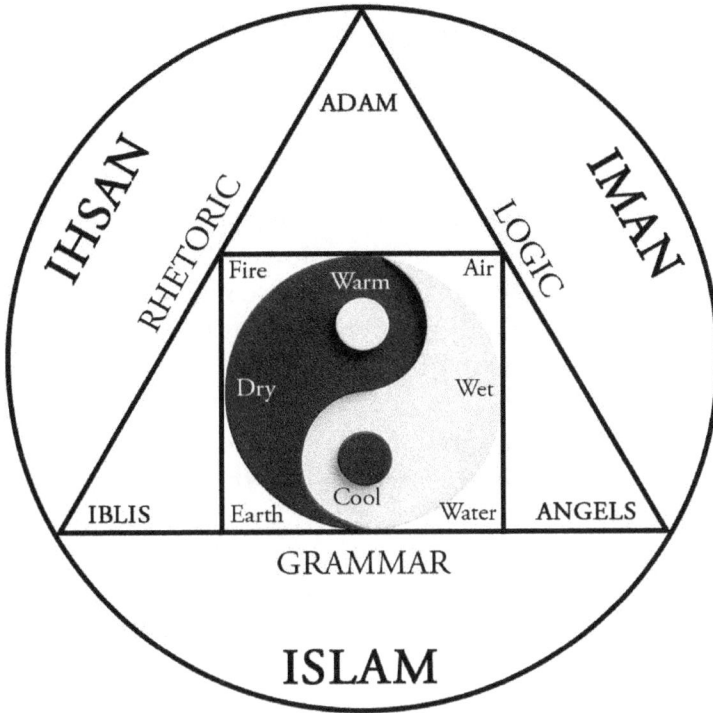

Fig. 22 - Summary of the Trivium.

1. First Circle (Spirit in the Physical World):

Symbolizes our spirit in the physical world.

The goal is to use Free Will to develop our personalities (temperaments) through knowledge and practice, attaining peace and harmony by aligning thoughts, emotions, and actions with Allah's will.

2. Square (Finite Physical World):

Encloses the first circle, representing the material body and the physical universe governed by Natural Law (discussed in the next chapter).

The body is the vessel for consciousness, and understanding natural laws like gravity, cause and effect, and morality is essential. The aim is to align perceptions with reality and avoid illusions.

147

3. Triangle (Unity and Higher Consciousness):

Represents the union of masculine and feminine energies to create offspring, the integration of mind, body, and spirit, the contrast between pride (Iblis) and humility (angels), and the embodiment of wisdom (Adam), as well as the foundational principles of Grammar, Logic, and Rhetoric.

Symbolizes the Trinity of Consciousness: thought, emotion, and action. Serves as a bridge to higher consciousness, fostering an elevated understanding of reality and connecting to the ultimate macro-circle of "spirit."

4. Final Circle (Higher Spirit):

Represents ultimate unity with the Higher Will and realization of the True Self.

This signifies living in harmony with Allah's divine will through practicing the five pillars of Islam, believing in the six pillars of Iman, and achieving Ihsan (excellence in worship and action).

The Meaning of the Divine Trivium

The Divine Trivium offers a roadmap for intellectual and spiritual evolution, equipping us to navigate life with clarity, purpose, and faith. It encourages aligning our thoughts and actions with Allah's will, fostering personal transformation and harmony with creation.

Archetypes of Knowledge:
* Iblis: Represents Material Knowledge
* Angels: Symbolizes Intuitive Understanding
* Adam: Embodies Spiritual Wisdom

Language Subjects for Intellectual Liberation:
- Grammar: The study of language structure and rules.
- Logic: The science of reasoning and critical thinking.
- Rhetoric: The art of persuasive and effective communication.

Dimensions of Islam:
- Islam: The practice of submission to Allah through actions and rituals.
- Iman: The belief in the core tenets of faith.
- Ihsan: The pursuit of excellence in worship and moral conduct.

In conclusion, the Divine Trivium provides a comprehensive perspective of our inner world and our place within it.

This framework enhances our understanding of both our intellectual and spiritual realms, encouraging us to align our thoughts and actions with divine purpose. It allows us to appreciate the mysteries of our inner life more profoundly and recognize the interconnectedness of our internal experiences. This holistic approach equips us to navigate life with a balanced and spiritually fulfilling existence.

In the next chapter, we will examine the natural laws as taught by Idris and examine the societies that have been impacted by his teaching.

PART 2:

EVOLUTION OF
ESOTERIC EDUCATION

CHAPTER 3
THE DIVINE LAWS

SECTION 0

THE FATHER
OF ESOTERIC WISDOM

﴿ وَٱذْكُرْ فِى ٱلْكِتَـٰبِ إِدْرِيسَ إِنَّهُۥ كَانَ صِدِّيقًا نَّبِيًّا ﴾

﴿ وَرَفَعْنَـٰهُ مَكَانًا عَلِيًّا ﴾

"And mention in the Book O Prophet, the story of Idris.
He was truly a man of truth and a prophet.
And We raised him to an honourable status."
(19:56-57).

﴿ وَإِسْمَـٰعِيلَ وَإِدْرِيسَ وَذَا ٱلْكِفْلِ كُلٌّ مِّنَ ٱلصَّـٰبِرِينَ ﴾

"And remember Ishmael, Idris, and Dhul-Kifl, who were
all steadfast"
(21:85).

151

IDRIS: THE PROPHET & MESSENGER

Before Adam passed away, his third son, Seth (Shayth/ Sheeth), inherited the mantle of Prophethood. To prepare him for this role, Adam taught him the natural laws that govern the earth, such as the movement of day and night and the acts of worship tied to these cycles.[45] Allah revealed 104 psalms, granting Seth fifty of them as guidance for his people (Bukhari).

After Adam's death, Shaytan found new ways to lead humanity astray. Disguising himself as a young man, he enticed the descendants of Qabil (Cain) with audible distractions by introducing music via the invention of the flute. He used it to lure them into dance, intermingling, and ultimately, *zina* (unlawful sexual relations).

Seth warned his people against these evil practices for the remainder of his life. He lived to the age of 912, and upon his death, his son Enosh (Anush/Enosch) succeeded him. Enosh was then succeeded by his son Kenan (Qinan/Cainan), who was followed by Mahala'il (Mahabil/Mahlabeel).

Ancient Persians claim that Mahabil was the King of the 7 Regions. He cut down trees, built large forts, cities, and castles, and established the cities of Ancient Mesopotamia.[46]

He built the city of Babylon, the "Gate of the gods," and the furthest city of Sus. He defeated Iblis and his armies, killing many of them and pushing the rest into mountains and valleys. He ruled for 40 years.

His duties were taken over by his son Jared (Birad/Yard), who was then succeeded by his son Khonoukh (Akhnukh/ Khanukh/Uhnukh), more widely known as Idris (Enoch), the

---

45   Narrated by Muhammad Ibn Ishaq

46   Note: The Sumerians founded the first cities around 4000 BC and Babylonians founded cities around 1000 BCE in Mesopotamia. The Babylonian empire lasted until 745 BC.

7th great leader.[47]

In the 7th generation after the Prophet Adam, Prophet Idris (عليه السلام) was sent on a mission to call two separate nations to the truth.[48] Idris was born and raised in Mesopotamia approximately 4,400 years after the birth of Adam, around 5,300–4,935 BC. Mesopotamia was a civilization centered between the Tigris and Euphrates rivers. When Idris was young, he was taught by Prophet Seth, who prepared him for initiation into the elite chain of Prophets and Messengers. In adulthood, Idris was devoted to studying the sacred books passed down by Adam and Seth.

At the age of 40, Idris received Prophethood and was sent on a mission to call his people back to the moral conduct of their forefathers, Adam and Seth. They blatantly disobeyed the laws that were established. Idris's teachings were ignored by most. Although *shirk* (associating partners with Allah) did not exist in Babylon, the people were engulfed in sin. Idris was directed to take his followers to Babylon and migrate to Kemet to guide the people there. The ancient Egyptians referred to the land where they lived as Kemet/Kmt. Kemet (Kmt), meaning "the black land" or "the black place," which refers to the fertile black soil that was washed down from Central Africa.

Idris's followers were disturbed by this decision because they believed they could not find a better home than Babylon.

Idris responded, "If you endure the inconvenience for

---

47   Note: It is the author's opinion that an approximate birth timeline for Adam and his early descendants is as follows—dates reflect prophetic lifespans preserved in Islamic tradition and are not precise archaeological correlates:
9,700 BC – Adam
9,560 BC – Seth (Shith)
9,455 BC – Anoush (Enosh)
9,365 BC – Qinan (Cainan)
9,295 BC – Mahlabeel (Mahalalel)
9,230 BC – Yard (Jared)
5,300 BC – Idris (Enoch)
4,935 BC – Idris raised

48   A) Note: the English version of the names are listed after their Arabic names.
    B) Note: Additionally, it is believed that during this era, a generation spanned approximately 100 to 200 years, significantly longer than the modern concept of a generation, which is typically around 25 to 30 years.

Allah's sake, then His Mercy is very encompassing. So, do not despair but bow yourself before His command."

Fig. 23 - Kmt in Hieroglyphics.

Idris's followers agreed to migrate to Egypt. Upon arrival, they witnessed the massive Nile River and the surrounding lush, fertile land. Idris responded to the beauty of the river by saying, "Babylon," which in Syrian refers to something that means "a river like yours." Idris likened the Nile River to what became known as the Euphrates River. The Messenger of Allah ﷺ told us that both "*Seehaan* and *Jeehaan*" (the Euphrates and the Nile) are rivers from *Jannah*, Paradise (Muslim). In time, the people began to refer to the Mesopotamian civilization as Babylon.

Idris and his followers settled along the Nile and established a new home. In Egypt, however, they were met with a lot of resistance. The Egyptians had created a gnostic sect called the Sethians.[49]

They believed their forefather, Seth, was divine, and erected statues in his memory and honor. These statues became objects of worship. Idris called the various tribes to the pure teachings of Adam and Seth, and advised them to return to upright moral conduct.

At the time, 72 languages were spoken, and Idris was said to have known them all, speaking to the various groups of people in their own language. He taught the Egyptians the tenets of religion, medicine, astronomy (and astrology), civics, etiquettes, and a civilized way of existence. He taught them

---

49   Gnosis: knowledge of spiritual mysteries.

prayers and instructed them to fast on certain days and to give a portion of their wealth to the poor. Idris set a noble example for all by being truthful and patient (86-21:85 ;57-19:56).

IDRIS: THE KING

As a ruler, Idris divided his land into four regions and appointed a leader for each. These leaders were responsible for their territories' political and day-to-day governmental affairs. It was their duty to observe the rule of Shari'ah (Islamic law) above all other laws, and Idris conveyed the Shari'ah injunctions to them as they were revealed to him by Allah. Idris categorized the people in his land into three types: **clairvoyants**, **kings**, and **laymen**. The clairvoyants were considered the most important because they were answerable to Allah, the king, and the laymen. Kings were responsible for their own actions and the people's affairs, while laymen were answerable only for themselves. Idris established these laws and responsibilities until he was taken from this earth.

The Ancient Egyptians honored Idris as a ruler. Statues and effigies were permissible in that age, so statues and temples were constructed for him in the city of Khemennu, also known as Hermopolis, which became the main cult center of Thoth.

TRISMEGISTUS: THE THRICE-GREAT SAGE

As time passed, Idris became intertwined with mystical wisdom and his legacy shaped spiritual thought across different civilizations. His tripartite model influenced various philosophical traditions, and even contributed to the concept of the Christian Trinity.

The title "Trismegistus", meaning "Thrice-Great", became linked to Hermes Trismegistus, a fusion of the Greek god Hermes and the Egyptian deity Thoth. There are various opinions as to why he was referred to as the "Thrice-Great". Some say it refers to his mastery in three realms of wisdom: **Prophethood, kingship**, and **philosophy**. Others suggest that it reflects his embodiment of the three fundamental aspects of existence: **body, soul**, and **spirit**.

Thoth, the Egyptian god often associated with wisdom and writing, was said to be self-created or born from the seed of Horus and the forehead of Set, symbolizing the balance between order and chaos. Horus represented order, kingship, and stability, embodying justice and rightful rule. Set, on the other hand, was the god of chaos, representing the desert, storms, and disorder. Their prolonged struggle for the throne of Egypt reflected the ongoing conflict between order and chaos. Thoth's birth from these two deities signified his role as a mediator and harmonizer, balancing the opposing forces of the universe. He became the god of equilibrium and balance, closely associated with Ma'at, the principle of divine order. As the scribe of the gods, Thoth ensured that the principles of Ma'at were maintained, preserving cosmic stability.

Abu Ma'shar Ja'far ibn Muhammad al-Balkhi (787-886), in his book *Kitab al-Uluf*, described three versions of Hermes. The first Hermes was the grandson of Adam who lived before the flood. He was an astrologer, instructed in the universal knowledge passed down from Adam, particularly concerning the division of the hours of the day and night. He is credited with erecting pyramids and cities in Upper Egypt, where he resided. To preserve knowledge from being lost in the flood, he built the temple of Akhmin and had all the wisdom inscribed on its walls in hieroglyphics (holy writing). The term *hieroglyph* comes from the Greek *hiero* ("holy") and *glypho* ("writing"), but the ancient Egyptians referred to it as *medu netjer*, meaning "the gods' words." This concept reflected their belief that nature and its laws were divine expressions communicated through sacred symbols. Over time, as cultures like the Greeks and Romans reinterpreted these ideas, the sacredness of nature transitioned into personifications like Gaia and Demeter, eventually evolving into the modern concept of "Mother Nature" as a nurturing force symbolizing the earth's life-sustaining systems.

The second Hermes, known as Hermes of Babylon, lived after the flood. He established temples and a mystery school where Pythagoras is said to have learned, subsequently bringing philosophy back to Greece. This version of Hermes is noted for his role in preserving and transmitting ancient wisdom.

The third Hermes, identified with the Egyptian tradition, was a teacher of alchemy who imparted his knowledge to Asclepius. This Hermes is particularly associated with the Hermetic traditions of alchemy and mystical wisdom.

IDRIS: THE SAGE

As a sage and educator, Prophet Idris (عليه السلام) is celebrated as one of humanity's greatest teachers. His name comes from the root د-ر-س, which in Arabic can mean "to study" (دَرَسَ) or "to teach" (دَرَّسَ). Some scholars believe Idris means "the one who studies," to highlight his love of learning, while others see it as "the one who instructs" to emphasize his role in revealing divine mysteries. In Islamic philosophical and metaphysical works, Idris is often referred to as Abdu'l-Hukama (Servant of the Wise). Many philosophical and esoteric sciences are attributed to his teachings.

Idris had students from all walks of life. He trained them in various subjects until they achieved mastery, after which they returned to their tribes as expert philosophers. These students established cities and settlements, governing them with civic principles. It is said that they founded between 88 and 200 cities throughout North and Western Africa, marking the first civilizations.

The 'Hermetic chain' of adepts included great thinkers like the Greek philosopher, mathematician, and astronomer Pythagoras (570-495 BCE), who influenced Plato (424/423 - 348/347 BCE). Pythagoras and Plato played significant roles in sparking the Scientific Revolution. Aristotle, who studied

157

at Plato's Academy, taught Alexander the Great. Alexander founded Alexandria, a hub for alchemy and Hermeticism, where Greek wisdom, rooted in Egyptian knowledge, flourished.

Idris's oral chain of knowledge has permeated nearly all ancient traditions and has been revived in various societies and eras. His teachings offered pupils a way to gain experience in the spirit world. To acquire this knowledge, a pupil must become an initiate, joining the chain of transmission from master to pupil. In the East, this practice is known as *Satsang*, which translates to "association with truth" or "being in the company of truth." Satsang involves sitting in the presence of a spiritual teacher or guru, engaging in community gatherings, receiving spiritual discourse, participating in meditation and chanting, and reflecting on sacred texts. It is a holistic process where truth is experienced through words and a transformative mind-to-mind connection. This profound transmission of knowledge is more than mere instruction; it is an almost hypnotic process that deeply influences the initiate's spiritual journey.

Idris is credited with many firsts in education: writing with a pen, practicing medicine, studying natural laws and astronomy, developing mathematics, creating civilization, and sewing cloth from animal skins. His students became the first scientists, alchemists, astrologers, and psychologists. Idris is also credited with designing many of the world's ziggurats, pyramids, and monuments. He is believed to have traveled and influenced civilizations such as the Olmecs and the Mayans. In short, all pre-flood sciences were taught by Idris.

The number of texts attributed to Idris remains unknown. Andalusian scholar Imam Al-Qurtubi states Idris had 30 scrolls from which he taught. Syrian philosopher Iamblichus claimed Hermes wrote over 20,000 books and Egyptian historian Manetho increased this to 36,000. Most of these works, known as the Hermetica, have been lost to time. Clement of Alexandria noted 42 secret books in Egypt containing essential knowledge, with 36 covering philosophy, laws, hymns, rituals, astrology, cosmology, and geography, and 6 on medicine.

Three major texts contain Hermetic doctrines. The *Corpus*

Hermeticum, with 18 chapters, features dialogues between Hermes and others, including a chapter where Poimandres (God) teaches Hermes the secrets of the universe. The *Emerald Tablet of Hermes Trismegistus* is a short work beginning with "That which is Below corresponds to that which is Above..." and refers to the three parts of universal wisdom: **Alchemy**, **Astrology**, and **Theurgy**. *The Perfect Sermon* (or *The Asclepius*) is a Hermetic work similar to the *Corpus Hermeticum*, written in the 2nd or 3rd century.

Although it is claimed that these writings go back to the grandson of Hermes, they are actually influenced by later thought, including Plato and Aristotle, and their followers, as well as Hebrew writers known as the Gnostics. There was no original form of an Egyptian language from which these texts were derived, and they could not have been written without the conceptual vocabulary and rhetoric of Greek philosophy. Most of the writings of the Gnostics have been erased from human history by the early Church, which regarded them as blasphemous.

Thoth served as the bridge to Hermetic traditions that emerged over a millennium later, preserving strands of Idris's wisdom in concise symbolic systems like the 78-card Tarot deck. Divided into Major and Minor Arcana, the deck reflects the hidden and revealed aspects of reality; through these cards, Thoth came to represent the sage of sorcerers, embodying the wisdom and power to navigate unseen forces. The Tarot's path mirrors the initiatory progression of the soul—from ignorance to illumination—as the seeker learns to wield divine laws. More than a divination tool, it is a metaphysical book without words, revealing the hidden structure of the universe to those who can decipher its symbols.

Fig. 24 - A relief carving of the Egyptian god Thoth from the throne back of a seated statue of Ramesses II (1279-1213 BCE), Luxor.

NAMES OF TAHUTI

Tahuti / Djehuty is revered in Ancient Egypt as the "first great educator," deified as the scribe of the Neteru who invented hieroglyphs and transmitted knowledge of **language, science,** and **magic**.[50] In Egyptian hieroglyphs his name was written ḏḥwty (pronounced "Djehuty" or "Tahuti"), meaning "He who is like the Ibis." When the Greeks encountered his cult in the Ptolemaic period, they Hellenized ḏḥwty into Θωθ (Thoth), adapting the foreign name into Greek phonetics.

Some Sufi and Hermetic sources identify him with the Quranic Prophet Idris (عليه السلام), "raised to a high station" (19:56–57), and early commentators such as al-Tabari, al-Thaʿlabī, and Ibn ʿArabi even equated him with al-Khidr. In Judaic lore, Idris is often linked to Biblical Enoch—renamed Metatron in the Midrash and Zohar as the prototype who "walked with God" before being exalted. Later Hellenistic tradition fused Thoth with the Greek Hermes to create Hermes Trismegistus, the "thrice-great" sage whose Hermetic writings shaped **alchemy, astrology,** and **early science**. Later mythic and esoteric traditions worldwide developed their own "first sage" archetype, demonstrating that Tahuti/Idris left an enduring imprint on humanity's quest for wisdom.[51]

---

50   Note: Gods (or Neters, as the Egyptians referred to them) were recognized as archetypes or symbols representing powerful patterns within the collective mind of the human race. Thoth was the psycho-spiritual archetype of science, magic, and civilization.

51   Note: Variants of this "first great sage" archetype also appear under other guises—Imhotep (Egypt); Kukulkan and Quetzalcoatl (Mesoamerica); Ningishzidda and Marduk (Mesopotamia); Odin (Norse); Jamshid (Persia); and Hanuman (Hindu)—reflecting a recurring motif of the primordial educator rather than literal identifications with Prophet Idris.

ENOCH: INTERDIMENSIONAL PROPHET

The Book of Enoch describes Enoch's amazing travels beyond the earthly realm. The very name "Enoch", from the Hebrew root חָנוֹךְ (Chanokh), means **"the initiated one,"** **"the insightful one,"** or **"the skillful one."** It was preserved for centuries in the Ethiopian Orthodox canon, though it disappeared from most European traditions after the early Church debates on scripture. It was never part of the Biblical canon because it was regarded as a pseudepigraphal text. The work resurfaced in Europe in 1773 when the Scottish explorer James Bruce returned from Ethiopia with several complete Ge'ez manuscripts, sparking renewed study and translation. It is believed to have been written by either the Hasidim or early Pharisees.

The first part of the Book of Enoch recounts how, in the "days of Jared," Samjaza (Satan) led a group of 200 angels who descended on Mt. Hermon (in present-day Israel). "From afar, they lusted after the daughters of men and later took them as wives" (1 Enoch 7:1-11). These fallen angels, known as the Watchers (shayateen in Islamic tradition), taught their wives forbidden knowledge such as magic and astrology, resulting in the birth of giant humanoids known as Nephilim (Gen 6:4).[52] The Nephilim were a warlike tribe with deep-seated hatred, causing violence and bloodshed. They introduced cannibalism by consuming their victims. Later, they became known as "the sons of Anak" (Numbers 13:33). According to some accounts, God eradicated them, while the Archangel Michael imprisoned the Watchers in deep chasms within the earth. The remainder of the book details Enoch's celestial journeys, visions, dreams,

---

52 Note: Some Islamic scholars draw parallels between the tribes of 'Ad and Thamud, described in the Quran as giants with immense strength, and the Nephilim of the Bible. The term "jabbarin" (26:130), used to describe 'Ad, is linked by some to the Hebrew "gibborim," referencing powerful beings. These tribes, like the Nephilim, were destroyed by divine punishment for their defiance.

and revelations.

During Enoch's time, humanity possessed clairvoyance (the ability to see the Astral worlds) and could communicate with spirits (angels and jinn). However, this spiritual clarity was rapidly diminishing due to widespread sin, corruption, and material indulgence. Enoch's father, Jared, belonged to one of the last generations capable of perceiving the spiritual beings existing between the heavens and the earth. Enoch's mission was to preserve heavenly knowledge of the arts and sciences on marble and brass pillars for future generations.

At the age of 365 (corresponding to the number of days in a solar year), Enoch was taken up into the heavens, either in body or spirit (Genesis 5:23). Because he did not experience death on Earth, Enoch is not bound by the same rules of time and space as other humans. Some apocryphal and mystical traditions believe that he has returned to earth many times and will return in the future.

HERMES: THE FATHER OF HERMENEUTICS

Before the European "Age of Enlightenment" in the eighteenth century,[53] Hermeneutics was a popular branch of knowledge that dealt with the theory and practice of interpreting scriptures, especially the Bible and classical texts. Over time, hermeneutics expanded to include **literary theory**, **law**, and **philosophy**, encompassing broader questions of **meaning**, **language**, and **understanding**. This interpretive practice is analogous to the methods of *Tafsir* (exegesis) and *Taweel* (Interpretation). A hermeneutical reading of scripture is a mystical experience that opens the "doors" of consciousness in the reader's mind, enabling them to experience a personal 'union with God.' Such readings reveal that texts can transform the reader by dismantling previous beliefs and replacing them with new self-understanding, transmuting one's character and daily life.

In time, hermeneutics evolved into an umbrella term that encompassed various methods of theorizing about human interpretation. This included understanding books, works of art, architecture, verbal communication, and nonverbal communication. Hermeneutics now applies to all branches of knowledge within the social, human, and natural sciences. It has moved beyond the interpretation of sacred literature to become a universal method of clarifying the conditions of all human understanding.

Understanding the 'original' meaning or 'truth' embedded in a text or other medium is more of an art than a science grounded in rules. It involves the interpretive act of integrating **signs**, **words**, and **events** into a meaningful whole. We only really understand an **object**, **word**, or **fact** when it resonates within our own life context and speaks to us meaningfully.

---

53   Note: It was during this period that European writers began rewriting narratives of the past to conceal many truths of their history to hide the truth that Europe was deeply in-debited to the people of Kemet for their intellectual and cultural contributions.

Hermeneutic thinkers are concerned with the universal conditions for human understanding in three areas: the **nature of consciousness**, the **nature of truth**, and the **importance of language**. While scholars have not reached a universal and unambiguous definition of hermeneutics, the term traces back to the ancient Greek verb *hermeneuein*, which means to utter, explain, interpret, or translate. Initially, it was used to discuss how divine messages or mental ideas are expressed in human language.

Hermeneutics begins with Hermes, son of Zeus, the mythological Greek deity who was the 'messenger of the gods,' responsible for communicating their messages in a way that mortal humans could understand the meaning. Hermes translated divine messages into human language, contextualizing them within human experience to ensure understanding by connecting **history**, **culture**, and **concepts** to make sense of things. Similarly, hermeneutics interprets the deeper significance behind texts and actions, acting as a bridge between different **eras**, **cultures**, and **languages**. By integrating new information with existing knowledge, hermeneutics makes the unfamiliar comprehensible and maintains the relevance of historical texts. Thus, Hermes' role symbolizes the essential function of hermeneutics in connecting and understanding diverse expressions of human thought.

According to Greek mythology, Hermes was the inventor of language and speech, an interpreter, as well as a liar, a thief, and a trickster. These multifaceted roles made Hermes an ideal representative figure for hermeneutics because they highlight the complex nature of communication and interpretation. Words can **reveal** or *conceal* the truth, guide, misguide, enlighten, or obscure. Just as Hermes could skillfully navigate between honesty and deception, clarity and confusion, hermeneutics explores how meaning is constructed, interpreted, and sometimes distorted. This discipline has become a way of describing our self-understanding as historical beings, acknowledging that our interpretations are influenced by our own contexts, biases, and experiences. Hermeneutics recognizes that the act of understanding is not straightforward

THE FATHER OF ESOTERIC WISDOM

but involves a dynamic interplay of revealing and concealing, much like the dual nature of Hermes himself.

What is hermeneutics? Simply put, it is what we are doing right now. It is our way of understanding the meanings on this page, a process through which truth is revealed as we combine our previous experiences and understandings.

THE HISTORY OF THE HERMETICA

The Hermetica, or Hermetic philosophy, is a collection of philosophical and symbolic ideas and texts that describe the true nature of reality. Understanding and harnessing the power of nature has been the primary mission of the Persian Magi, Babylonian Chaldeans, Greek philosophers, and Jewish Kabbalists throughout the ages. The Hermetica is divided into two parts: the **practical**, encompassing **astrology**, **magic**, and **alchemy**, and the **theoretical**, known as the Corpus Hermeticum, which addresses theological and philosophical questions. Central to the Hermetica is the belief that a spirit unifies all things and that humans are miniature versions of the universe. It suggests that nature is built on certain principles, with laboratory alchemy being the science that studies these natural processes, making it the mother of all arts and sciences. The Hermetica separates the spiritual-subatomic realms from the material-earthly realms, suggesting that the spirit is good and noble while the material is often seen as evil.

While later Hermetic authors ascribe these teachings to the Egyptian deity Tehuti (Thoth) and claim a pre-diluvian transmission, our focus here is on the corpus that first crystallized in Hellenistic Alexandria.

The earliest traces of Hermetic knowledge are believed to stem from the priesthoods of ancient Egypt and Sumer (Mesopotamia), where priests served as guardians of scientific knowledge and education. These priesthoods claimed to possess well-preserved accounts of civilization during the first

Egyptian dynasty (around 3500 BCE).[54] According to their records, there existed a lineage of wisdom that traced back more than 30,000 years. Central to these traditions was the figure of Tehuti, a great Priest-King who, according to legend, came to ancient Egypt and founded a society after the mythical sinking of Atlantis. During Tehuti's rule, it is said he composed numerous letters revealing divine truths, which were taught in secret to a disciple who then passed them down through an unbroken chain of transmission. These teachings, preserved in dialogues, guided disciples toward higher consciousness by revealing knowledge of the **divine**, the **cosmos**, the **mind,** and **nature**. While these stories are steeped in myth, they emphasize the revered role of Thoth in raising the intellectual and spiritual level of ancient Egyptian civilization.

Throughout history, Hermetic traditions occasionally resurfaced, reawakening the consciousness of those who studied them. For instance, after Alexander the Great's conquest in 332 BCE, Egypt transformed from a land of pharaohs and pyramid builders into a Hellenistic intellectual hub and bustling cosmopolitan center.[55] Alexander founded the city of Alexandria, which became home to the largest and most renowned library in the ancient world. The Library of Alexandria represented every branch of hidden knowledge due to the congregation and cultural exchange of scholars from various backgrounds.

Between the 2nd and 3rd centuries, Egyptian knowledge began merging with occult wisdom from early Gnosticism and Plato's pagan Greek philosophy.[56] The Hermetica and Greek philosophy differ in the sense that the former is *revealed*, and

54   Note: Historians divide Ancient Egypt into 30 dynasties and then group them into 3 periods. Pre-Dynastic Period (4500 to 3500) the Old Kingdom (3500 to 2400), the Middle Kingdom (2400 to 1600), and the Empire Period (1600 to 1100).

55   Note: The Hellenistic age is the period between the death of Alexander in 323, to the conquest of Rome in 31 BC.

56   Note: Gnosticism refers to a group of ancient heresies emphasizing escape from the material world through the acquisition of esoteric knowledge. Also, Neoplatonic and Neopythagorean thought consisted of most of the Greek philosophy.

the latter is *argued* (deductive vs inductive). Plato believed that truth was arrived at by dialectic reasoning, not formal or ritual prayer. Hermeticism teaches the internal experience of worship and prayer to guide the initiate toward spiritual heights. Hermetic initiations create a moral contract between the aspirant and the Adept to **walk, teach,** and **complete the path** toward spiritual illumination.

Later, the Hermetica became influenced by Jewish Kabbalah and Christian Gnostic traditions, along with Persian, Roman, and Arab cultures. This diverse mix of influences produced an exotic mode of thought. However, this blend of ideas contributed to today's confusion regarding its core principles and authenticity. Much of the Hermetica was destroyed by Christians, beginning with Emperor Constantine and his successors from 312 CE until the 6th century, putting to death thousands of Hermetic pagans, destroying their temples and sacred papyri texts. The Library of Alexandria was destroyed multiple times, leaving only a small handful of texts that survived until today.

By 480 CE, the Western Roman Empire had fallen, ushering in what later became known as the "Dark Ages." Over the ensuing centuries, Church leaders quietly rounded up Hermetic and other occult manuscripts, hiding them in monastery scriptoria and episcopal vaults. In 1475, Pope Sixtus IV finally gave those once-secret texts a permanent address— the newly founded Vatican Apostolic Library. There they remain, sealed behind thick walls and locked away from public eyes, preserved for a day when their mysteries might at last be revealed.

From the early Middle Ages (6th century) onward, Church authorities recognized that esoteric thinking—**Hermeticism, alchemy, Neoplatonism**—undermined the Church's strict doctrinal frameworks. As occult students began producing literature and art to help people expand their consciousness and perceive patterns beyond rote doctrine, the clergy systematically suppressed these works and monopolized education within cathedral schools and monastic universities. By the late Middle Ages (13th–14th centuries), scholars of the Western mystery tradition were forced underground. It was then—from roughly 1300 to 1500 CE—that secret brotherhoods began to form to preserve and circulate esoteric knowledge in secret networks.

These organizations used **enigmas, symbols**, and **allegories** to keep their knowledge public while simultaneously keeping it secret. In the comfort of temples and lodges, they taught the allegorical thinking required to understand Hermetic **signs**, **symbols**, and **writings**.

In 639 CE, the 2nd Caliph Umar ibn al-Khattab رضي الله عنه directed an invasion of Egypt, ushering in the Islamic Age. Between the 8th and 15th centuries, Arab scholars sought out Greek knowledge and heritage and then expounded on it with fundamental techniques. It was during this period that the article "al" became affixed to the word "chemia,"[57] giving rise to "alchemy." This marked the beginning of alchemy as a systematic science, as Arab scholars integrated Greek, Egyptian, and Indian knowledge with their own innovations, laying the foundation for modern chemistry.

The first of the great Arab contributions came in the 8th century when the oldest and most famous Hermetic text of all, *Lawh al-zumurrudh*, The Emerald Tablet, was composed. Although the tablet is only one paragraph long, it became the foundational text for Arab and Latin alchemists and scholars due to it containing the one formula that describes the structure and dynamics of any system in nature: animal, vegetable, mineral, matter or energy, physical, psychological, or spiritual, on any level in existence.

The *Emerald Tablet* and the formula it contains are credited with being the source used to create the Philosopher's Stone; the legendary substance used to turn lead into gold through laboratory alchemy. The stone has three uses which correspond to the three main goals of alchemy: firstly, the transmutation of base minerals into precious gems; secondly, the Elixir of Life, which preserves health, cures disease, and extends life; and thirdly, spiritual illumination.

The origins of the Tablet are obscure. It came centuries after

57 Note: *kimiya* in Arabic means alchemy.

the Hermetica, and there is no evidence of an earlier version. It first appeared in a complex text which itself has obscure origins, *Kitab sir al-khaliqa*, the Book of the Secret of Creation, falsely attributed to Apollonius of Tyana (Balinus). However, it is likely that the text was produced by Jabir ibn Hayyan, who is known in the West as Geber, from whom we get the word "gibberish."[58] Jabir's works, translated into Latin in the twelfth century AD, formed the foundation for Western alchemists and justified their search for the Philosopher's Stone. Some claims suggest the original document was written in ancient Syriac or Phoenician and produced at least 2500 years before its rediscovery, which, if true, would make it one of the oldest revealed texts in history.

Around 900 CE, Europe began emerging from the Dark Ages due to knowledge acquired from the Muslim world, then at the zenith of its Golden Age. Modern historians agree that this era marked the true beginnings of Western Hermetic occult tradition. Clerics affiliated with the Christian Church were sent to the Islamic-dominated East in search of knowledge lost due to the fall of the Roman Empire. The Greek and Arabic texts they acquired were rapidly translated into Latin for a European audience. Among these were several salvaged copies of the Hermetica from the Eastern Roman Empire.

The Italian scholar, astrologer, and Catholic priest Marsilio Ficino (1433-99) was commissioned by the papal banker Cosimo de' Medici to prioritize the translation of fourteen Greek Hermetic texts into Latin in 1462, pausing his work on Plato's complete works. These texts represented the ancient pagan mystery teachings of the Chaldeans, Egyptians, and Platonists. The antiquity of the Hermetic texts excited Medici, who was intrigued by rumors that Hermes was a combination of two ancient sages, Hermes and Zoroaster and that he was a contemporary of Moses. It is believed that Hermes and Moses met during Moses's exile from Egypt. If true, Hermes would be a key figure in merging ancient philosophy with Judeo-

---

58 They called Jabir's (Geber's) works 'Geberish' because they thought he was writing in his own language. In time, the word 'gibberish' became the denotative for 'to talk in no known language.' In essence, his writings were so advanced, they could not understand anything.

Christian concepts. Medici desired to read Hermes' writings, which trace back to the origins of the two major intellectual influences of the time: Christianity and Ancient Greek philosophy.

Ficino's translations included two treaties: the *Asclepius*, which contains material regarding ritual magic, and the *Poimandres*, which included passages on astronomy-cosmology. These texts became known as the *Corpus Hermeticum* or the *philosophical* Hermetica. Afterward, the Hermetic corpus began to influence European scholars who made scientific advances that inspired the birth of the Italian Renaissance, which was a revival of both humanism and esoteric traditions.[59] The ethos of this philosophy is captured in Hermes Trismegistus' assertion: "What a great miracle is man." Scientists of this era were impressed with Hermeticism's theoretical and practical aspects. Practical Hermeticism, or 'natural magic,' involved testing nature through experiments, while theoretical Hermeticism helped scientists understand the universe. Renaissance thinkers built on these foundations, searching for hidden and allegorical links between all things. In this sense, the 'occult' was positive, revealing hidden aspects of reality.

Ficino's translations firmly established Hermes Trismegistus as the founder of a philosophical tradition with followers including Orpheus, Pythagoras, and Plato. Philosophers of the Italian Renaissance viewed Hermeticism as the only legitimate source of Adamic primeval knowledge. However, many northern European scholars saw Hermeticism as un-Christian and inspired by the devil, unsuitable for understanding nature or penetrating its true essence.

Between the sixteenth and early eighteenth centuries, during the Scientific Revolution, the Hermetica experienced both its peak and decline. This era, beginning with the Renaissance, marked a shift from faith-based cosmological

---

59   Note: The spiritual de-evolution of European thought went through several critical stages beginning with the Crusades when they began rejecting religious superstition and reviving classical learning which led to the Renaissance which led to 18th century Enlightenment culminating in the American and French Revolutions and the creation of a new government which separates Church and State.

views of the Classical period and the Middle Ages to an embrace of empiricism, reason, and open inquiry. Despite this shift, many scientists of the time were deeply influenced by Hermetic principles. Notable figures include Nicolaus Copernicus (1473–1543), who developed the heliocentric theory with Hermetic ideas about the cosmos; Johannes Kepler (1571–1630), who advanced planetary motion theories blending Hermetic mysticism with geometry and astrology; Robert Boyle (1627–1691), the father of modern chemistry, who incorporated Hermetic principles into his experimental approach; Isaac Newton (1642–1727), who unified physical and spiritual worlds and extensively wrote on alchemy; and Francis Bacon (1561–1626), the father of empiricism, who reflected Hermetic beliefs in his emphasis on observation and experimentation. These figures demonstrate Hermeticism's profound impact on modern science's development.

During the Age of Reason, part of the Hermetic tradition was rejected as modern science and psychology emerged. Scholars debated the authenticity of the Hermetica, arguing that the Greek language used in the texts appeared after the time of Christ. Some claimed the Hermetica was a forgery by different authors, and others believed Hermes never existed. They argued that ancient Egyptian innovations were based on superstitions and were vastly superseded by Greek advancements. Some contended that true mystical theology began with Abraham and entered Egypt via Joseph. Consequently, the Hermetica was no longer seen as complementary to revelation but was condemned as magical superstition

The Scientific Revolution separated the visible and the invisible. Science was separated from religion and the spiritual world, leading to a mechanistic view of nature focused on logical and rational thought.

By the 18th century, during the Age of Enlightenment, religious superstitions were replaced with a revival in classical learning. The American and French Revolutions brought new freedoms, and a distinct European civilization began to emerge. Europeans led the world in scientific discoveries fueled by the global acquisition of material resources, culminating in the Industrial Revolution.

Aside from esoteric groups like the Freemasons, which preserved the memory and teachings of Hermes, the history of Hermeticism disappeared at the beginning of the nineteenth century. In 1798, Napoleon's invasion of Egypt opened the door to Egyptology. After the discovery of the Rosetta Stone, Ancient Egypt could speak for itself, revealing little connection to Hermeticism.

By the 20th century, Hermeticism was revived through the writings of magicians such as Franz Bardon (1909-1958) and Hermetic philosophers like Helena Blavatsky (1839-1891), along with other groups calling themselves Hermetic. In the 1960s, the New Age Movement emerged as a counterculture to established beliefs and religions. Like Hermeticists, New Agers are pantheistic, seeing the presence of God everywhere and accepting that all religions have their own truth.

In the 21st century, the internet has reawakened Hermetic concepts in the consciousness of millions. A large increase in websites, blogs, and social media sites has enabled the occult movement to thrive, providing access to resources for like-minded people in virtual communities. Hermeticism and occult themes have also penetrated mainstream media, with movies and TV shows exploring magic, alchemy, and esoteric wisdom. These shows often incorporate occult symbols and ideas, introducing broader audiences to concepts once considered niche, further mainstreaming occultism and its related philosophies into popular culture.

In summary, the *Corpus Hermeticum* has traversed through various cultural periods, from the Greco-Egyptian era to the Arab Islamic period and into Latin European history, continuing to influence thought today. These texts have inspired philosophers, alchemists, mystics, magicians, poets, playwrights, writers, and members of secret societies such as the Rosicrucians, Freemasons, the Hermetic Order of the Golden Dawn, New Age movements, and Wicca.

Today, the Hermetica is regarded as a type of divine revelation, foundational to all fundamental occult teachings, **magic**, **astrology**, and **alchemy**. Practically every sage and mystic from antiquity has looked to Hermes Trismegistus as the source of their wisdom. The mystical allegories found in ancient doctrines, initiation rituals in mystery cults, sacred writings in ancient ruins and temples, and symbolic paintings on monuments worldwide all contain remnants of Hermetic influence. In summary, Hermes has been credited as the author of most esoteric wisdom with unclear origins.

The occult philosophy attributed to Hermes has influenced all religions, encapsulated principles of all sciences, conveyed paths for human progress, and shaped the growth or decline of various civilizations. It continues to provoke curiosity and fear today.

The practical branch of the Hermetica teaches students how to apply universal laws and achieve higher levels of consciousness and states of being. Transmutation, a core concept, involves changing one element or form of energy into a more valuable one. As mentioned in Chapter 1, traditional alchemists aim to turn base metals into gold, while mental alchemists strive to master mental forces and attract golden opportunities by changing their vibrational states. Mental alchemists can transform internal states from fear to hope, cowardice to bravery, and victim mentality to victor mentality.

Hermeticists believe that magic is a psychological process where invoked powers exist in the mind and are energized by the will. They change their habits of thought and action to manifest desired biochemical or mental conditions, embodying the practical aspect of the Hermetica: changing reality by changing one's mind.

A history of education would be incomplete without conveying the prominent teachings of the Hermetica regarding the principles governing the heavenly and earthly realms from an Islamic perspective. Although popular in occult circles, these principles are not inherently "evil" or "demonic"; they are universal truths recognized by all true religions. These principles describe reality and govern human behavior, applicable for bettering humanity or, conversely, enslaving it. They do not contradict Islam; rather, they help people understand the unseen dimensions of life that influence our external and internal worlds.

Throughout history, only a select few have understood these principles. Students proving their moral purity and trustworthiness gained access to these universal truths. Over time, as humanity degenerated into barbarism and cruelty, this divine knowledge survived in isolated pockets worldwide. Classical works, such as Shakespeare's plays, Krishna's teachings, and the Christian Gospels, all veil the truth of the great arcanum (secret knowledge).

Arrogant leaders have historically suppressed occult teachings about human consciousness and the unseen Universal Principles governing human behavior. They created governments with man-made laws dictating the physical, emotional, and mental conditions of the masses, which is an abuse of truth. Occult groups like the Freemasons have played a role in reviving the Hermetica in recent generations. Masonic rituals borrow from mystery school teachings connected to Hermes, with nearly all Masonic symbols being Hermetic. However, Masons are not the rightful owners of this knowledge. Like the Masons, Muslims should help revive the teachings of Idris and find parallels between those teachings and core Islamic concepts.

Arguably, the most significant text from the Hermetica is the *Kybalion*, published in 1908. Although there is no evidence of its existence prior to this publication, it is a collection of axioms and maxims taught and practiced in occult circles.

The *Kybalion*'s 7 Principles are based on the Hermetic idea of the individual's identity with the divine mind. Attributed to three anonymous initiates, it is believed to have been written by William Walker Atkinson, who learned from Baba Bharata, a student of the Indian mystic Yogi Ramacharaka. Before its written form, the *Kybalion*'s truths were passed down orally from teacher to student. The text suggests that knowledge is only imparted when the student is ready, emphasizing the need for openness and willingness to accept that there is more to the physical world than meets the eye.

These 7 Hermetic Principles are "Hermetically sealed" in the sense that they are eternal and unchanging, much like a sealed container that remains impervious to external influences. Just as the laws of nature are constant, these principles are universally applicable, governing all aspects of existence, physical, mental, and spiritual, across time and space. This sealed nature of the principles affirms their reliability as foundational truths that have guided sages and seekers throughout history and continue to do so in the present day.

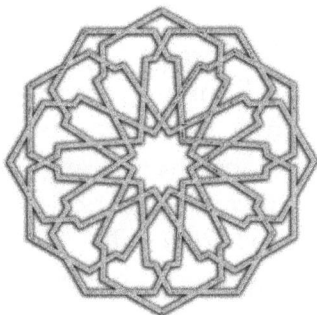

SECTION 1

THE PRINCIPLE OF MENTALISM

﴿ وَأَنَّ ٱللَّهَ قَدْ أَحَاطَ بِكُلِّ شَىْءٍ عِلْمًا ﴾

"...Allah encompasses all things in His knowledge" *(65:12).*

"THE ALL IS MIND; The Universe is Mental."
~ The Kybalion

"The gift of mental power comes from God, Divine Being, and if we concentrate our minds on that truth, we become in tune with this great power."
~Nicola Tesla

THE PRINCIPLE

Mentalism states that an unseen, supreme intelligence, beyond time, space, and matter, brought all physical and metaphysical reality into existence. In essence, all reality originates in the 'mind' of the Creator. This 'mind' that is beyond the cosmos unites all facets of the universe toward a common destiny. *The Kybalion* calls the creator of all reality "The ALL." "The All is everything, and everything is part of 'The ALL.'"

In Islamic thought, "The ALL" is none other than Allah, the Supreme Creator. Every phenomenon, seen and unseen, unfolds by His divine will and infinite knowledge. It is important to note that while the concept of "The ALL" in Hermetic thought is associated with a "mind," Islam makes a distinction: Allah's reality is beyond human comprehension.[60] As mentioned in Chapter 2, all that would ever occur was written and preserved in the *Lawhul-Mahfoodh*, the Preserved Tablet. However, all ideas, beings, and events contained in that book were known by Allah before being written. Moreover, the *Lawhul-Mahfoodh* and all its knowledge is itself a mental creation of Allah. This principle unifies all others, and all other phenomena are multiple manifestations or transformations deriving from this single principle. Mentalism is the law that governs the universe in perfect equilibrium. There is no LAW other than the ALL.

Allah's "mind" is the creative force that propelled the heavens and the earth into existence after pronouncing the command "*Kun*," Be! In short, everyone and everything that exists, has existed, or will exist is encompassed within the

---

60 Note: In The *Kybalion*, and other Hermetic texts, "The ALL" is characterized as a cosmic Mind. Islamic theology, however, holds that Allah does not possess a "mind" in human terms. References to His knowledge ('*Ilm*), awareness (*Khabir*), and will (*Iradah*) are ways to convey His attributes, not to liken Him to created intellects.

"mind" of Allah. Just as Allah's decree brings all of existence into being, our own thoughts shape our perception and experience of reality. While we do not create from nothing as Allah does, we influence how we engage with the world He has designed.

The "idea" of creation was a divine command that transformed the unseen into the seen. Allah is One, and through His pronouncement of Kun, multiplicity came into existence. Yet, His essence remains beyond human comprehension. No power or force can change Allah. He is *Al-Matin* (The Firm, The Ever Constant), unchangeable in His essence, yet all that is contained within His creation is in a state of flux. Likewise, the minds of humans are always changing, reflecting the constantly shifting nature of existence.

The "All is Mind" concept can also be understood as it relates to people on their physical plane of being. Allah created all material that exists within the macrocosmic realm of the Universe. People have the ability to co-create their reality by building objects using matter prepared for them within the microcosmic realm of the earth. Allah creates from the mind without using any material. For there was nothing except for Allah before He created immaterial and material objects. Humans can only create new physical objects by manipulating material that Allah mentally created for our usage.

~ The art and practice of creating something on the physical plane begins with generating thoughts and ideas on the mental plane; once the thought occurs, the rest follows. ~

In the astral realm, there is a higher and lower mental plane. After an idea has been developed, the 'thinker' holds onto it for some time until it becomes a desire. The desire settles in the heart and eventually becomes a will. The will is the decision to commit to a course of action. Consistent actions are made until a goal is manifested in the world. That manifested goal is the product of a mental creation. To bring forth another goal, one must generate a new idea and begin the process again. Every object, tool, and structure around us was once just a

179

thought, an idea formed in someone's mind before it became a reality. A towering skyscraper, a handcrafted chair, even a simple cup, all began in the unseen world of thought before taking physical shape. This reflects a fundamental truth: **the mind precedes matter**. Just as Allah's knowledge existed before creation, human thought is the seed from which all inventions, innovations, and creations emerge.

An individual's mental forces can change physical reality by altering their perception. One who desires to bring forth some change in their lives or within the world must first change that which is within themselves (13:11). We have the power to change our perception of all things, from gross physical objects to subtle feelings to even subtler thoughts. For example, one can react to the sudden jolt of cold water on our bare skin, or remain calm and feel empowered that they can embrace the cold and reap the internal benefits generated by the cardiovascular system.

Likewise, we have the potential to control our feelings when receiving troubling news or when witnessing a distressing event. We can optimistically choose to believe that one door will close for another to open, or we can resort to sadness and depression. Finally, we have power over our thoughts. We can choose to cultivate thoughts that are empowering or thoughts that are disempowering. Our character is a product of our thoughts. When we learn to master our thoughts, we are able to mold our character, allowing us to shape our environment and move towards our destiny with conviction. The inner world of thought shapes the outer world of circumstance.

We have the power to direct our thoughts toward either fleeting worldly pursuits or eternal success in the Hereafter. As Allah says:

مَّن كَانَ يُرِيدُ ٱلْعَاجِلَةَ عَجَّلْنَا لَهُۥ فِيهَا مَا نَشَآءُ لِمَن نُّرِيدُ ثُمَّ جَعَلْنَا لَهُۥ جَهَنَّمَ يَصْلَىٰهَا مَذْمُومًا مَّدْحُورًا

﴿ وَمَنْ أَرَادَ ٱلْآخِرَةَ وَسَعَىٰ لَهَا سَعْيَهَا وَهُوَ مُؤْمِنٌ فَأُوْلَـٰئِكَ كَانَ سَعْيُهُم مَّشْكُورًا ﴾

Whoever should desire the immediate - We hasten for him from it what We will to whom We intend. Then We have made for him Hell, which he will [enter to] burn, censured and banished.
But whoever desires the Hereafter and exerts the effort due to it while he is a believer - it is those whose effort is ever appreciated [by Allāh].
(17:18-19)

This verse highlights the fundamental truth that our **intentions and efforts shape our reality.** If we focus solely on short-term gains, we may achieve them, but at the cost of our eternal well-being. However, if we channel our mental energies toward a higher purpose, such as striving for the Hereafter, then our efforts will be recognized and rewarded by Allah.

The changing of one's perception can change our response and consciously change how that subject or object is understood. Our opinions, beliefs, and attitudes can color our experience of reality.

One of the most popular examples is the perception of a cup of water being half-full or half-empty. This simple analogy reflects a greater truth; our perception is the gateway to our emotional and spiritual state.

While we may not control external events, we hold power over how we interpret and respond to them. A refined mind sees wisdom in trials, while a heedless mind drowns in negativity. Therefore, our perceptions shape our journey through life.

In Islam, the believer is encouraged to perceive all occurrences optimistically, for everything is occurring according to Allah's plan.

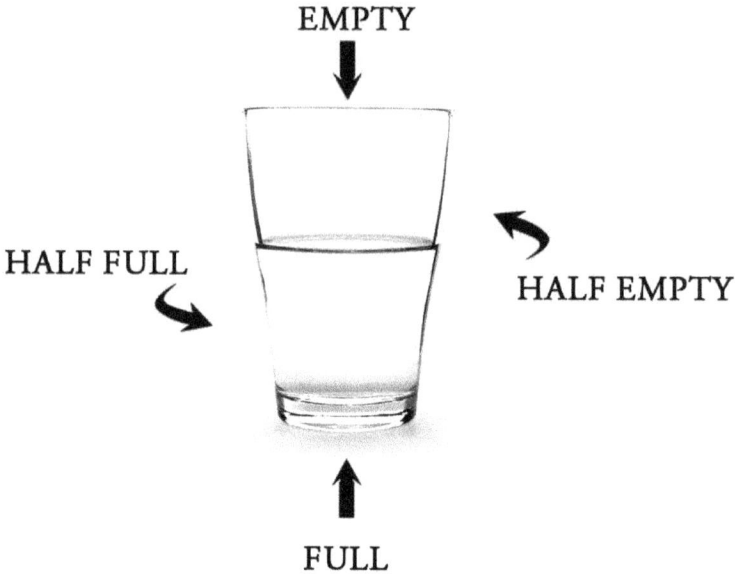

Fig. 25 - Is the glass "half full" or "half empty"? Or is it both? Or neither? The conclusive answer is often "Depends on who you ask."

> *Narrated Suhaib: The Prophet ﷺ said, "Amazing is the affair of the believer. Verily, his affair, all of it, is good. And not is this the case with any but the believer. If something of goodness happens to him, he is grateful, and that is good for him. If something of harm befalls him, he is patient, and that is [also] good for him (Muslim).*

This knowledge empowers the believer with the psychological strength to escape the pain of living on lower emotional planes, and instead encourages him to generate thoughts that vibrate on higher mental planes. The highest vibrating thought is dhikr (remembrance of Allah), which involves the silent recitation of Allah's names, *du'a* (supplications) from hadith texts, and verses from the Quran. As Allah teaches, "Remember Me, and I will remember you" (2:152), and He further exhorts us to "disperse within the land and seek from the bounty of Allah, and remember Allah often that you may succeed" (62:10). This practice of continual remembrance not only opens us up to divine attention but also grants profound inner peace: "Those who have believed and whose hearts are assured by the remembrance of Allah. Unquestionably, by the remembrance of Allah hearts are assured" (13:28). Through dhikr, then, we both fulfill our Lord's command and discover the serenity and success He has promised.

The ability to vibrate at a higher mental plane is an honor Allah has bestowed upon mankind to prepare us for the responsibility of serving Him as commanded. Since "ALL IS MIND," Allah had humans in mind when preparing the material conditions of the earth. Upon examining the earth closely, we see that Allah created the inanimate realms to serve the animate realms, with humans being the most honored of these creations. A divine pattern of 7 exists on Earth:

- dust (minerals) in service of...

- water in service of...

- fire in service of...

- plants in service of...

- proteins in service of...

- animals in service of...

- humans.

Humans were created to be the earth's leaders in service of (∞) Allah. From Allah's divine intentions was His desire to create and to be known. Likewise, Allah intends for His

183

creation to evolve from ignorance towards greater self-awareness and awareness of Him. To prepare mankind for their service to Allah as leaders of the earth, we were provided with the most intricate, powerful, and adaptable combination of features more than any other created being. We are physical bodies animated through 5 spiritual components:

- Ruh, (subconscious spirit),

- Nefs (conscious soul),

- Aql (intellect),

- Fitrah (innate disposition),

- Qalb (physical and spiritual heart, container of emotions, and intellect).

A more detailed analysis of each component follows:

Ruh (Subconscious Spirit).

As mentioned in Chapter 2, mankind is distinguished from the rest of creation by the **ruh**. The ruh enables life and activates the senses. Plants, animals, and humans all possess a ruh, but the ruh of the human being is superior to that of animals, and the ruh of animals is superior to that of plants. Proof of the Ruh in animals is their instincts. Proof of the ruh in plants is their intricate mycelium network, an underground web of fungal threads connecting plant roots and trees.

The first aspect of the ruh relates to its role in sustaining life through its influence on the physical body. This ruh is described as originating in the heart and spreading through the arteries to reach all parts of the body. It enables vital functions such as breathing and circulation, ensuring the body remains alive and capable of perceiving through the five senses. When this ruh departs, the body ceases to function and dies.

The second aspect of the ruh is its spiritual dimension, which is connected to the qalb and possesses a luminous nature derived from *Nur* (light). This ruh transcends the physical and serves as the essence of a person's spiritual being, perceivable only through an understanding of its divine origins. Its characteristics and changes are connected to the soul's journey through its various stages of existence, originating from Allah and returning back to Allah.

Stage 1: Our journey begins in the company of Allah in the *Alam Arwah* (the world of spirits). Here, all souls were created and entered into a covenant with Allah, promising to worship none but Him (*Alam al-Dharr*, the Realm of the Seed, where souls were pre-temporally gathered before earthly life.). When we perform dhikr, we reconnect with this primordial moment, reviving the memory of our closeness to Allah.

Stage 2: *Alam Arham* (**World of the Womb**). The next phase of the journey is the merging of the ruh with the body during its formation in the womb. This transformation unfolds in six stages, beginning at the atomic level with lifeless matter (**dust, water,** and **fire**). From this humble beginning, a human being is meticulously crafted within the mother's womb (3:6).

- *Nutfah* (**Sperm-drop**). The ruh enters the body at this stage, where the mix of male and female genetic material forms the basis of a human being. This fusion determines every characteristic of the individual, encoded in the chromosomes, XY for males and XX for females (22:5, 23:13).

- *Alaqah* (**Clinging Clot**). By day 15, the zygote clings to the uterine wall, growing rapidly until day 23–24 (96:2).

- *Mudghah* (**Chewed-like Substance**). Between days 24–40, the body takes on a shape resembling chewed flesh, alternating between formed and unformed states (23:14).

185

- *Idtham* (**Bone Formation**). By the 6th week (42 days), bones form, giving the fetus its human framework (23:14).

- *Lahm* (**Flesh Development**). Between weeks 7–8, the bones are clothed with flesh, and the embryo transforms into a human shape.

- *Khalaqan Akhar* (**Another Creation**). From weeks 9–38, the fetus develops rapidly, its gender becomes clear, and its unique features emerge. At week 17 (120 days), an angel records the child's decree: deeds, sustenance, lifespan, and ultimate fate as blessed or cursed (23:14; Sahih Muslim).

Stage 3: *Dunya* (Temporal material world). Emerging from the womb, the ruh enters the *dunya*, a physical realm marked by trials and impermanence. This stage is a testing ground, and it begins with the legacy of Adam and Hawwah, who descended from the garden due to disobedience. Life in this stage typically spans 60–70 years.[61] For believers (*mu'min*), the dunya is a prison, while for disbelievers (*kafir*), it is like paradise.

Stage 4: *Barzakh* (The Intermediate Realm). After death, the ruh transitions to the *Barzakh* (the interim between *dunya* and the Hereafter). Here, souls reside until resurrection. Depending on their deeds, they may experience peace or torment. Some souls dwell in Jannah, others in the *nar* (fire) or other states, awaiting the Day of Judgment.

Stage 5: *Qiyyam* (Day of Judgement). The Day of Judgment is the grand culmination of the ruh's journey. This day will last 50,000 years and begins with the blowing of the trumpet,

---

61   "The lifespan of my Ummah is between sixty and seventy years, with few surpassing it." (Tirmidhi, Ibn Majah, Ibn Hibban)

where all of creation will rise from their graves, uncircumcised and naked, to stand before Allah for judgment (Muslim). It is the most significant day all souls will experience, so much so that it is known by many names in Islamic tradition, each highlighting its gravity and challenges.[62] On this day, all souls will be judged for their actions in the dunya. The righteous will anticipate meeting Allah with joy, while the sinners will face terror. The day will test everyone based on four fundamental questions:

- How they spent their lifetime.

- The knowledge they acquired and how they acted upon it.

- The wealth they earned, how they acquired it and how they spent it.

- How they used their body and its faculties (Tirmidhi).

Amid the stress and terror, some will find refuge in Allah's shade, protected from the sun, which will be brought near to the earth. Among these fortunate ones are 7 types of people, as mentioned in authentic Hadith:

- A just leader.

- A youth who grew up worshiping Allah.

- A person whose heart is attached to the mosque.

---

62   For instance: *Yawmul Ahkir* "The Last Day" (2:62), *Yammul Deen* «Day of Recompense» (1:4), *Yawm al-Jami* «Day of Gathering» (64:9), *Yawm ad-Fath* "Day of Decision" (32:29), *Waqia't* «The Event» (56:1), *Yammul Fasl* «Sorting» (77:13), *Sakhkhah* «Deafening cry» (80:33), *A-Taamatu Kubra* "Great Catastrophe" (79:34), *Al-Qari'ah* "The Striking" (101:1), *Al-Haaqaqah* "The Reality", *As-Saa'ah* "The Hour" (31:34), *Al-Hasra* "Regret" (19:39).

- Two people who love each other for the sake of Allah, meeting and parting only for His pleasure.

- A man who is tempted by a woman of beauty and position but says, "I fear Allah."

- A person who gives charity so secretly that their left hand does not know what their right hand gives.

- A person who remembers Allah in private and their eyes overflow with tears (Bukhari and Muslim).

This special group will enjoy Allah's protection while most others endure the unbearable heat and trials of the day. This stark contrast emphasizes the immense importance of righteous deeds and sincerity in this life, as they determine one's ultimate standing on that day.

Stage 6: *Jannah* or *Jahannam* (Paradise or Hellfire). The final stage of the ruh's journey leads to eternal abode. Souls will inhabit either Jannah, the garden from which we originated, or Jahannam, the Hellfire, depending on their deeds.

In general, the ruh is an aspect of ourselves that we have little knowledge of.

$$ \text{﴿ وَيَسْأَلُونَكَ عَنِ ٱلرُّوحِ قُلِ ٱلرُّوحُ مِنْ أَمْرِ رَبِّي وَمَآ أُوتِيتُم مِّنَ ٱلْعِلْمِ إِلَّا قَلِيلًا ﴾} $$

*"And they ask you, [O Muhammad], about the spirit. Say, "The **spirit** is by command of my Lord. And you **have not been given of knowledge except a little**" (17:85).*

Nafs. The nafs is the soul, mind, self, conscious desires, impulses, appetites, personality, and ego. The ruh and the nafs are two different aspects of the same thing, except the the former is masculine (in language), and the latter is feminine. The former makes us inclined towards good; the latter tempts us towards evil. This is what the Western world refers to as the psyche. As Chapter One mentions, the nafs is located in our lungs and can influence our entire body. When the nafs is low, it resides within the belly and the genitals. However, with discipline, we can elevate it to a higher, more enlightened state. It is a non-material "hard disk" that stores our memories, desires, fears, and ambitions. The Nafs is the new entity created when the earthly body joins with the heavenly ruh. It serves as the bridge linking the metaphysical to the physical and conscious energy to physical matter.

Aql.[63] The aql refers to reason and intellect, which the Western world calls the 'mind.' It encompasses our mental ability to learn, understand, and act rightly based on knowledge. The aql governs our will, wit, power of judgment, perception, foresight, imagination, communication, and other cognitive experiences. When humans use their intellect to acquire a portion of the ilm (knowledge) that Allah has revealed, they gain insight into the "mind" of Allah.

Fitrah. Fitrah is our natural, inborn disposition to discern right from wrong and submit to Allah. Prophet Muhammad said, "Every new-born child is born in a state of fitrah. Then his parents make him a Jew, a Christian, or a Magian, just as an animal is born intact. Do you observe any among them that are maimed (at birth)?" (Muslim). This represents the natural disposition of the mind and body before any external alterations or influences. The fitrah is a part of the Nafs, which was discussed in the previous section.

---

63   Note: Al-'aql in Arabic is related to the root 'ql which means 'to bind'.

Qalb (heart). The *Qalb*, or heart, is where rational thinking, sensual experience, and moral judgment merge. There are two aspects to the *Qalb*. One is the physical heart, located towards the left side of our chest, containing blackish-red blood and acting as the source of the spirit of life. This physical heart beats around 100,000 times a day and pumps over 100 gallons an hour throughout our vascular system, keeping us alive. The second aspect is a subtle, spiritual substance that enables us to 'know' and to 'perceive.' This spiritual essence of the heart is the repository for our Nafs, *Fu'ad* (emotions, as mentioned in the Quran 17:36), Aql, and *Shu'ur* (inner awareness or perception). It is this second aspect of the Qalb that is being referred to in this text.

The Quran indicates that the heart has an intellectual function, acting much like an energetic gateway that allows us to resonate with and interpret external energies, particularly when the heart is aligned with truth and free of falsehood. When the heart is clean, it can guide and enlighten other faculties about the truth and reality of all things and how we should relate to them. One must constantly work on their heart, mind, and consciousness to protect them from falsehood. If one consistently mistakes falsehood for truth, they will develop a habit of mind that prevents them from distinguishing the real from the fake. When this happens, the heart can become 'sealed' and lose its consciousness (2:7). In that sense, the Aql and Qalb are one and the same.[64]

Contrary to common belief, thinking originates in the heart, where intent forms the foundation of thought. The heart's intent sets an energetic frequency that resonates throughout the body, often detecting subtle cues and 'vibes' before the brain does, which leads to actions in the limbs and speech on the tongue. Intelligence is using one's energy to store or release knowledge. Orienting one's intent (qalb) and brain towards a noble aim is using one's Aql. In several locations in the Quran, Allah commands people to use their Aql and warns against those who do not.

---

64   Note: There are other aspects of the *qalb,* such as *al-sadr,* the chest, *al-fu'ad,* the inner heart, and *al-lubb,* the innermost intellect.

The root of Qalb (*qaf lam ba*) means something that turns around, about, and upside down. When negative emotions dominate our hearts, they turn towards our lower Nafs. Over time, the lower Nafs may gain complete control over our Qalb, causing us to behave like or worse than animals. When positive emotions and intentions are in harmony, the heart resonates at higher frequencies, activating the Aql and attracting similar positive influences from the environment. When the Aql gains full mastery over the Qalb, we can elevate our actions and behavior to align with, or even surpass, the qualities of angels.[65] The process of using one's Aql to consciously change behavior is mental transmutation from an Islamic perspective. *Mental transmutation is the process of using higher principles to overcome the effects of lower principles.*

---

65   Note: Ibn al Qayyim wrote: Qataadah said: "Allah created angels with reason and no desires, animals with desires and no reason, and man with both reason and desires." So if a man's reason is stronger than his desire than he is like an angel, and if his desires are stronger than his reason, then he is like an animal. (Uddat As Sabireen, 2/7).

IS ALL REALLY MIND?

The more we have *Husn ad-Dhann Billah* (good opinion of Allah), the more we will recognize His wisdom manifesting in our lives. On the other hand, if an individual consciously chooses to disbelieve in Allah, then they will find that which appears to be evidence to support their disbelief. Allah guides those who consciously desire guidance and misleads those who choose misguidance. Allah eases the way for each of his servants without any compulsion. Allah is wise and just, giving all human beings the intellectual freedom to choose their desired path, and He assists them on their chosen path.[66] Our conditions and circumstances in life are created because of our freedom of choice; we are free to choose which ideas we want to generate within and respond to. This means the reality of Allah will manifest in the world of those who desire to know Him. Be conscious of Allah, and Allah will be conscious of you.[67] The Principle of Mentalism calls us to **elevate our thoughts**, to align our minds with divine wisdom. When we understand that all creation flows from Allah's will, we become more conscious of our own **thoughts**, **actions**, and **intentions**. By refining our inner world, we shape a better outer reality, in this life and the next.

---

66   "As for he who gives and fears Allah, And believes in the best [reward], We will ease him toward ease. But as for he who withholds and considers himself free of need. And denies the best [reward], We will ease him toward difficulty. (92: 5-10).

67   Abdullah ibn Abbas said: One day, I was behind the Prophet ﷺ so he said to me: "O young man, I am going to teach you some words. Be mindful of Allah, and He will protect you. Be mindful of Allah, and you will find Him facing you. If you ask, then ask of Allah. If you seek aid, then seek aid in Allah. Know that if the entire Ummah were to gather in order to benefit you with something, they could not benefit you with anything except with that which Allah has written for you. And if the entire Ummah were to gather in order to harm you with something, they could not harm you with anything except with what Allah has written against you. The pen has been lifted and the pages have dried." (at-Tirmidhi).

The significance of having consciousness of Allah is conveyed through the following *hadith qudsi*:

The Prophet ﷺ said, "Allah the Most High said, 'I am as My servant thinks (expects) I am. I am with him when he mentions Me. If he mentions Me to himself, I mention him to Myself; and if he mentions Me in an assembly, I mention him in an assembly greater than it. If he draws near to Me a hand's length, I draw near to him an arm's length. And if he comes to Me walking, I go to him at speed." (Bukhari)

Allah will grant you that which you expect from Him—and more. If we desire forgiveness, we will be forgiven; if we ask, it will be accepted; if we have hope in Him, we will obtain what we desire. On the other hand, those who believe they have bad luck, are victims of their circumstances, or feel they don't deserve what they get are people who are not content with their fate. The heart of the believer must always be in a state of assuming the best about its Lord and expecting the best from Him in times of both ease and hardship. Through the link of the Ruh, the Qalb is never cut off from the flow of good that Allah sends down. So if the heart doesn't disconnect itself, neither does the good. Some of the righteous people of the past would say, "Whenever a crisis comes your way, utilize your good expectations of Allah to repel it. This will bring you closer to relief."

Humanists, atheists, agnostics, and others who disbelieve in or have doubts regarding the existence of Allah will find this principle of Mentalism to be the most problematic of the 7 that we shall discuss later. All people of intellect acknowledge that intricately designed objects must have had an intelligent creator. At the same time, many will deny that an intelligent creator exists who is responsible for bringing all things into existence. *Kufar* (disbelievers) will perform elaborate mental gymnastics before they submit to the reality that there is a conscious Creator of all.

For Hermeticists, Occultists, Jews, Christians, and Muslims, this concept is the absolute truth. Our mission should be to understand the mental nature of all reality. By consciously shaping our thoughts, we align ourselves with divine wisdom, transcending lower states of existence and reaching toward higher consciousness. When we harness the power of our minds in service of truth and faith, we take full advantage of the physical and mental resources we have access to and strive to manifest our greatest ideals and aspirations on the physical plane. The following principles explain how Hermeticists attract what they desire and manifest their visions into the world.

SECTION 2

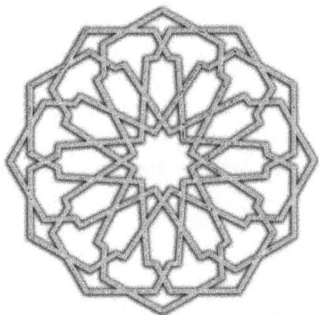

THE PRINCIPLE OF CORRESPONDENCE

PART I

﴿ ٱللَّهُ ٱلَّذِى خَلَقَ سَبْعَ سَمَٰوَٰتٍ وَمِنَ ٱلْأَرْضِ مِثْلَهُنَّ يَتَنَزَّلُ ٱلْأَمْرُ بَيْنَهُنَّ لِتَعْلَمُوٓا۟ أَنَّ ٱللَّهَ عَلَىٰ كُلِّ شَىْءٍ قَدِيرٌ وَأَنَّ ٱللَّهَ قَدْ أَحَاطَ بِكُلِّ شَىْءٍ عِلْمًۢا ﴾

"It is Allâh Who has created seven heavens and of the earth the like thereof. His Command descends between them (heavens and earth), that you may know that Allah has power over all things, and that Allah surrounds (comprehends) all things in (His) Knowledge (65:12)."

﴿ وَفِى ٱلْأَرْضِ ءَايَٰتٌ لِّلْمُوقِنِينَ وَفِىٓ أَنفُسِكُمْ أَفَلَا تُبْصِرُونَ وَفِى ٱلسَّمَآءِ رِزْقُكُمْ وَمَا تُوعَدُونَ فَوَرَبِّ ٱلسَّمَآءِ وَٱلْأَرْضِ إِنَّهُۥ لَحَقٌّ مِّثْلَ مَآ أَنَّكُمْ تَنطِقُونَ ﴾

195

"And on the earth are signs for the certain [in faith]. And in yourselves. Then will you not see? And in the heaven is your provision and whatever you are promised. Then by the Lord of the heaven and earth, indeed, it is truth - just as [sure as] it is that you are speaking (51:20-23)."

"As above, so below; as below, so above."—*The Kybalion*

THE PRINCIPLE

Correspondence teaches that there is a constant and meaningful relationship between all levels of existence, the macrocosm and the microcosm, the heavens and the earth, the physical and the spiritual. The entire Hermetic philosophy arises from the formula "as above, so below," a phrase found in the earliest Arabic version of the Emerald Tablet, dated between the sixth and eighth centuries.[68] This idea is found in all mystical traditions, including the *Sefer Yetzirah*, an early Kabbalistic text that describes six spatial dimensions—above, below, east, west, north, and south—all converging toward a sacred center. Such teachings affirm that by studying one realm, we may come to understand others, for all planes of reality reflect one another in structure, purpose, and design.

This concept is not merely abstract; it encompasses both a theoretical and a practical component, together forming a comprehensive path to understanding and enlightenment.

In theory, the human microcosm mirrors the greater macrocosm. If you *know your natural self, you will know natural law.* This principle suggests that the laws governing the cosmos

---

68   Translated into Latin from the Arabic:

لَوْح الزُّمُرُّذ : حق لا شك فيه صحيح إن الأعلى من الأسفل والأسفل من الأعلى

عمل العجائب من واحد كما كانت الأشياء كلها من واحد بتدبير واحد

are reflected within the human mind, body, and soul. By studying the inner world of thoughts, emotions, and spiritual states, one can draw analogies to comprehend natural and divine laws.

In practice, the seeker must be guided by a mentor or teacher to help climb up the spiritual ladder to have a direct experience with the Divine Presence. This path requires one to have inner purity during the physical journey toward enlightenment. This body-mind-spirit integration is the practice of yoga or meditation practices.

This principle also expresses the idea that there is harmony between the physical, mental, and spiritual planes of existence. The phenomena that exist on one plane reflect those that exist on another plane. The physical world of earth reflects the spiritual realm of the heavens, following a precise order set by the Creator. Just as gravity and thermodynamics regulate the material universe, spiritual laws govern the unseen world. However, while physical laws can be measured and observed, spiritual laws require discernment and faith. These laws can only be understood through analogy, drawing parallels between what is seen and what is beyond human perception.

The Kybalion divides the major physical, mental, and spiritual plane into 3 groups each with each subdivided into 7 minor planes. All the layers of reality are interconnected to form the whole of creation. Each plane is distinguished by its vibrational frequency. Vibration is the oscillatory motion of an object around a reference position. Frequency is the number of cycles of vibrational movement per unit of time. Everything down to the atomic level has energy; therefore, everything vibrates. The higher the frequency of vibration, the faster the atoms move. The spiritual planes have the highest and fastest vibration, while the physical objects on the lower material plane vibrate slowly. By understanding the inner workings of the microcosm (lower planes of physics and metaphysics), one can come to understand the macrocosm (higher planes of astronomy and astrology).

'As above, so below' lies at the heart of every revealed religion and esoteric teaching that exists throughout the world,

197

for each teaching aims to purify man's inner core to help him obtain more elevated states of consciousness and spiritual growth. In the following paragraphs, we will provide a brief overview of some prominent examples of how this principle is taught and applied in the various dominant religious and spiritual traditions.

ISLAM

In Islam, this principle applies to the realms above us and the realms below us, evidenced both by the Quran and Sunnah. For instance, we know that at the end of the seventh heaven, the *Sidrat al-Muntah* (the Lote-Tree of the Boundary) is to the right of Allah's Throne (53:14). This tree is believed to receive the water of purity that descends from above, along with Allah's *nur* (spiritual light) and Allah's *wahy* (speech). From below, the tree absorbs all that comes up from the heavens and earth. Its branches can be likened to the arteries and veins of the heavens and the earth. Beside the Lote-Tree are four rivers: two hidden and two visible. The two visible rivers are the Nile and Euphrates (Bukhari).

It is named thus, with Sidr, meaning 'Lote' and Muntaha, meaning 'at the furthest boundary.' It is unfathomably great, with immensely wide leaf-spans. Marking the boundary of the 7th heaven beyond which all human and angelic forms of knowledge, all aspects of rationality and intuition accessible by creation cease to exist. What lay beyond is believed to be purely the Divine Presence, untouched, incomprehensible. Its significance is such that even as it pertains to the Lote and Cedar trees of the earth, the Prophet ﷺ is reported to have said that whosoever shall cut down a lote tree, Allah would bring him headlong into Jahannam Hell.

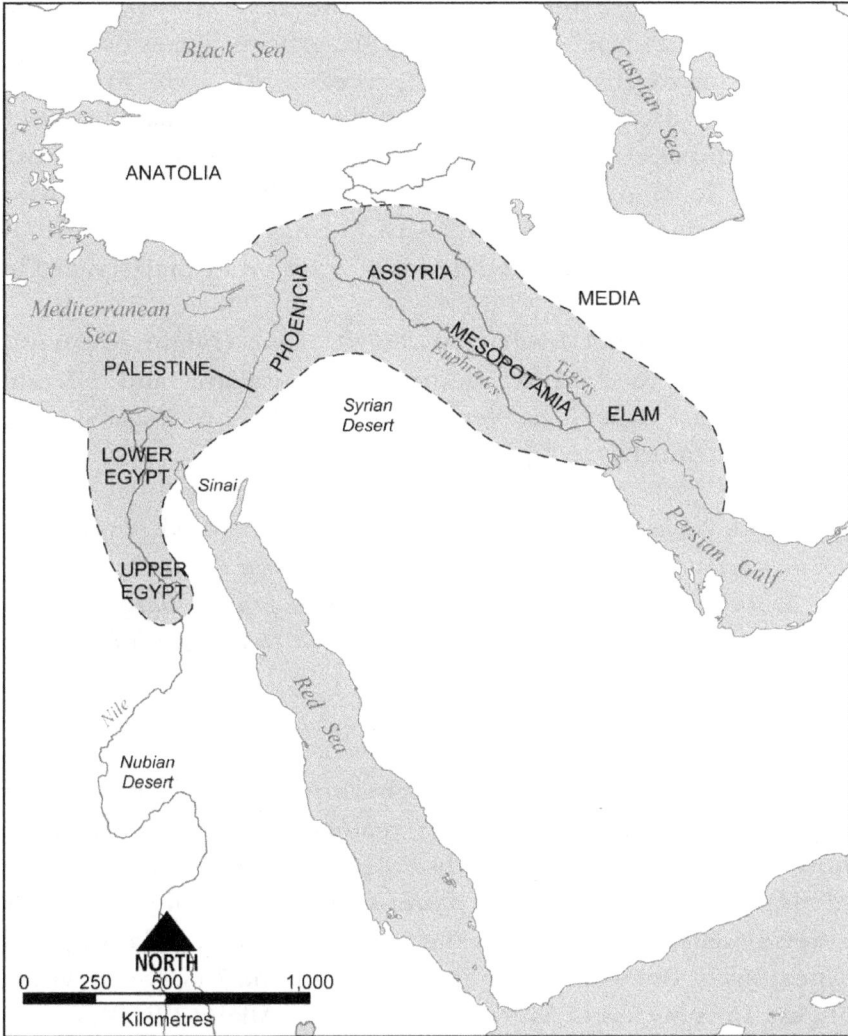

Fig. 26 - Map of the Fertile Crescent, a region shaped like a quarter moon that extends from the banks of the Euphrates and Tigris rivers in Mesopotamia through the Levant and down to the Nile River in Egypt. This fertile zone is bordered by the Persian Gulf and Zagros Mountains (Media) to the east, the Taurus Mountains (Anatolia) to the north, the Mediterranean Sea to the west, and the Syrian Desert to the south. Often called the "Cradle of Civilization," this region was home to some of the earliest complex societies. The civilizations featured on the map span from approximately 4100 BCE to 70 CE.

Beyond Sidrat al-Muntaha lies the *Bait al-Ma'mur*—the "Frequented House" of Allah (52:4). Above it stands Allah's *Kursi* (Footstool), which itself precedes the *'Arsh* (Throne). Both are of inconceivable magnitude: the Kursi extends over and encompasses all the heavens and earth, while the Throne surpasses it many times over.[69] The 'Arsh is Allah's greatest creation, upheld by eight angels of unimaginable size (69:17). Above it all, Allah – exalted be He – is seated in majesty, as He has Himself declared (7:54).

During Prophet Muhammad's ﷺ *Israa* (Night Journey), from Mecca to Masjid al-Aqsa in Jerusalem, and Mi'raaj (Ascension) to the 7 heavens above (17:1), he described the Bait al-Ma'mur by saying the following:

> *"Then I was shown Al-Bait al-Ma'mur (i.e. Allah's House). I asked Gabriel about it and he said, This is Al-Bait al-Ma'mur where **70,000** angels perform prayers daily and when they leave they never return to it (but a fresh batch comes into it each day)."*
> *(Bukhari and Muslim).*

This narration gives us insight into the vast number of angels that exist in the heavenly realms. We can only imagine how many angels there are in existence. From the beginning of time until the end, this pattern of a new group of angels entering daily to pray and make tawaf (circumambulation) will repeat itself. Below the Bait al-Ma'mur are the 7 heavens, where angels, Prophets, and Messengers worship Allah (22:18).

We are given very little knowledge regarding the details as to what exists in the 7 heavens. Science cannot reach the discovery of the first heaven, for it lay beyond physical and observable phenomena. It cannot be measured by any material instrumentation, nor does it abide by physical dimensions.

---

69   Note: The seven heavens in comparison to the kursi are like no more than a ring thrown out into an empty field, and the superiority of the Throne in relation to the kursi is like the superiority of that field in relation to that ring." (Narrated by Muhammad ibn Abi Shaybah in Kitaab al-Arsh).

Furthermore, we have no scientific knowledge regarding a material reality beyond the observable universe.

However, Prophet Muhammad's ﷺ heavenly ascent in the 7th month of the Hijri calendar, during Israa and Mir'aaj, gives us insights into the heavens:

- In the first heaven, Prophet Muhamad ﷺ met **Adam** ﷺ, who had the believing souls of his offspring to his right and the disbelieving souls of his offspring to his left.

- In the second heaven, he met the two cousins, Prophet **Yahya** bin Zakariya ﷺ (John the Baptist) and Prophet **Isa** bin Maryam ﷺ (Jesus).

- In the third heaven, he met Prophet **Yusuf** ﷺ (Joseph).

- In the fourth heaven, he met **Idris** (the middle of the seven heavens) ﷺ.

- In the fifth heaven, he met Prophet **Harun** (Aaron, the brother of Musa) ﷺ.

- In the sixth heaven, he met **Musa** ﷺ (Moses).

- On the seventh level of heaven, Prophet Muhamad ﷺ met **Ibrahim** ﷺ resting against the Baitul Ma'mur.

The Isra and Miraj chart [*next page*] reinterprets the Tree of Life structure within an Islamic framework, showing a spiritual hierarchy centered on Prophets.

Adapted from Kabbalistic traditions, the chart maintains three pillars—Mercy (right), Severity (left), and Balance (center)—each associated with specific Quranic verses and Prophetic qualities. Reimagined through the Prophet Muhammad's ﷺ celestial journey (Israa and Mi'raj), the

Fig. 27

اَهْدِنَا ٱلصِّرَاطَ ٱلْمُسْتَقِيمَ

صِرَاطَ ٱلَّذِينَ أَنْعَمْتَ عَلَيْهِمْ غَيْرِ ٱلْمَغْضُوبِ عَلَيْهِمْ وَلَا ٱلضَّآلِّينَ

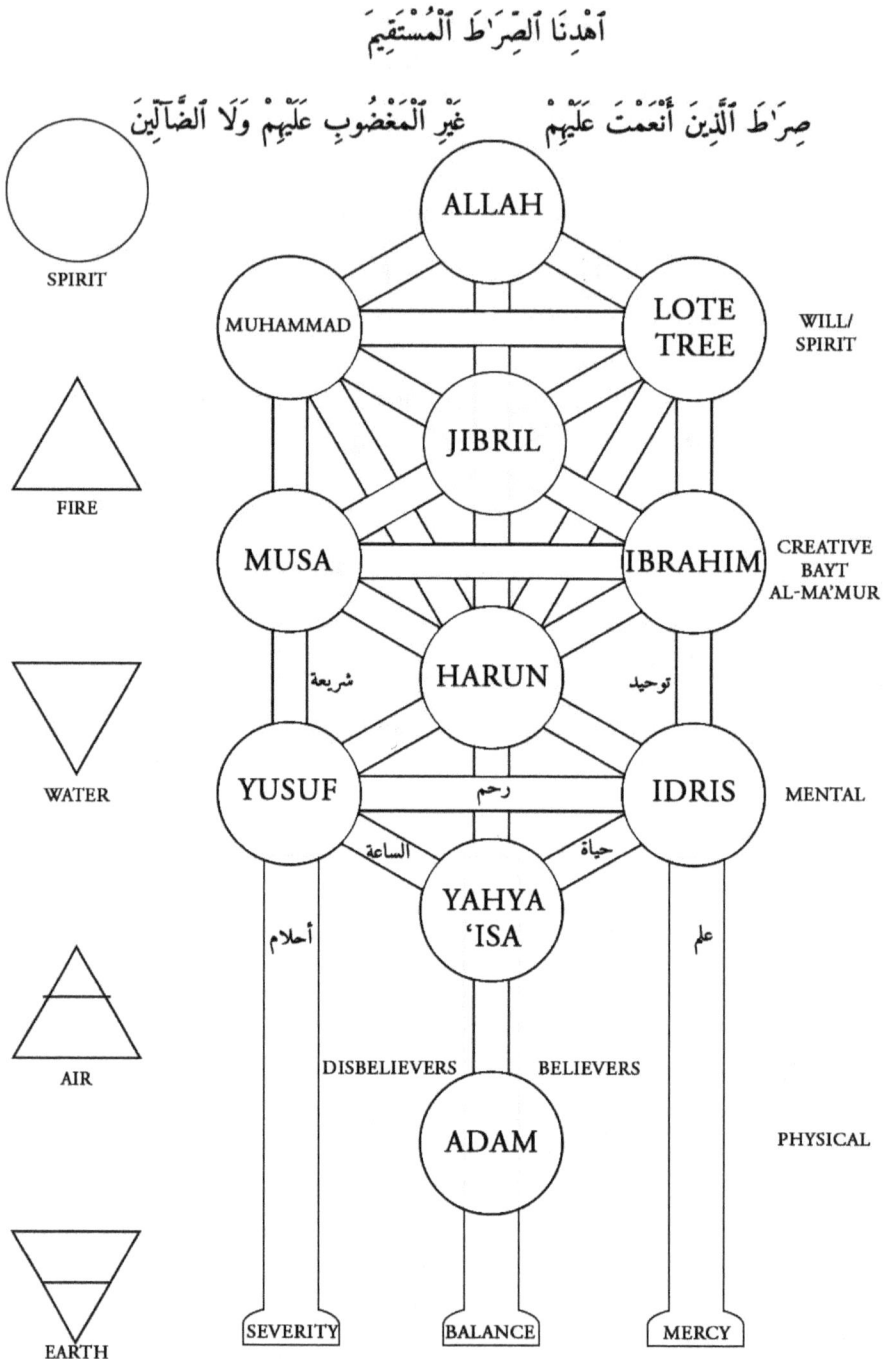

diagram becomes a vertical map of spiritual ascent—each pillar reflecting a prophetic archetype and a stage in the soul's journey toward Allah.

Right Pillar – Mercy (الرحمة)

Quranic Link: صِرَٰطَ ٱلَّذِينَ أَنْعَمْتَ عَلَيْهِمْ

"The path of those whom You have bestowed favor"

(Al-Fatiha 1:7)

This pillar represents **compassion, divine favor,** and **spiritual ease**—the path of those uplifted by grace and nearness to Allah.

- *Idris:* Elevated through wisdom and sacred knowledge, Idris reflects the seeker lifted by clarity of thought and inner illumination.
- *Ibrahim:* The embodiment of unwavering Tawhid and deep trust—his journey speaks of creative faith and intimate friendship with the Divine.
- *The Lote Tree (Sidrat al-Muntaha):* Marks the furthest limit of creation and the threshold of divine presence—a symbol of celestial beauty and favor, beyond which none passed except Muhammad ﷺ.

Left Pillar – Severity (العدل)

Quranic Link: غَيْرِ ٱلْمَغْضُوبِ عَلَيْهِمْ وَلَا ٱلضَّآلِّينَ

"Not of those who have incurred [Your] wrath, nor of those who have gone astray"

(Al-Fatiha 1:7)

This pillar reflects **divine justice, trial,** and **the purification of the soul through hardship.** It honors those prophets whose lives were marked by struggle and spiritual resilience.

- *Musa:* Bearer of divine law and leadership under fire, Musa's life reflects confrontation with falsehood, divine discipline, and steadfastness.
- *Yusuf:* His journey—through betrayal, temptation, and imprisonment—teaches patience, moral clarity, and the refinement of the soul through adversity.

Middle Pillar – Balance (الاستقامة)

Quranic Link: ٱهْدِنَا ٱلصِّرَٰطَ ٱلْمُسْتَقِيمَ
"Guide us along the Straight Path"
(Al-Fatiha 1:6)

The middle pillar signifies **moderation, inner alignment, and the Prophetic path that unites heaven and earth**. It is the road between extremes—mercy and severity—walked by those who embody wholeness.

- *Adam (Base):* The first prophet, symbolizing human origin and the dual potential of belief or denial. His story marks the beginning of the soul's journey and its longing for return.
- *Yahya & Isa:* Signs of purity and divine spirit—Yahya through his austere, principled life; Isa through miraculous birth and spiritual depth.
- *Harun:* A gentle and wise leader, reflecting the power of compassion in guidance and balance in responsibility.
- *Jibra'il:* The mediator of revelation, bridging the unseen and the human heart—his role represents divine communication and sacred order.
- *Muhammad ﷺ (Above):* The seal of prophethood and the perfect embodiment of balance—he alone passed beyond the Lote Tree, ascending to divine nearness and completing the spiritual journey.
- *Allah (Apex):* The source of all light and being, beyond comprehension, reached only through Tawhid, sincerity, and Prophetic guidance.

Elements and Inner Qualities:
The Hidden Structure of the Soul

Beyond vertical ascent, this chart also reveals the inner structure of the soul, formed through the balance of cosmic elements and prophetic qualities.

On the left side are the elements of the soul's journey:
- *Earth (Adam):* physical grounding and moral capacity
- *Water (Isa):* purity, renewal, and divine breath
- *Air (Yusuf):* emotional clarity, dreams, and intuition

204

- *Fire (Musa):* passion, confrontation, and purification
- *Spirit (Muhammad ﷺ):* unity, completion, and ascension

On the right side are the inner attributes of the prophetic path:

- *Idris:* elevated intellect and sacred insight
- *Ibrahim:* creative trust and unwavering faith
- *The Lote Tree:* divine will, surrender, and celestial nearness
- *Adam:* human responsibility and physical consciousness.

This chart is more than symbolism—it is **a living map of the soul.** Each prophet's life reflects a stage in our own journey: from Adam's grounding to Musa's trial, from Isa's purity to Muhammad's ﷺ perfection. These aren't just stories, they are **archetypes alive within us.** When we align the elements with prophetic qualities, we begin to walk the Miʿraj within, ascending from dust to divine light, guided by balance, clarity, and faith.

Below the 7 heavens is our known universe, a vast expanse structured with divine precision. Within it, the **Sun** orbits the center of the Milky Way in a "G" shaped spiral motion, following the same counterclockwise movement observed in planetary orbits and even the rotation of electrons. This recurring circular motion is a signature of divine order, embedded in the fabric of existence. Likewise, the **Moon** follows this cosmic rhythm, completing a counterclockwise orbit around the Earth every 29 days.[70] This celestial motion governs the tides, ensuring the delicate balance of life on our planet. Below the Moon lie the 7 **Earths**—a concept interpreted by scholars as either the Earth's physical layers or symbolic representations such as the 7 continents.[71]

---

70   21:33: "And He is the One Who created the day and the night, the sun and the moon-each travelling in an orbit;
36:40: "It is not for the sun to catch up with the moon, nor does the night outrun the day. Each is travelling in an orbit of their own.

71   Note: Ibn Kathir and al-Tabari read "seven earths" as seven strata or dimensions; al-Qurtubi records opinions of seven physical layers or seven continents; Fakhr al-Razi affirms seven earths but warns against overly literal speculation.

This divine pattern extends throughout our solar system, where Mercury, Venus, Mars, Jupiter, Saturn, Uranus, Neptune, and even Pluto all orbit the Sun in a counterclockwise direction.[72] This motion is not arbitrary but rather intrinsic to the cosmic order—mirroring the design observed at every scale, from subatomic particles to vast galaxies.

On **Earth**, this cosmic rhythm finds its ultimate reflection in sacred worship. Directly aligned with the heavenly Al-Bayt al-Ma'mur stands the Ka'aba, the earthly House of Allah, located in Mecca. Just as angels in the heavens perform Tawaf around Al-Bayt al-Ma'mur, so too do Muslims on Earth circumambulate the Ka'aba 7 times in an act of devotion. This counterclockwise motion unites believers with the divine order, embodying the correspondence between the heavens and the Earth.

The Quran beautifully expresses this theme of constant, harmonious motion in Surah Al-Anbiya:

$$\text{﴿ كُلٌّ فِى فَلَكٍ يَسْبَحُونَ ﴾}$$

"...each one is swimming in its own orbit" (21:33; 36:40).

Remarkably, this phrase is a palindrome in Arabic, meaning it reads the same forwards and backward. This palindromic structure mirrors the circular orbits of celestial bodies, reflecting the balance and cyclical nature of the universe. Just as the phrase can be read in both directions, celestial bodies continuously move in their designated paths, each orbiting in a perpetual cycle that aligns with the divine order, silently praising Allah through their motion.

This motion extends even within the human body. Approximately 37 trillion cells work together to sustain life, with each cell containing molecules made up of atoms, and within each atom, electrons rotate continuously around the nucleus in a counterclockwise direction. Additionally, blood in the human body circulates in a vortex-like motion, often

---

72 Note: this is in accordance with the Heliocentric model, according to classical Islam, the sun and moon orbit the earth and the earth is stationary.

flowing in a counterclockwise pattern as it moves through the heart and veins. This intricate system ensures that oxygen and nutrients reach every part of the body, maintaining the life-giving cycle that sustains us.

On multiple levels, creation reflects this divine rotation and orbit—from the atomic to the cosmic—mirroring the sacred movement of the seven cycles of Tawaf around the Ka'aba. Through Tawaf, worshippers align their bodies and souls with the natural rhythm of the universe, embodying harmony with all that glorifies Allah.

In this sacred motion, Tawaf becomes more than ritual; it is a lived symbol of cosmic unity. From the spin of subatomic particles to the orbit of galaxies, everything moves in devotion. Even the blood within us flows in submission to divine order. Tawaf reminds us that the entire cosmos exists in perpetual dhikr, glorifying the Creator with every rotation.

Between these levels of existence lies a subtle partition known as the *Barzakh*. Literally meaning "isthmus" or "barrier," a place in between two things, separating and connecting one realm to the next. In Islamic cosmology, the Barzakh is the intermediate state where the soul resides after leaving the body and before the Day of Judgment. It is neither fully this world nor the next, but a distinct domain awaiting final reckoning.

As a transitional boundary, the Barzakh also serves as a bridge between life and death. It is a medium of interaction where visions, dreams, and divine intimations can take shape. Classical scholars liken it to the *'Alam al-Mithal*—an "imaginal" realm in which spiritual realities can take on symbolic, perceivable forms. Thus the Barzakh is both a separator and an active zone of **transformation, translation, and transmutation**.[73]

In life we glimpse this "between" state whenever we sleep or dream. Sleep is a minor form of death, a nightly crossing of thresholds before returning to consciousness. In the true

---

73   Note: Although distinctively Islamic, the Barzakh resembles Plato's intermediary realm of Forms, the Hindu subtle-body plane (*sukṣma sharira*), and the Jungian unconscious.

Barzakh, every soul awaits its outcome: the rewards or the punishments for the actions that we committed during our state of biological existence. Good actions will earn Allah's mercy and enable us to rise above. Bad actions in disobedience to the divine laws will earn Allah's wrath and justify our descent below.

Above the Barzakh, in an undefined location, lies *Jannah* (Paradise). The obedient and righteous who are granted this lush garden will have the choice to enter through one of eight gates, depending on their earthly deeds.

These are the gates of:

- *As-Salaat* (prayer),
- *Al-Jihad* (struggle),
- *As-Sadaqah* (charity),
- *Ar-Rayyaan* (fasting),
- *Al-Hajj*, (Pilgrimage),
- *Al-Kaazimeen Al-Ghaiz wal Aafina Anin Naas* (people who could control and suppress their anger),
- *Al-Iman* (steadfast in faith),
- *Dhikr*, (remembrance of Allah).

Below both Jannah and the Barzakh, in an undefined realm of reality, lies *Jahannam* (Hellfire). Jahannam has 7 levels; each level is filled with specific types of disbelievers (15:44). *Jahannum, Ladha, al-Hutamah, al-Sa'ir, Saqar, al-Jahim*, and finally *Haawiyyah*.[74] Prophet Muhammad ﷺ advised us to avoid the 7 destructive sins, which make can us deserving of entry into one of these 7 gates.

Seven destructive sins:

- *Shirk* - Associating anything with Allah,

- *Sihr* - magic and witchcraft,

---

74 Note: *Jahannum* is mentioned 77 times in the Quran, *Ladha* (once), al-*Hutamah* (twice), *al-Sa'ir* (20 times), *Saqar* (4 times) *al-Jahim* (25 times) *Haawiyyah* (once).

- *Qatl* - killing a soul that Allah has sanctified except for a just cause,

- *Riba* - consuming usury,

- *Aklu Māl al-Yatim* - usurping the wealth of an orphan,

- *Tawalli Yaum al-Zahf* - fleeing the battlefield,

- *Qadf al-Muhsanat* - slandering chaste women. (Bukhari and Muslim).

At the bottom of *Jahannam* lies the roots of the tree of *Zaqqum*. Its branches rise to the various levels of *Jahannam*, its fruits are shaped like the heads of *shayateen* (devils) (37:62-68), and it burns and tears apart the bodies of those who eat from it. *Below is an inversion of that which is above.*

Moreover, all significant dates in the Islamic lunar calendar are based on specific times and cosmological events that occurred in human history. Allah mentions,

$$ \text{﴿ ... وَذَكِّرْهُم بِأَيَّامِ ٱللَّهِ ... ﴾} $$

"... and remind them of the days of Allāh." (14:5).

The "days of Allah" are days when we must work to be more conscious of Allah through dhikr (remembrance), dua (supplication), *sawm* (fasting), and good acts towards others. The month of Ramadan is when the Quran descended from beyond the heavens to the heart of Prophet Muhammad ﷺ on the mountain of Hira in Mecca. All able-bodied Muslims must fast during this month and are encouraged to seek the night when the Quran was revealed through dedicated worship.[75] Additionally, Muslims are encouraged to fast on Mondays,

---

75 Note: Whoever establishes the prayers on the night of Qadr out of sincere faith and hoping to attain Allah's rewards (not to show off) then all his past sins will be forgiven. (Bukhari).

Thursdays, and three days when the moon is full each month. On Monday and Thursday, angels descend to collect the book of deeds of all humans and present them to Allah, so it is encouraged to fast on those days. [76] Conversely, on the white days (*al-ayam al-bayd*), when the moon is at its fullest, Muslims are encouraged to fast, for the reward for fasting on these three days is equivalent to fasting the whole month (Lunar month).

Another dimension of this principle of Correspondence is the concept "As within, so without." The "within" is one's internal state—the thoughts, emotions, and desires. The "without" is the outer reality, the "real life," the realm of working, living, and interacting with people.

This idea aligns with the Prophet Muhammad ﷺ saying:

> *"Truly in the body there is a morsel of flesh, which, if it is sound, all the body is sound; and if it is diseased, all of the body is diseased. Truly, it is the heart"*
> *(Bukhari and Muslim).*

The qalb determines one's actions, their state of being, their contentment or ingratitude, shaping their path in life. Thus, cultivating a virtuous internal state is not only a moral imperative but is also essential for achieving harmony in the external world.

Similarly, the principle of "as within, so without" highlights the connection between one's inner state and their external reality. It suggests that true mastery of the outer world begins with cultivating harmony and clarity within oneself. When thoughts, emotions, and actions are aligned with divine wisdom and guidance, one can achieve a heightened sense of awareness and fulfillment. This inner alignment of mind, heart, and behavior empowers one to live a life that is balanced, meaningful, and intentionally directed toward a higher

---

76   Abu Huraira reported: The Messenger of Allah ﷺ said, "The deeds are presented on Monday and Thursday. Thus, I love for my deeds to be presented while I am fasting." (Tirmidhī).

purpose.

When a student desires to master something in the external world, they must first master their internal dimension. Unlike the body, which is bound by physical constraints, the mind can move freely—forward and backward in time, imagining the past or projecting into the future. This ability to mentally transcend time and space allows one to envision potential outcomes and align their inner state with clarity and intention, directly impacting the outer world. Mastery from within not only opens doors of opportunity but also elevates the seeker to higher ranks reserved for the virtuous. In this sense, *the inner world is the cause, and the outer world is the effect.*[77]

The aspiration to attain *Ihsan* is the noblest aim a Muslim can pursue. Ihsan is reached when one purifies the self from lowly attributes that lead away from Allah and embraces virtues leading toward divine harmony. This state of purity connects the self with Allah, aligning one's actions with a higher purpose. For the *Muhsin* (one who practices *Ihsan*), this journey involves cleansing the heart, guiding others, and striving continually toward self-transformation.

The path to Ihsan involves elevating the nefs. Islamic scholars in the past have looked at various types of nefs so that we can be conscious about reflecting on where we are at vs. where we want to be.

The lowest level of our Nefs is:

1. ***al-ammara bi'l-su'*** (12:53), **the commanding soul, or the passionate soul**: This is the soul that inclines to evil actions without a second thought. Those who embody this state are like animals, addicted to the material world and constantly seeking to fulfill their base desires, lusts, and greed. The *ayah* (verse) where this term is used is in the context of the story of Yusuf (Joseph), who resisted the sexual seduction of the Egyptian king's wife. The **fire** of this nafs can be weakened by eating, sleeping,

---

77   Note: The inner world corresponds to *'Alam al-Amr*, and the outer world to *'Alam al-Khalq*, with the *Amr* giving rise to the *Khalq*.

and drinking less. To completely rise beyond this state, one must strive to suppress their ego, shed themselves of blameworthy attributes, and adorn themselves with praiseworthy traits.

2. *al-lawwama* (75:2), **the blaming soul**: This is the soul that discerns good from evil, feeling guilt and shame when it yields to evil instead of choosing good. Those who embody this state recognize their addictions and consciously desire to change for the better. Despite wanting to act for Allah's sake, it also desires for its actions to be seen by others; their sincerity needs sincerity. Like **air**, this nafs can quickly turn hot or cold, for it is the soul caught in the tension between right and wrong. It strives to do good, but often lapses, despite which, unlike the commanding soul (*al-ammara*), it is eager to recover from its wrongdoing. It can be weakened or strengthened depending on how it regulates the six habits of eating, sleeping, talking, entertaining, dhikr, and *fikr* (reflection). To completely rise beyond this state, one must first be sincere in their desire to escape the trappings of this world and focus entirely on their Lord.

3. *al-mulhama* (91:7–9), **the inspired soul**: This soul struggles internally between good and evil. Though aligned with our fitrah (primordial nature) (30:30), it retains the freedom to choose its course. Having tasted faith, it can distinguish the suggestions of angels from the whispers of devils. Like water, it is malleable— capable of flowing toward righteousness or veering into wrongdoing. Yet divine inspiration channels it, guiding the nafs back to its intended path. If the soul embraces this guidance, it ascends to higher stations, marked by emotional maturity, justice, and dignity. But if it ignores the inspiration, it may descend into a lower

state. To rise beyond, one must live with values such as gentleness, compassion, and creativity—ideally under the mentorship of a trusted guide or shaykh.

4. *al-mutma'inna* **(89:27; 13:28), the peaceful or tranquil soul**: This is the soul that experiences gratitude, peace, and certainty even in times of hardship and difficulty. It possesses true knowledge, or *ma'rifah* (gnosis). Those who realize this state have defeated the struggles of the earlier stages and are not addicted to any former desires or attachments. They are firm like the **earth**. The ego has been subdued, and they are now approaching the Divine. They embody the Laws of the Shari'ah and the Laws of Nature, acting in harmony with both. This soul has replaced all blameworthy traits with praiseworthy ones such as generosity, trust in Allah, wisdom, devotion, gratitude, and *rida* (contentment).

5. *al-radiya* **(89:28), the pleased soul**: This soul has replaced all its likes and desire with what Allah likes and desires. This nafs is content with all the trials and tribulations in life because it knows, with utmost certainty, that everything it encounters is decreed by Allah.[78] Some interpret this as the nafs that was with Allah in the garden before creation. The characteristics of this nafs are asceticism, sincerity, diligence, and detachment from everything that is not its concern. To rise above this level, the seeker must love to reach Allah and be grateful for all He has provided.

---

78   The Messenger of Allah said, "Whoever is concerned about the world, Allah will disorder his affairs, make poverty appear before his eyes, he will not get anything from the world but what has been decreed for him. Whoever is concerned about the Hereafter, Allah will settle his affairs, make him content in his heart, the world will inevitably come to him" (Ibn Maajah).

6. *al-mardiya* (89:28), the self-pleasing to Allah: This is the soul that experiences the higher levels of Ihsan. It no longer fears anything, nor does it ask for anything. According to Ibn 'Arabi, this is the level where the nafs and the ruh intermarry, where the inner nature and the external world become one unified whole.

7. *al-kamila* (89:29), the perfected soul: This is the soul of the saint, the enlightened soul. These are the spiritual elite who have transcended their lower souls, making every breath an act of worship. They do not have a drop of pride within. They have completely annihilated their ego and are ready to return to Allah.[79] Very few masters on earth are at this level. These ranks are reserved for the Prophets, Messengers, and those promised paradise while they were living.[80] They experientially realize that "there is no God but Allah" and that only the Divine exists. According to Hermetic thought, they know "All is mind" and any sense of individuality or separateness is an illusion.

These 7 levels of the nafs correspond to the 7 heavens and the 7 layers of the universe. Picture the nafs as an onion with 7 skins, each layer deeper than the one before, and the universe as an enormous, reversed onion whose outer heavens enfold the inner realms. When we pass from this world, our soul begins to peel away these layers one by one, first relinquishing the physical body, then shedding each subtler aspect, as gentle

---

79 Note: Muslim tradition recognizes three primary souls (*al-ammaara*, *lawwaama*, and *mutma'inna* corresponding to the commanding soul, the accusing soul, and the tranquil soul). In light of that understanding, *Nafs mutma'inna* may be thought of as the overarching nafs, while the remaining four nafs are sub-qualities which fall under its umbrella.

80 Narrated 'Abdur-Rahman bin 'Awf' that the Messenger of Allah said: Abu Bakr is in Paradise, 'Umar is in Paradise, 'Uthman is in Paradise, 'Ali is in Paradise, Talhah is in Paradise, Az-Zubair is in Paradise, 'Abdur-Rahman bin 'Awf is in Paradise, Sa'd bin Abi Waqqas is in Paradise, Sa'eed is in Paradise, Abu 'Ubaidah bin Al-Jarrah is in Paradise. (Tirmidhi).

angels guide it upward through the heavens. The lowest layer of the nafs remains in Barzakh, while the highest layer ascends, echoing how the universe's layers fold inward. In this way, the nafs not only unveils our inner moral journey but also mirrors the larger cosmic order, returning the soul, well-pleased and pleasing, to its Lord, as Allah says,

﴿ يَـٰٓأَيَّتُهَا ٱلنَّفْسُ ٱلْمُطْمَئِنَّةُ ﴾

﴿ ٱرْجِعِىٓ إِلَىٰ رَبِّكِ رَاضِيَةً مَّرْضِيَّةً ﴾

﴿ فَٱدْخُلِى فِى عِبَـٰدِى ﴾

﴿ وَٱدْخُلِى جَنَّتِى ﴾

"O reassured soul. Return to your Lord, well-pleased and pleasing [to Him]. So enter among My [righteous] servants. And enter My Paradise." (89:27-30)

While Islam grounds the Principle of Correspondence in divine revelation and prophetic experience, this concept has also been explored across ancient civilizations. In some cases, these traditions preserved insights that aligned with divine wisdom; in others, they strayed into mystical speculation or occult manipulation.

The Ancient Egyptians, Ancient Indians, Jewish Kabbalists, Christians, Hermeticists, and other followers of astrology and esotericism developed distinct interpretations of this principle—often within secret oral traditions passed down in symbolic or coded from the mouths of scholars, sages, and wise men to the ears of select initiates.

215

ANCIENT KEMET

After leaving Babylon, Idris established his learning centers in Kemet (ancient Egypt) where he and his students studied the universe and its rhythms and cycles, which enabled them to develop calendars and mathematics. Kemet quickly became a center of advanced study, contributing significantly to various fields of life and academics, and is considered the source of many human inventions. The priests of ancient Kemet began keeping written records between 4000 and 3000 BCE. In contrast, the Phoenician alphabet was developed around 1000 BCE, and is responsible for influencing the Greek writing system, which in turn both directly and indirectly influenced European (through Latin) and Cyrillic (through Russian and Slavic) writing systems. The Phoenician alphabet evolved from the Proto-Sinaitic script (from the Sinai peninsula ca. 1800–1500 BCE), which itself was influenced by Egyptian (Kemetic) hieroglyphs. In this regard, the discipline of academia and sciences, in particular the mathematical sciences, Kemet is considered a proto civilization.

Historians have divided Egypt's early history into thirty-one dynasties and then grouped these dynasties into periods:

- Pre and Early Dynastic Period (Dynasties 0–2)
5500–2686 BCE

- Old Kingdom (Dynasties 3–8)
2686-2181 BCE

- 1st Intermediate Period (Dynasties 9-11)
2181-2055 BCE

- Middle Kingdom (Dynasties 11-13)
255-1650 BCE

- 2nd Intermediate Period (Dynasties 13-17) 1650-1550 BCE

- New Kingdom Dynasties (18-20) 1550-1069 BCE

- 3rd Intermediate Period (Dynasties 21-25) 1069-747 BCE

- Late Period (Dynasties 26-31) 747-332 BCE

- Greco-Roman Period 332 BCE to 395 CE

During the Fourth Dynasty of the Old Kingdom period, Kemet witnessed the construction of its most renowned pyramids, including the Great Pyramid of Giza. To this day, the pyramids are the only remaining monuments from the 7 Wonders of the Ancient World.[81] These structures exemplify the Hermetic principle of "As above, so below," particularly due to their alignment with celestial bodies. Some scholars theorize that the Great Pyramid aligns with the constellation of Orion, which was associated with Osiris, the Kemetic God of the afterlife. This alignment is believed to reflect the ancient belief in the direct influence of the heavens on earthly and human affairs. Furthermore, the pyramid's design is said to incorporate advanced mathematical concepts, including the golden ratio and Pi. These ratios are observed in the relationship between the pyramid's perimeter and its height, aligning with the proportions of the Earth. Such design choices suggest that the pyramid builders aimed to mirror the geometric harmony of the cosmos within their monumental architecture. These construction techniques and their celestial alignments indicate a sophisticated integration of astronomy, architecture, and spirituality in Kemetic culture.

---

81   Note: the other six are the Hanging Gardens of Babylon, Statue of Zeus at Olympia, Temple of Artemis at Ephesus, Mausoleum of King Mausolus at Halicarnassus, Colossus of Rhodes, Pharos Lighthouse at Alexandria.

Later, during the reign of Amenhotep III in the 18th Dynasty (1391-1353 BCE), the city of Waset (modern-day Thebes) was a significant cultural center. The Temple of Waset, often regarded by some scholars and esoteric traditions as the world's first university, reached its zenith during this period. It educated thousands of students within its walls, which were adorned with pillars depicting constellations and Zodiac signs. The design of each temple aimed to reflect a microcosm of the macrocosmic universe, embodying a celestial-earthly connection. This architectural philosophy has been passed down through generations and has influenced the designs used in modern-day Masonic lodges. Another key center of knowledge during this era was the Temple of Ipet-Isut (Karnak), a location that proves that there was a commitment to education and cosmic symbolism.

Many notable Greek figures studied in Egypt, although none completed the extensive 40-year education system that was the standard requirement at the time. For instance, Thales studied at the Temple of Waset, returned to Greece, and became famous for predicting solar eclipses. Hippocrates, considered the father of medicine, learned from Imhotep's diagnostic medicine teachings that were established 2,500 years earlier. Pythagoras returned to Greece after 22 years of study in mystery schools with Egyptian initiate priests and became the "father of mathematics." He learned calculus and geometry from the Kemetic priests based on millennia-old papyrus.

The Greek Historian and "father of history," Herodotus, stated, "During the reign of Cambyses in Egypt, a great many Greeks visited that country for one reason or another: some, as was to be expected, for trade, some to serve in the army, others, no doubt, out of mere curiosity, to see what they could see." In the 27th dynasty, Herodotus traveled to Kemet and described the people by saying, "It is in fact manifest that the Colchians are Egyptians...I myself guessed it, partly because they are black-skinned and have woolly hair" (Herodotus 2.104).

This perception of Egypt as a source of profound knowledge continued to influence subsequent Greek scholars and philosophers.

The Greeks modified the Kemetic mystery system by separating the physical from the spiritual. The Kemetic people believed that the physical and spiritual were intertwined, a concept embodied in Ma'at.[82] Ma'at represents truth, balance, order, harmony, law, morality, and justice. It was believed that the spirit of Ma'at infused creation, ensuring that the world operated rationally and in harmony. Life, based upon the 42 principles of Ma'at,[83] was considered essential for maintaining this balance, and failing to do so brought about self-inflicted consequences.

There are claims that Socrates, Plato, and Aristotle studied in Egypt for over a decade each; though the exact duration and nature of their studies are debated. Plato deviated from their teachings as explained in his *Republic*, wherein he argues in favor of reason over emotion. This later inspired the 17th-century philosopher Rene Descartes to create the modern scientific method, which sparked the rationalist 'Age of Enlightenment.' These examples show that Kemetic teachings deeply influenced Greece and all subsequent civilizations.

One of the central spiritual frameworks in the Kemetic way of life was the Tree of Life—a symbolic cosmology that charted the soul's journey toward divine realization. Though modern writers sometimes use the phrase "Tree of Divinity," the original structure expressed ancient teachings about the individual's spiritual ascent through successive stages of self-mastery. Rooted in the concept of Ma'at—truth, balance, and cosmic order—the Tree of Life provided a psycho-spiritual path through which seekers refined their character and aligned themselves with divine laws. In this tradition, enlightenment meant raising one's consciousness into harmony with the cosmic intelligence of the universe, leading to inner peace and an awareness of unity with the Supreme Being.

Ancient Kemetic spirituality taught that ten gods and goddesses operating in time and space emerged from the

82 Note: This concept first appeared in the Old Kingdom (2613 – 2181 BCE)

83 Note: These 42 principals are also known as the Negative Confessions from the Egyptian Book of the Dead.

Supreme Being, called a Neter. Each deity represented a different aspect of nature and embodied a different principle on the Tree of Life. Each principle relates to an element of an individual's personality and a cosmic aspect of Creation that must be discovered and mastered.

The journey through the Tree of Life begins at the bottom (number 10) and ends at the top (number 1). One moves up the path through theurgy ("white magic") by cultivating the cosmic energy of the gross physical deity Heru Ur (Master of Earth) to the highest deity, Ra, which is subtle. Climbing this ladder requires dedicated practice of rituals such as chanting, meditation, deep study, and teaching. Through this discipline, the seeker raises the "serpent power" from the base of the spine to awaken higher knowledge and open the divine eye.

KABBALAH

The Tree of Life philosophy deeply influences various religious and spiritual belief systems, including Kabbalah, which derives from the Hebrew term for "reception" or "correspondence." Rooted in Jewish mysticism, Kabbalah serves as a blueprint for understanding how the divine manifests into the physical world, guiding individuals on their journey from material existence toward spiritual unity with the Creator. The Tree of Life acts as a framework used to explore the esoteric aspects of the Torah through **names**, **numbers**, and **symbols**. [84]

Kabbalah is a complex mystical system that incorporates cosmology and eschatology to explain the creation of the universe and its ultimate purpose. It is rooted in ancient traditions such as paganism, Hermeticism and Greek philosophies like Gnosticism and Neo-Platonism. Kabbalah has significantly influenced Rosicrucianism, Freemasonry, and all other occult traditions. According to Gershom Scholem (1897-1982), who established the academic study of Kabbalah, Kabbalah begins with Merkabah mysticism and culminates with the messianic movement of Shabbetai Zevi, who helped change the perception of Kabbalah as a heretical practice into being one that helps develop Judaism's religious and national tradition. From there, it became infused with Reform and Conservative Judaism, which laid the foundations for the political movement of Zionism.

The doctrine of Kabbalah offers a multilayered, allegorical approach to understanding divine realities by making complex ideas accessible to all, but fully grasped by only a few. It reveals the scientific blueprint of creation. In turn, this knowledge teaches man how to understand his place in the universe and how to achieve unity with G-d[85] by understanding the secrets of

84   Note: The Torah means "The *Shariah*" or "the Law" in Hebrew.

85   Note: Judaism avoids writing down any name of God to prevent it being treated in any disrespectful manner. God is usually written as G-d.

221

divine revelations. It is believed that when the initiate embarks on this path, they gain—as Henrietta Bernstein explains in *Calabah Primer: Introduction to English/Hebrew Calabah,* "direct contact with the living powers and forces of the Universe, and through them, with the eternal source of all manifestation. In other words, you make contact with G-d."

Central texts of Kabbalah include the *Sefer Yetzirah* (Book of Formation), likely penned in Babylonia between the 3rd and 6th centuries CE, and the *Zohar* (Book of Splendor), authored in Aramaic in 1275 by Moses de Leon and traditionally ascribed to Shimon bar Yochai. Yochai is said to have hidden in a cave for several years and was supposedly inspired by Elijah to write the Zohar. These texts lay the foundational cosmology through the Hebrew alphabet and the sefirot (divine emanations), with the Zohar providing an allegorical interpretation of the Torah. The widespread dissemination of the Zohar following the expulsion of Jews from Spain in 1492 substantially impacted Renaissance Neoplatonism, influencing major European intellectual movements such as the Reformation and the Enlightenment.

The Zohar was inspired by earlier mystical texts and Bible commentaries written by medieval rabbis. Legends suggest that they may have been based on an earlier "Arabic Kabbalah" produced by the Brethren of Sincerity. This Sufi mystic group was inspired by the teachings of Ibn Arabi, who formulated many of the ideas that became central to the Zohar. For instance, his theory of the mystical importance of language, the concept that man was a complete microcosm of the macrocosmic God, and specific interpretations of grammar and prayer all became central to Kabbalah.

Occult traditions hold that hidden wisdom, or *hokmah nistarah*, has been secretly passed down through generations of initiates since the time of Abraham. Some European occultists trace this wisdom even further back, arguing that it predates the Great Flood and originates with the Watchers, fallen angels who, according to the Book of Enoch, descended to Earth and mated with women from the lineage of Cain, giving rise to the Nephilim (Genesis 6:1-4). From these Nephilim came the Anakim, giant inhabitants of Canaan referenced in Numbers

13:33 and Deuteronomy 9:2.

According to this tradition, these giants were part of the lineage of Ham, who was cursed and tasked with the burden of guarding this occult knowledge. The Book of Enoch also describes the 12 archangels, including figures like Michael and Gabriel, who serve as divine intermediaries and protectors of hidden wisdom, opposing the fallen Watchers and maintaining cosmic balance.

In line with these ancient traditions, Theosophy suggests that the descendants of those who guarded this hidden wisdom were later known as the Aryans, a race created on Atlantis where they taught all occult knowledge.[86] According to legend, these Aryans survived the flood by escaping to the highest mountains. After the waters receded, they descended to invade the known world, spreading the Indo-European language and culture as they moved forward.

Islamically, it appears as though Kabbalah comes from the angels Harut and Marut, who were sent to the Judeans during their Babylonian captivity. Their mission was to test the people by teaching them sihr, or magic. Allah says:

$$\text{﴿ وَلَمَّا جَآءَهُمْ رَسُولٌ مِّنْ عِندِ ٱللَّهِ مُصَدِّقٌ لِّمَا مَعَهُمْ نَبَذَ فَرِيقٌ مِّنَ ٱلَّذِينَ أُوتُوا۟ ٱلْكِتَٰبَ كِتَٰبَ ٱللَّهِ وَرَآءَ ظُهُورِهِمْ كَأَنَّهُمْ لَا يَعْلَمُونَ ﴾}$$

$$\text{﴿ وَٱتَّبَعُوا۟ مَا تَتْلُوا۟ ٱلشَّيَٰطِينُ عَلَىٰ مُلْكِ سُلَيْمَٰنَ وَمَا كَفَرَ سُلَيْمَٰنُ وَلَٰكِنَّ ٱلشَّيَٰطِينَ كَفَرُوا۟ يُعَلِّمُونَ ٱلنَّاسَ ٱلسِّحْرَ وَمَآ أُنزِلَ عَلَى ٱلْمَلَكَيْنِ بِبَابِلَ هَٰرُوتَ وَمَٰرُوتَ وَمَا يُعَلِّمَانِ مِنْ أَحَدٍ حَتَّىٰ يَقُولَآ إِنَّمَا نَحْنُ فِتْنَةٌ فَلَا تَكْفُرْ فَيَتَعَلَّمُونَ مِنْهُمَا مَا يُفَرِّقُونَ بِهِۦ}$$

---

86   Note: The term "Aryan" was coined by a Freemason, Friedrich von Schlegel, and was used to refer to the people of northwestern Asia and Europe.

بَيْنَ ٱلْمَرْءِ وَزَوْجِهِۦ ۚ وَمَا هُم بِضَآرِّينَ بِهِۦ مِنْ أَحَدٍ إِلَّا بِإِذْنِ ٱللَّهِ ۚ وَيَتَعَلَّمُونَ مَا يَضُرُّهُمْ وَلَا يَنفَعُهُمْ ۚ وَلَقَدْ عَلِمُوا۟ لَمَنِ ٱشْتَرَىٰهُ مَا لَهُۥ فِى ٱلْءَاخِرَةِ مِنْ خَلَٰقٍ ۚ وَلَبِئْسَ مَا شَرَوْا۟ بِهِۦٓ أَنفُسَهُمْ ۚ لَوْ كَانُوا۟ يَعْلَمُونَ ۞

And when a messenger from Allah came to them confirming that which was with them, a party of those who had been given the Scripture threw the Scripture of Allah [i.e., the Torah] behind their backs as if they did not know [what it contained].

And they followed [instead] what the devils had recited during the reign of Solomon. It was not Solomon who disbelieved, but the devils disbelieved, teaching people magic and that which was revealed to the two angels at Babylon, Harut and Marut. But they [i.e., the two angels] do not teach anyone unless they say, "We are a trial, so do not disbelieve [by practicing magic]." And [yet] they learn from them that by which they cause separation between a man and his wife. But they do not harm anyone through it except by permission of Allah. And they [i.e., people] learn what harms them and does not benefit them. But they [i.e., the Children of Israel] certainly knew that whoever purchased it [i.e., magic] would not have in the Hereafter any share. And wretched is that for which they sold themselves, if they only knew.

(2:101-102)

The practice of sorcery and witchcraft, though existent from the elder days of humanity, truly took shape, as a science in and of itself, after the reign of Sulayman (970 to 931 BCE).

The Israelites, like many who subscribe to the "power of supernatural phenomena" held the belief that the jinn had knowledge of the unseen. The methods and practices of witchcraft were compiled in books, and these books are believed to have been confiscated by Sulayman due to how dangerous they were, and buried beneath his throne. It is also believed that after Sulayman's death, these books were retrieved, perhaps by the Shayateen, and publicly circulated amongst the people.

A few hundred years later, during the Babylonian captivity (586 BCE - 538 BCE), Allah sent two angels from heaven, Harut and Marut, to guide the Israelites in differentiating pure knowledge from sorcery. Pure knowledge was extracted from the Torah, together with the Secret of the Attributive Names of Yahweh. The Israelites corrupted what they were taught, mixing the lawful with the unlawful (sihr), and used the knowledge of the Divine Names for evil, such as separating husband and wife.

These teachings became the sacred knowledge of the Magi (priests of the Persian Empire), who acquired this knowledge from the Chaldeans (Babylonian priests) after the Persian conquest in 539 BCE.[87] They blended what they learned from Babylonian magicians with their religion of Zoroaster and became a cult known as the Chaldean-Magi, spreading their empire to India, Egypt, and Greece. As these mystical traditions evolved and spread across cultures, they laid the groundwork for subsequent occult practices, drawing from the foundations of Kabbalah.

Kabbalah offers both a theoretical framework and a practical pathway for spiritual engagement and transformation. The initiatory journey begins with understanding creation as described in the Book of Genesis and the Sephir Yetzirah, where the universe is set into motion by the divine utterance "fiat lux" or "let there be light." Through God's speech, this act of creation suggests that all existence is manifested through dynamic energies of **vibrations**, **colors**, and **sounds**.

The Zohar expands on this understanding, explaining how the universe was created using the ten sefirot and the twenty-two Hebrew letters, and delves into the mystical interpretation of the 72 Names of God. These names, derived from Exodus 14:19-21, are formed by combining three consecutive verses of 72 letters each, then creating 72 triplets that symbolize divine

87　Note: The *magos* is "one of the members of the learned and Old Persian priestly class. This is from where we get the word 'magic'.

attributes and powers. In Kabbalah, these 72 names represent different aspects of God's presence and influence throughout the universe. They are often used in meditative and spiritual practices to connect with higher planes of consciousness. Unlike traditional biblical texts, which refer to God as Elohim, the Zohar refers to Him as Ein Sof, the Infinite, indicating a more abstract and boundless aspect of divinity beyond human comprehension. This mystical framework is a form of pantheism that directly contradicts monotheism by merging the Divine with the fabric of creation itself. In Kabbalah, the cosmos is depicted as a manifestation of God's inner being, erasing the boundary between Creator and creation and undermining the core belief that God is wholly separate from and above His creation. This view later shaped Western esotericism, Renaissance magic, and Freemasonry.

Mankind, created in the image of God as described in Genesis 1:27, is believed to possess the ability to harness cosmic energies. The sefirot—ten divine attributes that reflect human potential—serve as channels for either healing and transforming the world or bringing about destruction, depending on how they are engaged. These attributes are linked with the twenty-two letters of the Hebrew alphabet, creating channels of divine energy essential for both worldly creation and spiritual endeavors. This cosmic structure aligns with the number 33, a number that is symbolically associated with divine ascent in Kabbalah and Christian symbolism as it relates to the life of Jesus. This number is found by adding the 10 sephirot and the 22 pathways that connect them with the hidden sefirah *Da'at*. Together, these provide practitioners with a detailed path toward enlightenment.

Practitioners of Kabbalah ascend from the material realm of Malkuth to the sublime Keter through a variety of spiritual disciplines. These include specific postures, controlled breathing, dietary regimes, prayer, and study. Each practice is designed to help the seeker shed egoistic impulses and deepen their meditation.

This process fosters detachment, enabling practitioners to explore Kabbalah's four interconnected worlds: *Atziluth* (the world of Emanation), *Beriah* (the world of Creation), *Yetzirah* (the world of Formation), and *Assiah* (the world of Action). Each world represents different aspects of consciousness and divine manifestation, reflecting the holistic nature of Kabbalistic practice.

Kabbalah also offers a comprehensive understanding of the soul's properties through the sefirot. **Intellectual** properties like ***Chochmah*** (wisdom) and ***Binah*** (understanding) enhance cognitive processes, while **emotional** properties like ***Chesed*** (loving-kindness) and ***Gevurah*** (might) balance emotional states. **Behavioral** properties like ***Netzach*** (victory) and ***Hod*** (glory) influence actions, together guiding practitioners' everyday lives and spiritual journeys.

Kabbalistic scholarship highlights how the intricate correspondences within the Tree of Life—spanning the four worlds of Kabbalah, the ten sephirot, various human organs, the five elements (Fire, Air, Water, Earth, and Spirit), and the sacred name of G-d, YHWH—demonstrate the principle of "As above, so below." By aligning the four letters of the Tetragrammaton (Yod, He, Vau, He) in a vertical sequence that mirrors the human anatomy from head to hips, Kabbalah visually and conceptually unites the cosmic with the corporeal, emphasizing the interconnectedness of the universe and human experience. This synthesis embodies the essence of Kabbalistic wisdom, revealing a universal blueprint where the spiritual and physical realms reflect and inform each other, guiding practitioners toward a deeper understanding and alignment with the divine order.

Category	Sefirot	Organ	Element	World
Super-Conscious	1. Keter "Crown"	1. Skull	◯ Spirit	י Atziluth (תוליצא) Archetypal world Plane of Will/ Spirit
Conscious Intellect	2. Chochmah "wisdom" 3. Binah "understanding" Da'at "knowledge"	2. Right brain 3. Left brain Central brain	△ Fire	
Conscious Emotions	4. Chesed "Loving-Kindness" 5. Gevurah "Might" 6. Tiferet "Beauty"	4. Right arm 5. Left arm 6. Torso	▽ Water	ה Beri'ah (הָאיִרְב) Creative world/ Emotional Plane
Conscious Behavior	7. Netzach "Victory" 8. Hod "glory" 9. Yesod "Foundation"	7. Right leg 8. Left leg 9. Sexual Organ	◮ Air	ו Yetzirah (הָריִצְי) Formative World/ Mental Plane
	10. Malkuth "Kingdom"	10. Mouth (Feet)	◺ Earth	ה Asiyah (הָיִשֲׂע) Physical World/ Material Plane

Fig. 28 - Table of Correspondences
Categories of sefirot linked to body, elements, and worlds.

יהוה

H W H Y

Head

Neck

Shoulders

Arms/Hands

Torso/Spine

Legs/Feet

Pelvis

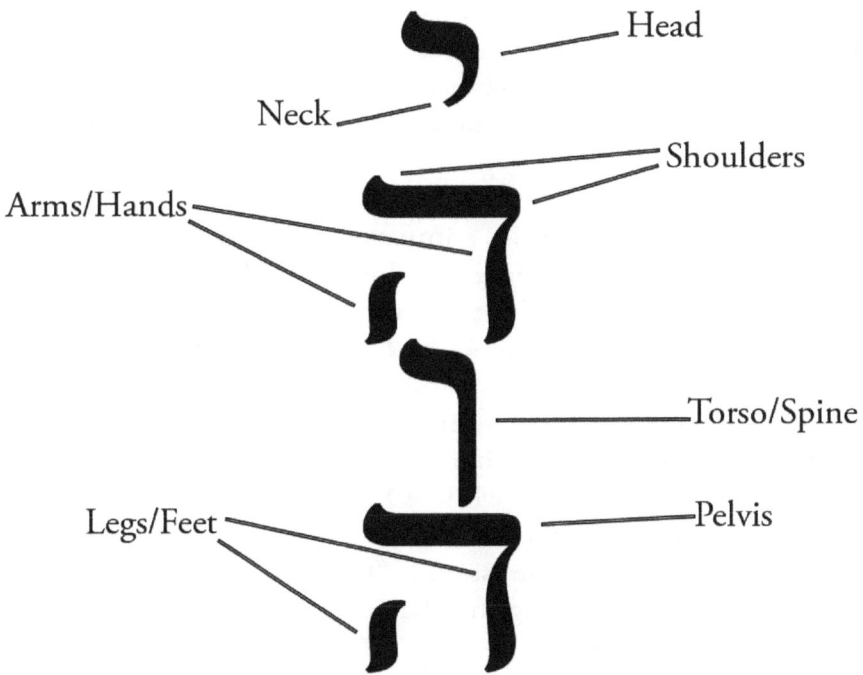

Fig. 29 - Divine Name and Human Form
YHWH mapped onto the body: Yod = head, Heh = arms, Vav = torso,
final Heh = legs.

KUNDALINI

Indian mysticism offers a practical expression of the Tree of Life philosophy through the Kundalini chakras. Kundalini chakras are latent energy centers within humans, often depicted as a coiled snake at the base of the spine. These areas are forms of consciousness and can be considered "mini-brains." This energy is known by various names across cultures, such as Chi in Chinese traditions or the Holy Spirit in Christian mysticism, and can be activated through practices such as meditation, *pranayama* (breath control), the chanting of *mantras*, and visualization of *yantras*.[88] The process of awakening Kundalini energy involves its ascent through the 7 chakras, each corresponding to the astral forces of the 7 classical planets. This journey activates 7 states of consciousness, which flow through the etheric body. Governed by these planetary influences, each chakra impacts specific organs, glands, and emotional states, harmonizing the physical, emotional, and spiritual dimensions of the individual.

Both mantras (sacred sounds) and yantras (geometric symbols) are key tools in stimulating and balancing the 7 **chakras**, allowing the energy to flow more freely throughout the body. A key mantra in this practice involves chanting the sequence of the 7 vowels: *A, E, I, O, U, Y,* and *M*—which harmonize with the chakras and the planetary energies they embody. Chanting these vowels harmonizes the body's energy, such as the vowel E activating the pituitary and pineal glands, enhancing clairvoyance, while O resonates with the heart chakra, promoting intuition. When these vowels are chanted together, they form the sound "OhM," believed to be a universal mantra unifying the chakras and promoting healing, peace, and cosmic unity.

Modern research complements this ancient understanding by highlighting how the pineal gland, when activated through

---

88   Note: Some other names are *"Barakah"* in Islam, *"Ka"* in Ancient Egyptian, *"Ruach"* in Hebrew, *"Prana"* in Hindu traditions, *"Ki"* in Japanese culture, "Psi" in parapsychology, *"mana"* in the Bible and many other examples.

meditation, pranayama, and visualization, can lead to the release of gamma brain waves. Gamma waves are associated with heightened states of awareness and consciousness, unlocking the brain's potential for transcendental experiences. As Kundalini energy rises to the crown chakra, stimulating the pineal gland, the brain enters a gamma state, creating bursts of creative insight, spiritual clarity, and a profound sense of oneness with the universe. This corresponds to the Indian mystic belief that Kundalini energy reaching the crown chakra leads to enlightenment and a sense of unity with all life.

In addition, preserving sexual energy and maintaining a healthy lifestyle, such as consuming an alkaline diet, avoiding alcohol, and balancing the chakras, are believed to help raise this energy. Once raised to the brain, Kundalini energy is thought to remodel the brain's capacity, unlocking dormant areas and expanding consciousness. This transformation can lead to heightened awareness, deeper spiritual insights, and even superhuman capabilities while aligning the **mind**, **body**, and **spirit**.

The medical symbol of the caduceus reflects the belief that raised Kundalini has healing properties through the activation of dormant cells and the regulation of bodily functions. As the energy reaches the crown chakra, it fosters unity, enlightenment, and a profound connection to the universe, transcending ordinary human limitations and bringing peace and fulfillment.

Fig. 30 - The caduceus, carried by Hermes in Greek mythology and later by Hermes Trismegistus, symbolizes balance and transformation. In the Kundalini tradition, it mirrors the twin energy channels (ida and pingala) winding around the central spine (sushumna) and rising toward spiritual awakening.

The journey of Kundalini from the base to the crown chakra passes through the central channel, impacting each chakra:

Root Chakra (*Muladhara*):

- *Location:* Base of the spine.

- *Element:* Earth.

- *Governance:* Survival instincts, grounding, physical identity.

- *Organs/Glands:* Adrenal glands.

- *Imbalance:* Manifests as anger and fear.

- *Balance Remedy:* Patience and grounding practices.

- *Sefirot Correspondence: Malkhut* (Kingdom). Represents physical existence and grounding in reality.

Sacral Chakra (*Svadhisthana*):

- *Location:* Lower abdomen, near the groin.

- *Element:* Water.

- *Governance:* Emotions, sexuality, creativity.

- *Organs/Glands:* Reproductive system.

- *Imbalance:* Manifests as lust and emotional instability.

- *Balance Remedy:* Chastity and emotional balance.

- *Sefirot Correspondence: Yesod* (Foundation) - Represents creativity, emotions, and the subconscious.

Solar Plexus Chakra (*Manipura*):

- *Location:* Navel area.

- *Element:* Fire.

- *Governance:* Personal power, willpower, subconscious mind.

- *Organs/Glands:* Pancreas.

- *Imbalance:* Manifests as sloth and lack of motivation.

- *Balance Remedy:* Prayer and cultivating personal strength.

- *Sefirot Correspondence: Hod* (Glory) Represents personal will and transformation.

Heart Chakra (*Anahata*):

- *Location:* Center of the chest.

- *Element:* Air.

- *Governance:* Love, compassion, peace.

- *Organs/Glands:* Thymus.

- *Imbalance:* Manifests as envy and lack of compassion.

- *Balance Remedy:* Gratitude and love cultivation.

- *Sefirot Correspondence: Tiferet* (Beauty) - Represents harmony, love, and compassion.

Throat Chakra (*Vishuddha*):
- *Location:* Throat.

- *Element:* Ether.

- *Governance:* Communication, creativity, expression.

- *Organs/Glands:* Thyroid.

- *Imbalance:* Manifests as gluttony and communication issues.

- *Balance Remedy:* Fasting and honest expression.

- *Sefirot Correspondence: Gevurah* (Strength) - Represents judgment, communication, and discipline.

Brow Chakra (*Ajna*, Third Eye):
- *Location:* Between the eyebrows.

- *Element:* Light.

- *Governance:* Intuition, insight, perception beyond the physical.

- *Organs/Glands:* Pituitary gland.

- *Imbalance:* Manifests as greed and lack of foresight.

- *Balance Remedy:* Charity and intuitive practices.

- *Sefirot Correspondence: Binah* (Understanding) — Represents insight, wisdom, and intuition.

Crown Chakra (*Sahasrara*):

- *Location:* Top of the skull.

- *Element:* Thought.

- *Governance:* Universal consciousness, spiritual connection.

- *Organs/Glands:* Pineal gland.

- *Imbalance:* Manifests as pride and spiritual disconnection.

- *Balance Remedy:* Humility and spiritual practices.

- *Sefirot Correspondence: Keter* (Crown) - Represents divine connection, enlightenment, and unity.

When Kundalini energy reaches the brain, it is said to unify the mind and body, aligning thoughts with actions and transforming a person's entire being. In tandem with the release of gamma waves, the individual becomes more attuned to the *Kala* (time-space) perspective of the universe, experiencing a profound sense of unity and oneness with all life. This transformation is believed to cultivate a sense of peace, fulfillment, and enlightenment, transcending ordinary human limitations and connecting with the divine essence of existence.

Fig. 31 - Modern Esoteric Tree of Life combining Egyptian Deities with the Kabbalistic Structure

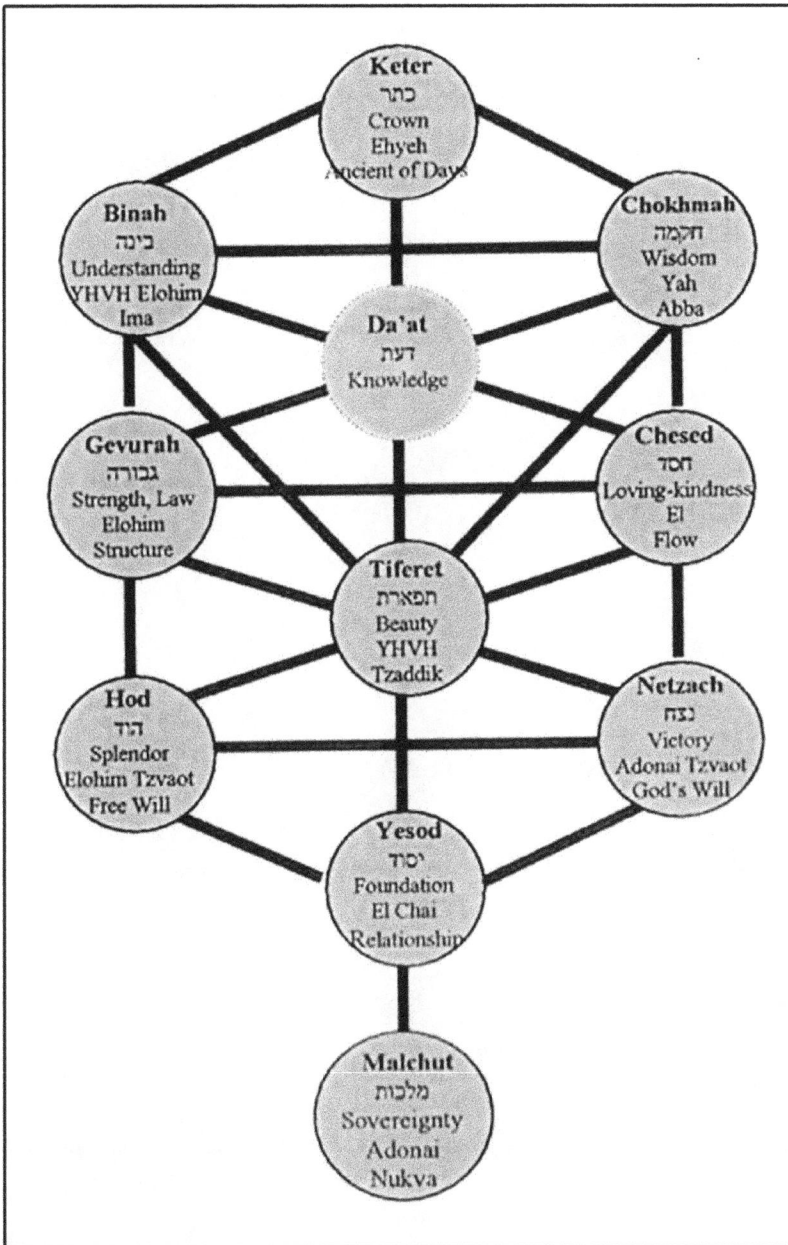

Fig. 32 - The ten sefirot as the Tree of Life

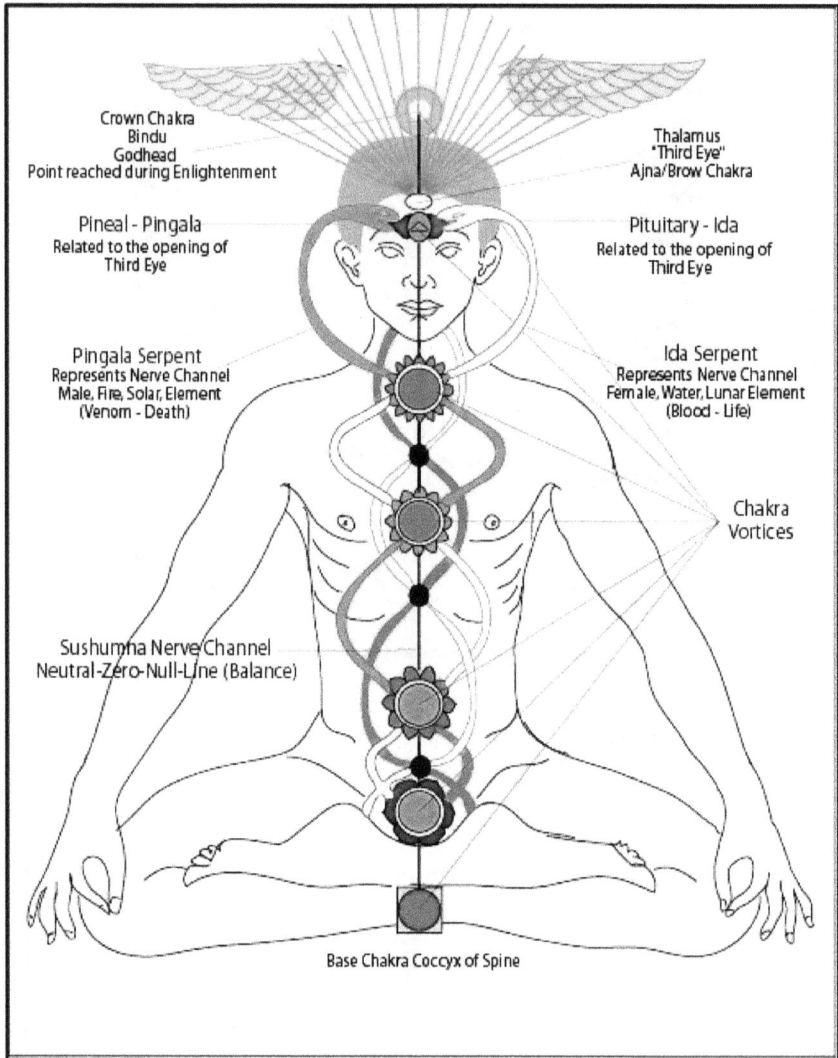

Crown Chakra
Bindu
Godhead
Point reached during Enlightenment

Thalamus
"Third Eye"
Ajna/Brow Chakra

Pineal - Pingala
Related to the opening of
Third Eye

Pituitary - Ida
Related to the opening of
Third Eye

Pingala Serpent
Represents Nerve Channel
Male, Fire, Solar, Element
(Venom - Death)

Ida Serpent
Represents Nerve Channel
Female, Water, Lunar Element
(Blood - Life)

Chakra
Vortices

Sushumna Nerve Channel
Neutral-Zero-Null-Line (Balance)

Base Chakra Coccyx of Spine

Fig. 33 - Chakras of Indian Kundalini yoga

CHRISTIANITY

Christians explore the 'As Above, So Below' concept by aligning the earthly realm with the heavenly in one of the most significant prayers in the Bible: The Lord's Prayer. This prayer, found in Matthew 6:9-13, is as follows:

"Our Father who art in heaven, hallowed be thy name.
Thy kingdom come.
Thy will be done, on earth as it is in heaven.
Give us this day our daily bread; and forgive us our
trespasses, as we forgive those who trespass against us; and
lead us not into temptation but deliver us from evil [or: the
evil one]."

The teachings of Jesus were initially passed along orally until the latter half of the first century, when various texts were written to preserve them. The Gospel of Matthew and other biblical texts record a version of the Lord's Prayer, which Jesus taught as a model for how his disciples should pray. The prayer consists of 7 petitions that aim to bring the flawed earthly realm into alignment with the perfect heavenly realm, emphasizing spiritual transformation and moral alignment.

The Lord's Prayer begins by addressing the Creator:
"Our Father who art in Heaven."

Fundamental Christian teachings characterize God as the Father and humans as His sons and daughters. Heaven is described as the kingdom of the spirit, the realm where the soul of man originates, and the realm towards which his life's mission is to ascend.

The First Three Petitions:
Connection to the Heavenly Realm

Hallowed be thy name:
This petition acknowledges God's holiness and calls on believers to honor and sanctify His name in their lives.

Thy kingdom come:
Here, the prayer envisions the manifestation of God's kingdom on earth, characterized by peace, justice, love, and compassion.

Thy will be done on earth, as it is in heaven:
This petition seeks to align human desires and actions with God's will, aiming to bring heavenly ideals to earthly existence.

The Last Four Petitions:
Addressing Human Needs and Challenges

Give us this day our daily bread:
This request concerns the physical sustenance necessary for life, reflecting a dependence on God for daily needs.

Forgive us our trespasses, as we forgive those who trespass against us:
This petition emphasizes the importance of forgiveness and the salvation of the soul through reconciliation with others.

Lead us not into temptation:
This request seeks guidance to overcome lower desires and avoid falling into sin.

Deliver us from evil:
This petition asks for protection from evil influences, including the ego's inclination towards sin.

The 7 petitions of the Lord's Prayer serve as a supplication, imploring the Lord to guide human nature towards alignment with the Divine Will. The principle of correspondence is evident in this prayer, as it directs followers to focus on the heavenly realm where God's name is revered and His will prevails. The prayer then calls on the individual to reflect on the state of the earthly world: our need for sustenance, our inclination to sin, and our battles with temptation and evil. The phrase "on earth as it is in heaven" unites these two realms. This union necessitates a transformation of the earthly realm. Christians must work to bring about on earth what they envision God achieving in the heavenly realms. God's kingdom cannot manifest if Christians are not actively pursuing righteousness. Similarly, the "Father's" will cannot be fulfilled on earth if Christians do not embody it in their daily lives.

SECTION 2

THE PRINCIPLE OF CORRESPONDENCE

PART II

ASTROLOGY

The doctrine of "as above, so below" is a foundational principle in the art of astrology (*tanjim*). This maxim found in the opening lines of the Emerald Tablet, suggests that events in the spiritual heaven (macrocosm) are mirrored in the physical world (microcosm) and vice versa. Ancient societies observed that occurrences on Earth often reflected conditions in the heavens. The pagans studied the stars, believing them to be living entities that influenced the destinies of nations, tribes and individuals. They were particularly fascinated by how the 7 moving planets shifted in regular patterns relative to each other and to the Earth against the backdrop of "fixed" stars. These observations have become codified in a pseudo-science (i.e., shir) called astrology.[89]

Astrologers make predictions by interpreting a person's horoscope, often with intuitive insights or through the help of shayateen (divination or *kahanah*). They focus on the future, but their predictions are rooted in analyzing past planetary positions, which they believe will recur.

Astrological History

Astrology was originally developed by the priestly class in Mesopotamia, encompassing Babylonia in the south and Assyria in the north. These priests, known as Chaldeans, studied the qualities and positions of stars and planets, believing they affected the entire nation. Initially, this knowledge was kept secret, granting the Chaldeans significant influence over rulers and laypeople. They even used their understanding of celestial events to threaten to block out the sun, leveraging solar eclipses to maintain control and ensure obedience from those who feared the wrath of the gods.

The Chaldeans invented the zodiac, explaining the relationship between the fixed stars and the moving planets, which followed a definite track. The zodiac was divided into twelve parts, known as constellations, each represented by an animal, mythological figure, or object. The twelve signs fall into four elemental groups: fiery, earthy, airy, and watery. These signs are further categorized by qualities: cardinal (predominant), fixed, and mutable. Other cultures have categorized the signs into male and female, human and animal, or land and water. Each sign was believed to influence the qualities and personalities of those born under it.

In Babylon, each city-state had its god representative and shifts in power among city-states reflected changes in the gods' relationships. Priests ruled their provinces, dispensing wisdom to followers. They observed the stars and planets from large

---

89   Ibn 'Abbās narrated that Allāh's Messenger ﷺ said: "Whoever acquires a branch [of the knowledge] of astrology has certainly acquired a branch [of the knowledge] of magic. The more one increases so does the other along with it" (Abu Dawood).

observatories or watchtowers (ziggurats), which also served as places for sacrifices to communicate with the divine. The ziggurats were designed as meeting places between heaven and Earth, where gods could converse with elite priests. Through their observations, they devised ways to divide the year into months, weeks, hours, minutes, and seconds.

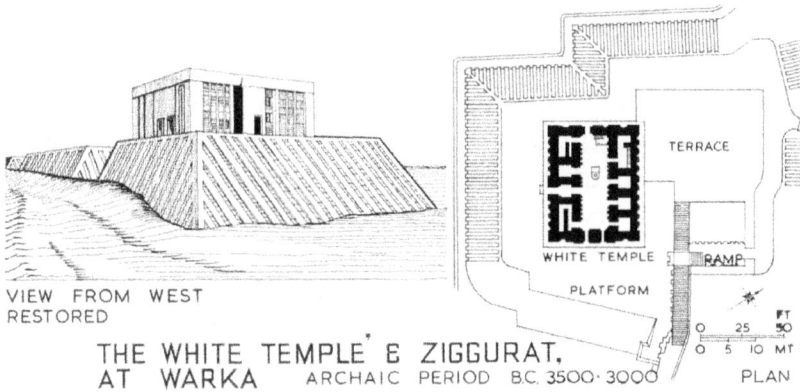

VIEW FROM WEST
RESTORED

THE WHITE TEMPLE & ZIGGURAT.
AT WARKA   ARCHAIC PERIOD B.C. 3500·3000

TERRACE

WHITE TEMPLE
PLATFORM
RAMP

PLAN

Fig. 34 - Schematic rendering of the Anu Ziggurat and White Temple at Uruk. The Anu Ziggurat was first constructed around 4000 BCE, and the White Temple was later built atop it circa 3500 BCE.

The astrological charts created by these priests enabled them to predict the recurrence of seasons and celestial events. The early Babylonian priests established the basic principles of astrology around 4000-3500 BCE and were refined during the reign of Nebuchadnezzar II (605-562 BCE), the longest-reigning ruler of the Babylonian Empire. During this time, the Jews were taken into captivity in Babylon, where their exposure to astrology likely influenced their own writings, as seen in the astrological allegories in the Old Testament. However, even prior to the enslavement in Babylon, they already worshipped the sun, moon, and planets as shown in II Kings 23:5. This idolatry and worship of celestial bodies were condemned by the Prophets as violations of the covenant with Yahweh, which is cited as a primary reason for the divine punishment upon the Judeans.

In the 4th century BCE, Babylonian astrology was introduced to the Greeks, who regarded it as a science. The Greeks added logical structures, such as naming signs after animals and objects, and shifted the focus from national destinies to individual fates.

The Greeks' influence reached India through the conquests of Alexander the Great. Later, Roman names for zodiac signs replaced those of Mesopotamian gods. These Roman names are still in use today. Finally, the Arabs spread "natal astrology" worldwide.[90]

Natal astrology is based on one's "horoscope" or "birth chart," which is the foundation of astrology.[91] It is a symbolic interpretation of a person's inner and outer life, both physical and psychological. A horoscope shows the positions of the planets relative to Earth and the stars at the time of a person's

---

90   Note: Astrology is divided into three categories:
- Natural astronomy- the foretelling of the motions of the heavenly bodies (now known as astronomy),
- Judicial astrology- interprets the motions of the heavenly bodies as it relates to terrestrial life.
- Natal astrology- the art of erecting and interpreting individuals' horoscopes.

91   Note: "*nature*" comes from the Latin *nasci,* "to be born"; *nasci* is also related to *nativity* and *natal*; "Horoscope" means "watcher of the hour"; it is also called a birth chart.

birth. An astrologer needs to know the exact time of birth to chart the positions of the sun, moon, and planets. The astrologer makes predictions by comparing these charts with what is known about a person's life and character.

Astrologers create a person's birth chart by determining where each planet was in the sky at the time of birth. Similar to how a geographer uses imaginary longitude and latitude lines to measure Earth's position, the zodiac determines the planets' positions in the sky.

The zodiac is divided into twelve equal sections, called houses or signs, with each sign consisting of 30 degrees. Viewed from Earth, the sun appears to move across the zodiac, completing the circle annually and spending approximately one month in each sign. According to astrologers, these signs influence how planets shape a person's character. The traditional planets and their influences are as follows:

1. **Sun**: Governs the inner self, influencing creativity, vitality, will, and ambition.
2. **Moon**: Governs the emotional self, affecting changes, growth, and personal relationships.
3. **Mercury**: Governs intelligence and communication, enhancing learning and expression.
4. **Venus**: Governs emotional makeup, shaping love, friendships, and aesthetic appreciation.
5. **Mars**: Governs assertiveness and drive, influencing ambition, comfort, and personal success.
6. **Jupiter**: Governs expansion and prosperity, encouraging growth, abundance, and fulfillment.
7. **Saturn**: Represents challenges, bringing lessons through obstacles and fostering resilience.

The discovery of new planets (Uranus, Neptune, and Pluto) over the last 200 years has complicated traditional astrological charts. Astrologers examine a person's sun sign first, as it is believed to dominate their basic character. However, the positions of the moon and planets also affect personality. The zodiacal position of a planet indicates its influence on character and life. As a result, astrological interpretations can vary, with different astrologers providing different predictions. These predictions often appear accurate due to the vagueness of the astrologer's language and cautious nature.

ASTROLOGICAL TIMELINE OF PROPHETIC HISTORY

In line with the principle of "as above, so below," humans breathe on average 25,920 times per day, mirroring the 25,920-year cycle of the "great Platonic year," which is the time it takes for the sun, moon, planets, and fixed stars to return to their starting point. The zodiac's full cycle, known as the precession of the equinoxes, is divided into twelve astrological ages, each lasting approximately 2,160 years and corresponding to a zodiac sign. These eras appear to align with major cultural, societal, and political changes on Earth.

The twelve zodiac constellations move linearly through the months of the year, but in the larger "Great Year" cycle, they appear to move backward. Currently, we are in the last 6 degrees of the Piscean Age. Since it takes Earth around 72 years to move through one degree, we will not fully enter the Age of Aquarius for another 130 years.

While astrologers do not agree on the exact dates for the beginning or end of these ages, the overarching patterns suggest significant shifts in human history aligned with the following celestial cycles. This timeline synthesizes astrological history, mainstream textual history, and Islamic history by linking Prophetic events, cultural developments, and societal changes with astrological ages, creating a unified narrative across different systems of knowledge.

Leo (Lion)
End of Summer

♌

10,800 - 8,640 BCE
or
10,000 -8,000 BCE

- The Age of Renewal and Personal Growth, ruled by the active sun. Represented by Leo which is a fire sign, symbolizing vitality, creativity, and self-expression.
- Marks the emergence of sun worship and solar deities.
- Cave paintings of the Sun-Lion symbolized the mind (Sun) before matter (Lion).
- Transition from the Ice Age to the Neolithic Revolution: agriculture and animal domestication.
- Considered a Golden Age for consciousness, this period is likely the era in which Prophet Idris lived.
- Transition from a purely mineral stage to a primitive plant stage of humanity, marked by creativity and ingenuity.
- Sun worship as a dominant religion, viewing the sun as a hero rescuing Earth from Saturn/Satan/ Saturday who ruled the previous "Mineral Age" age in which Adam and Seth lived.
- Sun is depicted as a proud young man, known as Krishna in India, Apollo in Greece, and Osiris in Egypt.
- Gold represents the sun in metal form.

The 'Age of the Sun' represents the Sunday era of existence.

Cancer (Crab)
Beginning and Middle of Summer

♋

8,640 - 6,480 BCE
or
8,000 BCE – 6000 BCE

The Age of the Great Mother, ruled by the passive moon. Associated with Cancer, a water sign, representing nurturing, fertility, and the feminine principle.

- Symbolizes moon worship and reverence for fertility goddesses.
- The continuation of the Neolithic Revolution and the further spread of agriculture in the Fertile Crescent, with societies forming along the Nile, Tigris, and Euphrates, led to structured civilizations and the domestication of animals. [92]
- Era of Prophet Nuh and the Great Flood.
- The 1,000 years before Nuh was the era of ignorance, marked by idol worship of figures like Wadd, Suwa', Yaghuth, Ya'uq, and Nasr.[93]
- Nuh advised and warned his people for 950 years before the flood.
- Rebuilding of civilizations by Nuh's sons Ham, Sham, and Japheth in Africa, the Middle East, and Europe.
- Widespread use of boats and vessels.
- Peak of matriarchal culture, with fertility figures and moon worship.
- Moon believed to regulate female cycles and thought.
- Silver represents the moon in metal form.

The 'Age of the Moon' represents the Monday era of existence.

---

92 Note: The first Biblical hunter in history is Esau "a cunning hunter, a man of the field" (Gen. 25:27)

93 And they said, 'Never leave your gods and never leave Wadd (manly powers) or Suwa' (woman beauty) or Yaghuth (Lion-brute strength) and Ya'uq (Horse-swiftness) and Nasr (Eagle-sharp sight) (71:23).

Gemini (Twins)
Beginning of Summer/ End of Spring

Ⅱ

6,480 - 4,320 BCE
or
6000 – 4000 BCE

- The Age of Communication, Trade, and Duality, ruled by the neutral planet Mercury. Represented by Gemini, an Air sign symbolizing communication, intellectual development, and duality.
- Marked by the rise of trade networks and the development of early writing systems like cuneiform.
- This is the second era associated with Prophet Idris.
- Development of proto-writing, cuneiform, wheel, and plow, advancing human intellect.
- In Egypt, the Gemini-like duality of Upper and Lower Egypt was formed.
- Mercury represents the planet Mercury in metal form.

The 'Age of the Mercury' represents the Wednesday era of existence.

Taurus (Bull)
Middle to late Spring

♉

4,320 - 2,160 BCE
or
4,000 BCE – 2000 BCE

The Age of Growth and Stability, ruled by the passive planet Venus. Represented by Taurus, an Earth sign symbolizing material wealth, stability, and fertility.

- Worship of the bull as a sacred symbol (e.g., Apis in Egypt).
- Transition from the Stone Age to the Bronze Age.

- Construction of pyramids in Egypt, Ziggurats in Mesopotamia, and other large monuments on earth.
- Worship of various deities like Apis, a sacred bull worshipped in the Memphis region of Egypt.
- Copper represents Venus in metal form.

The 'Age of the Taurus' represents the Friday era of existence.

Aries (Ram)
Beginning to Middle of Spring

♈

2,160 BCE – 1 BCE

or

2,000 BCE – 1 BCE

- The Age of Law, Conquest, and Patriarchy, ruled by the active planet Mars. Represented by Aries, a fire sign symbolizing action, war, and order.
- Transition through:
  Stone Age (500,000 – 2000 BCE) into the
  Bronze Age (2000 - 700 BCE) and the
  Iron Age (700 BCE - 43 CE).
- *1st Age:* Humans used primitive stone tools.
  2nd Age: Humans started working with metals.
  3rd Age: Humans smelted iron into swords.
- Creation of three Universal Systems:
  Invention of coins and banking - Universal Money.
  The Persian Empire – a Universal Political Order.
  Buddhism in India – a Universal Teaching
- This is the era in which Banu Israel rose and declined.[94] Aries signals the start of Spring.
- Several Prophets and Messengers established or upheld laws.

---

94 Note: Ibrahim's son Yaqub, Jacob was later renamed Israel and had 12 sons who became the 12 tribes of Israel. Later generations of Rabbis associated these 12 sons with the 12 signs of the zodiac. Like the zodiac they were divided into four camps of three in accordance with the four seasons and the four elements.

- Formalization of astrology.
- 2334 BCE First Empire- The Akkadian Empire of Sargon.
- 2150 BCE, Hammurabi ruled and established a 7-day week, with the last day a rest day or Sabbath. The Hebrews later adopted this idea and then transmitted it to the Greeks, Romans, and other Europeans.
- 2000 BCE Prophet **Ibrahim** leads a ram-like rebellion, mentally head-butting the world's leaders.
- Ibrahim argued against all the worshippers of the stars in the heavens above and the idols on the earth below.[95]
- Ibrahim becomes the father of Ismail, who became the ancestor of the Arabs, and of Ishaaq, who became the father of Yaqub (also called Israel), from whom the Children of Israel descended.
- The 18th century BCE Babylonian king Hammurabi established the first written codes of law in recorded history.
- 1800-1600 BCE: Hyksos take over Nile Delta & North Egypt.
- 1706 BCE Prophet Yusuf and his siblings (Banu Israel) settled in Egypt during the reign of the Hyksos in its Middle Kingdom.
- 1665 BCE - 538 BCE Biblical texts use the term "Hebrews".
- Egypt kicks out Hyksos, then Banu Israel is enslaved in the New Kingdom of Egypt, leading to the most brilliant three centuries of Egyptian history (1500-1200 BCE).
- In 1447 BCE, Prophet Musa led a Ram-like confrontation with Fir'awn, leading to the Israelites Exodus out of Egypt into the Sinai close to Canaan.[96]
- The Ten Commandments were revealed to Musa, then later established as a set of instructions and laws known

95   Stars Above: (Al-An'am, 6:75-83); Idols Below: (Al-An'am, 6:74-75)

96   Note: It is debated when Musa lived; some reports state he was born in 1540 BC, while others say between 1300-1200 BCE, and others say he lived during the 19th Egyptian dynasty from 1292 to 1189 BC.

as the Torah (five books)[97]

- While Musa was on Mount Tur receiving these commandments, the Israelites returned to their worship of the Golden Calf, representing the old familiar influence of Taurus that they knew in Egypt.
- Musa returned and punished the people by destroying the Golden Calf and keeping them in the desert until the entire older generation passed away.
- 1353–1336 or 1351–1334 BCE, King Akhenaton of the 18th dynasty of the New Kingdom in Egypt abandoned traditional polytheism and introduced monotheism.[98]
- 1200 - 900 BCE Bronze Age Collapse of Egypt, Hittites, Mitanni, Arzawa, Mycenean Empires.[99]
- Attack of Sea Peoples
- Invasion of Banu Israel in Canaan
- 1047 – 922 BCE: The United Kingdom of Israel was established and led by King Talut, Dawud, and Sulayman.
- 960 – 922 BCE: With the help of jinn, birds, and wind, Sulayman completes the greatest temple the world has ever seen in Jerusalem.
- 858 BCE: Elijah battles the false god Baal
- The Phoenician Alphabet was created.
- 722 BCE: The Assyrian Empire conquered Israel, and Greek city-states rose to power.[100]
- 600 BCE: The temple of Sulayman was destroyed by the Babylonians and the Banishment of 10 Tribes of

---

97 Note: The Pentateuch or Five Books of Moses are Genesis, Exodus, Leviticus, Numbers, and Deuteronomy.

98 Akhenaten is the strongest historical candidate to being Musa.

99 Note: The Bronze Age brought with it the three great Semitic cultural revolutions: Bronze, writing, and monotheism.

100 The period between 800-200 has been termed the Axial Age. This was a period wherein new ideologies were created that were crucial and formative up until today. Taoism and Confucianism in China, Hinduism and Buddhism in India, philosophical rationalism in Europe, Zoroaster in Iran, and the Hebrew Prophets in Israel.

Israel to the Lands of Medea

- Rise of Neo Babylonian Empire & Median Empire. *Nebuchadnezzar attacked Jerusalem and destroyed the temple of Sulayman, and the tribes of Israel were enslaved in Babylon.*
- In Babylon, the Jews adopted the corrupted teachings of Harut and Marut and the worship of the Dying & Rising God cult of the Canaanites (jinn worship).[101]
- In Egypt, astrology is developed.
- 600-300 BCE:
  Rise of Dhul Qarnayn/ Cyrus the Great
  1st Persian Empire that ruled over the Civilized World.
  Cyrus frees the Jews and returns them to Jerusalem.
  Jews built the 2nd Temple, which was destroyed during Roman rule in the 1st century.
- 538 BCE when the Persians overthrew the Babylonian Chaldeans. These Jews were ethnically European." with "The freed Judeans—now called Jews—returned from Babylonian exile with a mixed lineage of Israelite ancestry and neighboring peoples."
- *During the 2nd Temple period, the Bible was compiled, edited, and corrupted in the process.*
- Origins of what became known as the Zohar and Kabbalah (in secret).
- Spread of Judaic Kabbalah over the Civilized World.
- The sacred texts of Zoroastrianism - the Avesta- were written by Zoroaster and followed by the corruption of Zoroastrianism by the Magi.
- 500 BCE start of Buddhism.
- 550-330 BCE start of Greek Philosophy.
- 300 BCE start of Neo-Egyptian Hermeticism.
- 300-0 CE:
  Alexander the Great conquered the world, spreading Greek Hellenization.
- Era of the Sadducees, Essenes, Samaritans, Zealots, and Pharisees (forerunners to Rabbinic Judaism)

---

101 Note: The Bible was written during some 1,400 years (1300 BC-100 AD).

- 4th century Jerusalem Talmud was composed, followed by the Babylonian Talmud a century later.
- Rise of the Roman Empire (the most powerful empire ever known).

Powerful Empires:
- 900-600 BCE
  Assyrian/Babylonian Empire
- 600 BCE-300 BCE
  Dhul Qarnayn
  Persian Empire
- 400 BCE-100 BCE
  Greek Empire

- The four Sanskrit Vedas were established, laying the ground for the Hindu way of life.
- Worship of the ram/lamb, although there were many efforts to replace polytheism with monotheism.
- Many wars occurred during this time as nations expanded their empires.
- The ram/lamb was worshipped in this age.
- Iron represents Mars in metal form.

The 'Age of the Ares' represents the Tuesday era of existence.

Pisces (Fish)
Beginning of Spring/ End of Winter

♓

0 - 2,160 AD

- The age of Spirituality, Faith, and Illusion, ruled by the active Jupiter. Represented by Pisces, a water sign symbolizing faith, sacrifice, and mysticism.
- Rise of major monotheistic religions, including Christianity and Islam.

- We transitioned out of the:

256

Ancient Age (3000 BCE - 476 CE) into the
Medieval Age (476 CE – 1492 CE) into the
Modern Age (1492 – 1789 CE) and the
Contemporary Age (1789 CE – Present)

The Age of Pisces is also known as the "Age of Deception," with spiritual knowledge linked to illusions, confusion, frauds, schemes, secrets, and mysteries. The deception encompasses every aspect of our lives: our homes, entertainment, health, food, drugs, government, and religion.

- 0 – 33 CE Messiah Isa was sent with the Injil, Gospel. This was the last chance for Jews to return to the covenant and stop the corruption of the world.
- 0 – 325 CE:
  Spread of Isa's monotheism until the Council of Nicaea, where Church scholars decided which gospels to include in the Bible.
- Isa went from being a Prophet to being worshipped as the return of the 'Sun god,' to the Word.
- Emperor Constantine declared Christianity the official religion of the Empire.
- 27 BCE - 476 CE: Roman Empire falls
- Roman spread into Germanic and Celtic Lands
- Persecution of the monotheist from Romans and Jews
- In 70 CE, the Jewish 2nd Temple was destroyed, and Jews were banished from the Holy Land.
- 306 – 337 CE Emperor Constantine adopts Pauline Christianity
- 300 - 600 CE Roman Christianity spreads
- Invasion of the Huns and Germanic incursions into the Western Roman Empire; the seat of power moves to Constantinople.
- Sassanid Persian Empire rises
- 476 CE to 1492 CE Medieval Age: This began with the fall of the Western Roman Empire and ended with

Columbus discovering and colonizing America in 1492 CE.

- 600 - 1200 CE: Prophet Muhammad leads the Muslim Empire followed by the 4 rightly guided Khalifas.
- Islam ruled the world until the Mongol Invasion.
- 1200 - 1600 CE: Mongols/ Turks rule the East (Magog), while Christianity falls in the West (Gog).
- 1600 - 2000 CE: Rise of Germanic Empires aka Gog: (English, French, Spanish, Dutch, Italy, America).
- Scientific / Industrial Revolution:
  Globalization
  Electricity
  Atheism Scientism, and Democracy
- 2000 CE - Present: New Israel - Zionist Empire
  Tin represents Jupiter in metal form.
The 'Age of Jupiter' represents the Thursday era of existence.

Aquarius (Water jug)
Late to Middle of Winter

♒

2,160 - 4,320 AD
or
2,000 - 4,000 AD

The age of Technology, Innovation, and Humanitarianism is ruled by the active planet Saturn.

Represented by Aquarius, an Air sign symbolizing intellect, progress, and collective growth.

Features of this era:

- Global reset with new approaches to business, politics, and ecological concerns.
- Era of Imam Mahdi and the return of Isa (Jesus) to kill Dajjal (Antichrist) and lead the Muslims away from the test of yajuj and majuj (Gog and Magog).
- Peace and stability until Isa dies, which signals the

moments before the end of the world.

Features of this era:
- A Global Reset: new ways of doing business and politics.
- New Humanitarian principles amongst individuals and the collective.
- Addressing ecological concerns with innovative technology.
- Rational/ logical decision-making versus extremist fanaticism.
- Likely the age when the Day of Judgment occurs.

Lead represents Saturn in metal form.

The 'Age of Saturn' represents the Saturday era of existence.[102]

---

102 Note: Ibn Abbas (ra) said: "The world is seven days. Each Day is like a thousand years. And The Messenger of Allah ﷺ was sent at the end of that." (Suyuti).

Anas ibn Malik (ra) said that The Messenger of Allah ﷺ said: The life span of the world is seven days in the afterlife days. Almighty Allah said, "a day with your Lord is equivalent to a thousand years in the way you count". (Suyuti).

ASTROLOGY AND WITCHCRAFT

Astrologers are sorcerers, magicians, and fortune tellers who act as counselors guiding people toward happiness and success. Historically, they served in royal courts, interpreting divine signs to aid kings in aligning decisions with cosmic will. Today, they advise on compatible zodiac signs for relationships, ideal times for childbirth, and auspicious days for activities like business, planting, or healing. The practice is prevalent among elites; as a popular saying attributed to J.P. Morgan states, "Millionaires don't use astrology; billionaires do."

Astrology, when combined with alchemy, is practical Kabbalah. Astrologers channel planetary forces by meditating on each planet's qualities and symbols, sometimes using talismans to attract desired energies. Talismans, alongside symbols like animals embodying each planet's spirit, intensify ritual focus. Each planet carries distinct elements, metals, stones, plants, animals, birds, and fish, creating a multi-layered approach to harness celestial power:

Sun (Fire Element):
- Metal: Gold

- Stones: Diamond, topaz

- Plants: Heliotrope, citrus, ginger

- Animals: Lions, rams, baboons

- Birds: Eagles, hawks, phoenix

- Fish: Sea calves, jellyfish

- Symbolism: Represents vitality, courage, and ambition, often associated with creatures that embody strength and leadership.

Moon (Earth Element):
- Metal: Silver

- Stones: Pearl, crystal, quartz

- Plants: Hyssop, rosemary, olive tree

- Animals: Dogs, beavers, otters

- Birds: Geese, ducks, swans

- Fish: Crabs, oysters, shellfish

- Symbolism: Governs emotions, instincts, and intuition, influencing life rhythms and natural cycles.

Mercury (Water Element):
- Metal: Quicksilver

- Stones: Opal, agate

- Plants: Hazel, majoram, cinquefoil

- Animals: Foxes, apes, weasels

- Birds: Goldfinch, blackbird, lark

- Fish: Octopus, grey mullet

- Symbolism: Rules intellect and communication, associated with agility, intelligence, and adaptability.

Venus (Air and Water Elements):
- Metal: Copper

- Stones: Emerald, turquoise

- Plants: Lily, mint, rose

- Animals: Bulls, doves, cats

- Birds: Swans, sparrows, doves

- Fish: Dolphin, anchovy

- Symbolism: Represents beauty, harmony, and connection, with symbols of attraction, love, and unity.

Mars (Fire Element)
- Metal: Iron

- Stones: Ruby, bloodstone

- Plants: Garlic, hellebore, nettle

- Animals: Horses, wolves, serpents

- Birds: Falcons, hawks, kestrels

- Fish: Croaker, mullet

- Symbolism: Embodies assertiveness, aggression, and defense, reflected in resilient or combative creatures.

Jupiter (Air Element):
- Metal: Tin

- Stones: Sapphire, amethyst

- Plants: Oak, basil, violets

- Animals: Elephants, stags, bulls

- Birds: Pelicans, swallows, pheasants

- Fish: Dolphin, sheatfish

- Symbolism: Associated with growth, wisdom, and abundance, represented by noble and disciplined animals.

Saturn (Water Element):
- Metal: Lead

- Stones: Onyx, smoky jasper (dark and heavy stones).

- Plants: Cypress, asphodel, parsley (bitter-tasting plants)

- Animals: Moles, wolves, camels

- Birds: Ravens, owls, cranes

- Fish: Eels, dogfish, oysters

- Symbolism: Represents structure, limitations, and endurance, associated with creatures that embody resilience and patience.

To undertake the alchemical creation of the Philosopher's Stone, an initiate must first purify the soul, transmuting inner impurities—beginning with lead and culminating in gold.

Another way astrologers incorporate planetary influences into magical operations is by performing ceremonies on the day and hour governed by the appropriate planet. Each day and hour has its planetary ruler. The Earth was historically believed to be governed by 7 planetary spheres, which correspond to the 7 ancient planets.

The 7 days of the week are named after gods derived from the Latin equivalents of earlier Greek god-names, which themselves were named after Babylonian gods. Each of these planets was associated with a god who had unique attributes and myths. The Norsemen, a Northern Germanic people also known as Scandinavians, contributed to the naming of the days of the week in modern English through their mythological beliefs:

- **Sunday**: Derived from the Old English word "Sunnandæg" which means 'day of the Sun.' Sun Day was believed to be a feminine deity.

- **Monday**: From the Old English word "mōnandæg" which means "the Moon's Day." The moon was considered a powerful masculine god.

- **Tuesday**: Named after the Germanic god Tyr or Tiw, related to the Latin "dies Martis," meaning "day of Mars."

- **Wednesday:** This comes from Old English, which refers to "Wodan's day," referring to Wodan or Odin. In Latin, it's "dies Mercurii," or "day of Mercury."

- **Thursday**: Named for Jupiter, known to the Norse as Thor, the god of thunder. Thus, it is "Thor's Day."

- **Friday:** From Old English "day of Frigg," the Norse goddess of fertility and love, linked to Venus.

- **Saturday** is named after the Roman god and planet Saturn. Saturn is the Roman and Italic god of agriculture, justice & strength.

Originating in ancient Babylonia, later developed by the Greeks and Romans, and further elaborated by the medieval Arabs, the principles of Astrology have changed little in two millennia, and only since the seventeenth century has it been distinct from "scientific" astronomy.[103] For many, it continues to symbolize humankind's intimate connection with the cosmos.

TRUE CORRESPONDENCE
OR
FALSE MANIPULATION?

Across civilizations, the Principle of Correspondence has been recognized as a key to understanding all levels of reality (physical, emotional, mental, or spiritual). It states that the individual (microcosm) is a reflection of the greater universe (macrocosm), reinforcing the idea that inner transformation leads to external change. This principle is so profound that it became the foundation of both scientific inquiry and magic. Ancient priests and astrologers used correspondence to understand how the higher planes influence us and employed magic (practical correspondence) to manipulate these planes to affect the lower ones. The forcible manipulation of a lower plane is called sihr, encompassing poetry, music, sorcery, and

---

103 Note: Astronomy is the scientific study of the sun, moon and stars. Astrology is a pseudo-science interpreting the supposed effect of the heavenly bodies on human existence.

soothsaying.[104] Through the act of sihr, one draws closer to shaytan and learns tricks that can confuse and harm others.

Allah informs us that everything within the heavens above and within us below is a sign for us (41:53). Natural phenomena and cosmic events are signs of Allah that prove His existence. Allah invites us to ponder the patterns in creation, such as astronomical, meteorological, and other physical and technical sciences by directing us to 7 signs:

"Indeed, in the (1) creation of the heavens and the earth, and the (2) alternation of the night and the day, and the (3) ships which sail through the sea with that which benefits people, and what (4) Allah has sent down from the heavens of rain, giving (5) life thereby to the earth after its lifelessness and (6) dispersing therein every [kind of] moving creature, and [His] (7) directing of the winds and the clouds controlled between the heaven and earth are signs for a people who use reason." (2:164)

Heavens ↑ ↔ Earth ↓

Night ↑ ↔ Day ↓

Winds ↑ ↔ Clouds ↓

Rain ↓ ↔ Vegetation ↑

Ships ↓ ↔ Commerce ↑

Dispersal of Creatures ↓ ↔ Human Benefit ↑

Seas ↑ ↔ Lands ↓

---

104 Narrated Ibn Abu Hatim: I was told by `Isam Ibn Rawwad after Adam after Al-Mas'udi after Ziyad the freed slave of Ibn Mus'ab after Al-Hasan pertaining to Allah's Statement:
"They followed what the Shayatin (devils) gave out (falsely of the magic) in the lifetime of Sulaiman (Solomon)} ....as saying: one-third of poetry, one-third of sorcery (magic), and one-third of soothsaying.

Magicians from various esoteric traditions study the celestial signs above to influence the world below. For example, astrologers practice divination by interpreting the movements of stars, planets, and other heavenly bodies to foresee future events.[105] In addition to divination, some practitioners use psychokinesis, relying on imagination and willpower to affect physical objects. Others practice telepathy, the direct transmission of thoughts from one person to another, or engage in clairvoyance and precognition, perceiving future events through methods such as palm reading or gazing into a crystal ball.

Through deep study and practice, the *saahir* (magician) works in alignment with subtle and hidden aspects of natural laws. While these practices may appear supernatural, they are accomplished through profound knowledge and understanding. Although it may seem that the magician is performing these acts independently, Allah is the ultimate cause behind all actions. Even when one engages their mind, incantations, or influences from shayaateen (devils), they are still operating within forces created by Allah. Every natural force possesses specific properties, characteristics, and qualities that can yield results when understood. While Allah allows the existence of these natural phenomena through universal laws, He prohibits the use of magic according to His shariah (divine law).

Supernatural acts can occur through a *mu'jizah* (miracle) *Karaamat* (miracles of saints), or sihr. A mu'jizah is a direct act of Allah performed on behalf of a Nabi (Prophet).[106] For example, when the fire was made cool for Ibrahim, or when Nabi Musa turned his hand from black to white and transformed his staff into a large serpent before Fir'awn and his

---

105 Divination: Based on the Latin word divination meaning "the faculty of foreseeing." Divination is the art of uncovering the divine meaning behind chance events.

106 Note: Miracles happen by direct command of Allah. Evidence: So, it is not you who killed them, but in fact Allah killed them. And you did not throw when you threw but Allah did throw, so that He might bless the believers with a good favour. Surely, Allah is All-Hearing, All-Knowing. (8/17)

magicians.[107] Karaamat is similar to mu'jizah in that both are performed by men of high righteousness. At the same time, sihr is given to irreligious people who remain in states of impurity, filth, and sin for long periods in order to attract the assistance of shayateen. The character of a person determines the difference between a Nabi, a Wali, and a Saahir. Sihr is the ability granted only to a *faasiq* (flagrant violator of Allah's Laws).

Across time and civilizations—from Babylon and Kemet to Kabbalah, Gnosticism, Hindu mysticism, and Arab esoteric traditions—the principle of correspondence has served as a cornerstone of magical thought. While these traditions offer glimpses into the patterns of the cosmos, they also reveal a recurring human desire: to manipulate the divine order rather than submit to it with humility. At the heart of nearly every ancient and modern occult system lies the belief that all things are interconnected, and that the microcosm reflects the macrocosm. Yet Islam offers a sobering truth: recognizing the signs of divine order is not enough—those who know, understand, and contemplate these patterns are entrusted with the responsibility to align their actions with the will of the Creator who designed them. As Allah reminds us:

$$ \text{﴿ وَٱلَّذِينَ جَٰهَدُواْ فِينَا لَنَهْدِيَنَّهُمْ سُبُلَنَا ۚ وَإِنَّ ٱللَّهَ لَمَعَ ٱلْمُحْسِنِينَ ﴾} $$

And those who strive for Us - We will surely guide them to Our ways. And indeed, Allah is with the doers of good. (29:69).

---

107   And draw in your hand to your side; it will come out white without disease – another sign. (20: 22).
He said, "Rather, you throw." And suddenly their ropes and staffs seemed to him from their magic that they were moving [like snakes]. And he sensed within himself fear, did Moses. We [i.e., Allah] said, "Fear not. Indeed, it is you who are superior. And they intended for him a plan [i.e., harm], but We made them the greatest losers. (20: 66-70).

SECTION 3

THE PRINCIPLE OF VIBRATION

﴿ تُسَبِّحُ لَهُ ٱلسَّمَٰوَٰتُ ٱلسَّبْعُ وَٱلْأَرْضُ وَمَن فِيهِنَّ

وَإِن مِّن شَىْءٍ إِلَّا يُسَبِّحُ بِحَمْدِهِۦ وَلَٰكِن لَّا تَفْقَهُونَ تَسْبِيحَهُمْ

إِنَّهُۥ كَانَ حَلِيمًا غَفُورًا ﴾

"The seven heavens, the earth, and all those in them glorify Him. There is not a single thing that does not glorify His praises—but you ˹simply˺ cannot comprehend their glorification. He is indeed Most Forbearing, All-Forgiving" (17:44).

"Nothing rests; everything moves; everything vibrates."
~ The Kybalion

"If you want to find the secrets of the universe, think in terms of energy, frequency, and vibration."
~ Nikola Tesla

THE PRINCIPLE

Vibration teaches that nothing rests. Everything is in a perpetual state of motion, oscillation, and flow. All of creation—from the smallest atom to the grandest galaxy—exists within a sea of energy vibrating at different frequencies. Ancient wisdom and modern science both affirm this. Quantum physics shows that what appears solid is actually composed of energy in motion. Every sound, color, thought, and material form arises from these unseen vibrations. These subtle movements reveal a hidden unity behind the diversity of forms. The universe, then, is not static; it is alive with rhythm, resonance, and divine movement.

A vibration produces a wave. For that vibration to occur, something must move repeatedly over time. Waves, in essence, are disturbances that ripple through space. Whether it's light, sound, or electromagnetic energy, each moves in waves, each pulsing at its own frequency. Electromagnetic waves, for instance, consist of both electric and magnetic fields that oscillate at right angles to each other. These waves travel at the speed of light and do not require a physical medium to propagate. The frequency of their oscillations determines the type of electromagnetic energy: radio waves, microwaves, infrared, visible light, ultraviolet, X-rays, or gamma rays. Just as the physical world is governed by these vibrations, the spiritual and emotional realms are also shaped by vibrations that manifest in our thoughts, feelings, and actions.

The rate of vibration is what differentiates forms in the physical world. For instance, colors, sounds, and the difference between physical matter and unseen waves, such as radio signals, all depend on vibrational frequency. Energy travels in waves, which are expressed in curves: the movement of water in the ocean, the wave of light from the sun, the flow of air in the wind, the rumble of thunder, the wave of heat in the oven, and the wave of emotions that overcomes you, are all examples of energy in motion. As a principle, energy cannot be created or destroyed; it simply changes form.

Every action—such as breathing, eating, drinking, speaking, walking, or engaging in sexual relations—generates its own unique form of energy. In a metaphysical interpretation rooted in Islamic thought, energy is understood as a form of movement that produces heat. This heat can manifest as electromagnetic waves, which are said to be governed by the angel Jibra'il. These waves connect all elements of creation and are considered the lights of the heavens and the earth, originating from Allah, the ultimate source of light.[108] All of creation, whether physical or spiritual, is believed to emerge from this divine light. According to this view, low-frequency light condenses into matter, while high-frequency matter can transform back into light.

The nature and characteristics of all beings, including angels, jinn, humans, and even inanimate objects, are determined by their vibrational frequencies. Higher vibrations exist in more refined, spiritual forms, while slower vibrations produce denser physical forms. The higher the vibration, the purer the form, and the closer it aligns with Allah's divine presence.

On its most fundamental level, all energy is a form of praising Allah in a language we cannot understand (17:44). When humans purify their souls and listen to the wisdom of every animate and inanimate object, they become better prepared to be in contact with the supreme society and understand the hidden laws of the universe, as opposed to those who limit themselves to the physical world.

---

108 Allah is the Light of the heavens and the earth. His light is like a niche in which there is a lamp, the lamp is in a crystal, the crystal is like a shining star, lit from 'the oil of' a blessed olive tree, 'located' neither to the east nor the west, whose oil would almost glow, even without being touched by fire. Light upon light! Allah guides whoever He wills to His light. And Allah sets forth parables for humanity. For Allah has 'perfect' knowledge of all things (24:35).

ISLAMIC TRIVIUM

Allah sent Prophet Muhammad ﷺ with a trivium intended to perfect Islam on earth. In Islam, the principle of mentalism as it relates to this world is the knowledge that Allah is the infinite, unknowable, indescribable source of all energy. The principle of correspondence is energy's various scales of frequency. The principle of vibration is energy in its physical form.

The first three Kemetic principles correspond to the three dimensions of Islam, which align with the Trivium method of thinking and learning, influencing our disciplines, beliefs, and virtues:

Mentalism	Islam (*fiqh*)	Knowledge	Discipline
Correspondence	Iman (*Aqeedah*)	Understanding	Belief
Vibration	Ihsan (*Taswuf/ Tazkiyyah*)	Wisdom	Virtue

Islam

A Muslim (one who submits to Allah) enters Islam by knowing and acting upon the five pillars. These pillars can only be practiced with knowledge of the legal rulings related to required actions based on detailed proofs from the Quran and Sunnah. This is the science of *fiqh* (jurisprudence).

- **Shahadah (Declaration of Faith):** The individual enters into Islam by pronouncing the shahadah, the two testimonies of faith:

أَشْهَدُ أَنْ لَا إِلَهَ إِلَّا اللَّهُ

"I bear witness that none deserves worship except Allah,"

وَأَشْهَدُ أَنَّ مُحَمَّدًا رَسُولُ اللَّهِ

"I bear witness that Muhammad is the Messenger of Allah."

The first statement negates worship to anyone and everything other than Allah; while affirming that worship is for Allah, alone without partners. The second statement affirms that Muhammad is the messenger of Allah; thus, his statements are believed, and his commands are followed.

- *Salah* (**Prayer**): A Muslim must pray five times daily. *Salah* is the connection between a believer and their Creator. Prayer in congregation raises one's spiritual state higher and faster than prayer in solitude, while walking to prayer increases this spiritual elevation.[109]

- *Zakat* (**Charity**): Affluent Muslims must give *zakat* (charity) to the poor. Each year, Muslims must give 2.5% of their standing wealth to the needy within their community.

- *Sawm* (**Fasting**): During Ramadan, the 9th month of the lunar calendar, Muslims must fast from dawn to dusk. Fasting purifies the body, disciplines the soul, and increases empathy and compassion.

---

109 *"Salah (prayer) in congregation is twenty-seven times more rewarding than a Salah performed individually."*(Bukhari and Muslim); Hadith: It was narrated that Abu Hurayrah (may Allah be pleased with him) said: The Messenger of Allah (peace and blessings of Allaah be upon him) said: "Whoever purifies himself in his house then walks to one of the houses of Allah in order to perform one of the duties enjoined by Allah, for every two steps he takes, one will erase a sin and the other will raise him one degree in status." (Muslim).

- *Hajj* **(Pilgrimage)**: A Muslim must perform Hajj once in their lifetime if financially and physically able. Hajj offers many spiritual and social benefits, uniting Muslims of all races, colors, nationalities, and economic backgrounds in one place, dressed uniformly to worship their Creator.

Iman

A *Muslim* becomes a *Mu'min* (believer) when he understands and believes with both heart and mind in the six pillars of faith.[110] The science that defines and articulates these six pillars is called *Aqeedah*.

- **Belief in Allah**: *Mu'minun* (believers) believe in one incomparable God who created the universe and controls all affairs. Allah is the giver of life and causes death, and all affairs are in His hands. He has no mother, father, siblings, children, or wife. He has no equal and is the only one deserving of worship, with no intermediaries.

- **Belief in His Angels**: Angels are a creation of Allah, invisible to us, who worship Allah and never disobey Him.

- **Belief in His Books**: Allah has sent down many books (ordinances) to His messengers, including the Torah (revealed to Musa), the Psalms (revealed to Dawud), the Gospel (revealed to Isa), and the Quran (revealed to Muhammad).

---

110 The 'true' believers are only those whose hearts tremble at the remembrance of Allah, whose faith increases when His revelations are recited to them, and who put their trust in their Lord. They are' those who establish prayer and donate from what We have provided for them. It is they who are the true believers. They will have elevated ranks, forgiveness, and an honorable provision from their Lord (8: 2-4).

- **Belief in His Prophets**: There are numerous Prophets, including Nuh, Ibrahim, Dawud, Sulayman, Lut, Yusuf, Musa, and Isa.[111]

- **Belief in the Day of Judgment**: This is the day when all mankind will be resurrected and held accountable for their actions. Those who worshipped Allah as commanded will be rewarded with eternal bliss in Paradise, while those who refused will face eternal punishment in Hell. Those who were oppressed in this life will receive retribution against their oppressors on this day.

- **Belief in His *Qadr* (Divine Decree)**: Everything happens according to Allah's will. It is to believe in His absolute power and knowledge over all things and all outcomes, whether they appear, to us, as good or bad.

The Muslim who believes in these tenets, becomes eligible to earn Allah's mercy and enter Paradise. However, Iman is not confined to belief alone; it extends into every aspect of a person's character, speech, and actions. The Prophet Muhammad ﷺ explained that Iman consists of over 70 branches—rooted in the **heart**, expressed through the **tongue**, and manifested in **deeds**.[112] The goal of a believer is to cultivate these branches, strengthening faith and drawing closer to Allah.

Ihsan

A Mu'min becomes a Muhsin (one who obtains spiritual perfection) when they demonstrate Iman in their **thoughts, speech,** and **actions**. This individual lives as though they

---

111 First four beliefs expressed in this ayah: 2:285

112 Sahih al-Bukhari, Muslim, and Tirmidhi

see Allah,[113] or at least he knows that Allah sees him. This awareness leads to wisdom that permeates their entire attitude, turning every aspect of life into worship. Due to their conscious attitude, beliefs, and feelings, they are constantly rewarded.[114]

The science of Sufism (*Tasawwuf / Tazkiyah*) is associated with Ihsan. This is the science of transforming one's inner state and psychology from heedlessness of Allah to noble character, lofty states of heart, and pious devotion, enabling knowledge and love of Allah through a mystical, experiential vision.

In essence, Islam is the '**what**' you should do in Islam. Iman is the '**why**' you should do those actions. *Ihsan* is the '**how**' you should intentionally practice those actions. This is the Universal Trivium that Prophet Muhammad ﷺ was sent to mankind to offer the entire creation.[115]

Rate of Vibrations = Level of Iman.

Begin to see yourself as a soul with a body rather than a body with a soul.
~ Wayne Dyer

In Islam, the concept of Iman corresponds to the law of correspondence and the law of vibration. When angel Jibra'il questioned Prophet Muhammad ﷺ about Iman, the Prophet ﷺ defined it as the belief in Allah, His angels, His books, His Messengers, the Last Day, and His Decree (al-Qadr), both in its good and its bad aspects.

Scholars have explained that Iman is manifested in the **heart**, **tongue**, and **limbs**, increasing with good deeds and decreasing with bad deeds. Therefore, if a Muslim desires to

---

113 Note: "Seeing" in the sense of inner realization, not with physical sight.

114 Suhaib reported that Allah's Messenger ﷺ said: Strange are the ways of a believer for there is good in every affair of his and this is not the case with anyone else except in the case of a believer for if he has an occasion to feel delight, he thanks (God), thus there is a good for him in it, and if he gets into trouble and shows resignation (and endures it patiently), there is a good for him in it.

115 And We have not sent you, [O Muhammad], except as a mercy to the worlds. (21:107).

vibrate on higher spiritual planes (Ihsan), he must focus on raising their Iman.[116]

The Quran and Sunnah offer numerous examples of ways to strengthen one's Iman, such as praying regularly on time and, for men, praying in congregation. Another way to enhance one's faith is by praying during the last third of the night, a time when Allah descends to the lowest heaven to respond to those seeking forgiveness and making *du'a* (supplication). Interestingly, this special time of divine closeness aligns with the body's natural secretion of melatonin from the pineal gland, promoting spiritual and physical rest and renewal. Other ways include reciting the Quran and pondering its meanings, gaining deep knowledge of Allah's names and attributes, reflecting on Allah's universal signs, and consistently performing righteous actions. Each of these requires a combination of pure **knowledge** and righteous **action** for proper execution.

Our souls can change their resonance to match their immediate environment. The people we surround ourselves with can influence our level of Iman (rate of vibration). Scientifically, the principle of resonance—also known as sympathetic vibration—states that when one object vibrates at a certain frequency, it can cause a nearby object with the same natural frequency to begin vibrating as well. Prophet Muhammad ﷺ illustrated this in a parable:

Abu Musa reported, The Prophet ﷺ said, "Verily, the parable of good company and a bad company is only that of a seller of musk and a blacksmith. The seller of musk will give you some perfume, you will buy some, or you will notice a good smell. As for the blacksmith, he will burn your clothes, or you will notice a bad smell." (Bukhari and Muslim).

It is essential to be mindful of the company one keeps. Surrounding oneself with individuals who uphold similar or

---

116 Ahmad ibn Hanbal, may Allah have mercy upon him, was asked as to whether iman increases and decreases. He replied: "It increases until it reaches the highest part of the seventh heaven, and it decreases until it reaches the lowest part of the seventh plane."

even higher values and beliefs can significantly impact personal growth. Over time, such individuals naturally influence each other, shaping thoughts, beliefs, and behaviors. Remarkably, even their brain activity begins to align, as mirror neurons play a crucial role in facilitating learning through observation. This makes ideas, emotions, and habits highly contagious within close relationships.

When one's Iman is high, they 'vibrate' at a faster rate, allowing them to be more in tune with higher vibrational entities in the spiritual realms.

This is exemplified in a hadith about Hanzalah Al-Usayyidi, a scribe of Prophet Muhammad ﷺ:

> *"When we are in the company of the Messenger of Allah ﷺ and he reminds us of Jannah and Jahannam, we feel as if we are seeing them with our own eyes. But when we return to our families and attend to our affairs, much of this slips from our minds." The Prophet ﷺ responded, "If your state of mind remained the same as it is in my presence, the angels would shake hands with you in your beds and on your roads. But, Hanzalah, time should be devoted to worldly affairs and time should be devoted to prayer" (Muslim).*

The *Sahabah* (companions of Prophet Muhammad ﷺ) were people who operated at such an elevated spiritual level that they altered the spiritual frequency of the world. They were the first to recognize the truth and were unwavering in their faith. Their lives exemplify how people from diverse backgrounds can unite for a common purpose and transform the world within a single generation. However, even in such a spiritually united community, the lower energies of hypocrites could infiltrate and cause disruption.

The Sahabah's high vibrational state attracted angelic support during pivotal moments in their lives. This constant interaction between the heavens and the earth caused their generation to be the brightest collective example in human history. After that generation, the spiritual light began to diminish. Today, we are at the lowest vibrational frequency the world has ever seen; which carries strong indications of an approaching shift in the poles.

To every negative, there is a positive. Today's darkness ensures that there is an unprecedented number of opportunities for others to shine their light. Low vibrational energies are always in search of frequencies of truth. But that is only in the case of the **ignorant**.

The **arrogant** have low vibrational energies, and they hate the truth. They run from it, attack it, and demonize it. For them, good is evil, and evil is good. They come in various forms. They are wealthy and meek, optimistic and bleak, powerful and weak.

Defeating them is simple if one aligns oneself with proper frequencies and consciously adjusts to those vibrational experiences. To do this, one must be attuned to their energy and reflect on how their perception affects their experience. Once aligned with higher vibrations, it becomes easier to attract what one desires.

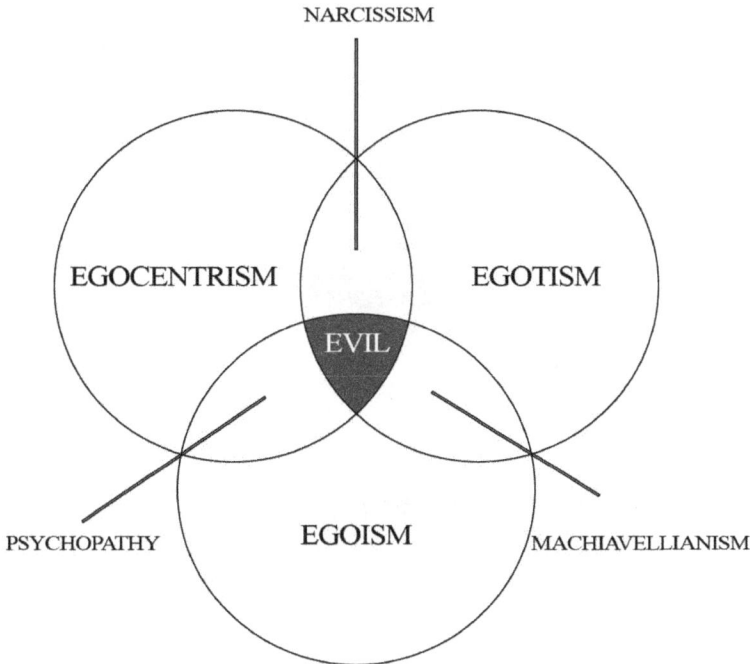

Fig. 35 - Depicting the resonance of self-driven psychological states.

VIBRATIONS & PHYSICS

The electromagnetic spectrum consists of 7 categories of radiation, each with distinct properties:

1. Gamma rays
2. X-rays
3. Ultraviolet
4. Visible light
5. Infrared
6. Microwaves
7. Radio waves

Gamma rays possess the highest energy and shortest wavelengths, allowing them to penetrate biological tissue. This ability makes them useful in targeted medical treatments, such as radiation therapy for cancer, though their high energy also makes exposure potentially harmful if not carefully controlled. At the other end of the spectrum, radio waves have the longest

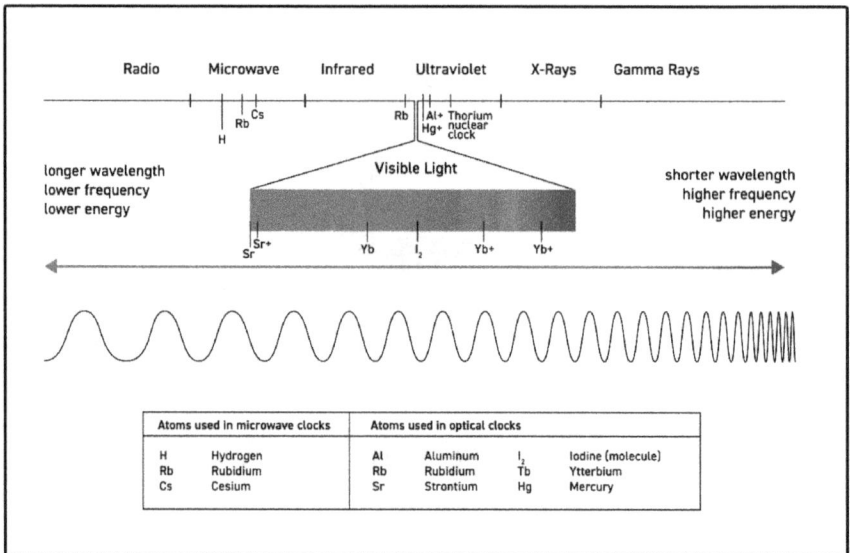

Fig. 36 - Wavelengths and frequencies cross the electromagnetic spectrum.

wavelengths and lowest energy. **Radio waves** play a key role in communication technologies, including television, mobile phones, and 5G networks. Devices must be tuned to specific frequencies to interpret the information carried by radio waves.

Visible light: The visible light portion of the spectrum is a small band of wavelengths detectable by the human eye. It includes 7 main colors:

1. Red
2. Orange
3. Yellow
4. Green
5. Blue
6. Indigo
7. Violet

Each color corresponds to a specific wavelength, with red having the longest and violet the shortest. When light of these wavelengths reaches our retinas, it stimulates cells that allow us to perceive color. For example, red has a lower frequency, while violet has a higher one. These physical properties of light define our visual experience. Light is the visible portion of the electromagnetic spectrum, and color is the brain's interpretation of different frequencies within that spectrum.

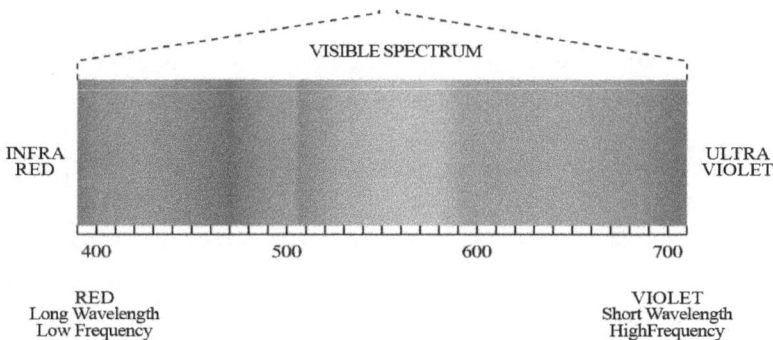

Fig. 37 - The visible part of the electromagnetic spectrum.

THE PRINCIPLE OF VIBRATION

Sound and Vibration: Sound is a form of mechanical energy produced by vibrating objects that create waves moving through a medium, like air or water. These vibrations cause nearby air molecules to move, generating pressure waves that travel outward. The frequency of these sound waves determines the pitch we perceive: low frequencies produce bass tones, while high frequencies create treble sounds. In Western music, the diatonic scale consists of 7 core pitches (**C, D, E, F, G, A,** and **B**), forming the foundation of most musical scales and harmonies. Each pitch corresponds to a specific frequency, creating a structured relationship between sound and tone.

The human voice functions similarly to a musical instrument. Vocal cords, located in the larynx, vibrate as air passes through them, creating sound. The pitch depends on the tension, length, and mass of the vocal cords; tighter, shorter cords produce higher pitches, while looser, longer cords yield lower tones. As sound waves travel through the throat and mouth, they are shaped by the movement of the tongue, lips, and mouth, enabling us to create a broad range of tones and express complex ideas and emotions.

Sound is not just something we hear, it's also something we feel. And sometimes, it's something that heals.

Impact of Sound on Well-being:

Sounds, including spoken words, can influence our emotions and even impact our physiological responses. While the extent to which sound directly affects cellular structures or DNA remains an area of ongoing research, evidence suggests that sound can significantly shape our psychological and emotional states. In Islam, the Quran has profound healing effects on both the body and soul, serving as *ruqyah* (spiritual healing). For instance, Allah states, *"And We send down from the Quran that which is a healing and a mercy for the believers..."* (17:82), affirming its healing capacity. Similarly, the Prophet Muhammad ﷺ approved of using *Surah Al-Fatihah* as *ruqyah* for physical ailments, as when a companion recited it over a chief who had been stung by a scorpion, and he was healed

(Sahih al-Bukhari). This example illustrates the Islamic belief in the healing power of the Quran when recited with faith and intention.

The impact of spoken words is also evident in the Prophet's interaction with Hazn bin Wahb. The Prophet ﷺ asked him, "What is your name?" and upon hearing his name, which meant "rough," he suggested he change it to Sahl, meaning "easy." Hazn declined, but his descendants noted that they continued to inherit a degree of roughness in character thereafter (Bukhari). This hadith highlights the belief that names and words can influence one's character and outlook.

Contemporary science confirms that sound can indeed influence mood and psychological states. Occultists have also long held similar beliefs about the transformative power of words. For instance, the term "abracadabra" originates from ancient Aramaic or Hebrew roots, meaning "I create as I speak," reflecting a belief that sound can alter material reality at a cellular level. Words can reshape one's world when a message is heard and the brain responds by creating neural pathways that reinforce the message. In both Islamic tradition and various cultural beliefs, words and sounds are acknowledged as having the power to influence us physically, mentally, and spiritually.

Comparison of Light and Sound Waves

While both light and sound exhibit wave properties, they interact with our senses differently. Light, studied in the field of optics, is an electromagnetic wave that can travel through a vacuum. Sound, explored in acoustics, is a mechanical wave requiring a medium such as air or water. Together, these fields help us understand the unique properties and applications of waves in daily life.

VIBRATIONS & BIOLOGY

Until the early 1900s, the scientific community believed that matter was solid and unchanging, consistent with the Newtonian view of the universe. This perspective shifted with groundbreaking discoveries in physics, particularly Einstein's theory of relativity and the development of quantum mechanics. Scientists discovered that atoms, once thought to be solid, are mostly empty space. Einstein demonstrated that mass is really just energy in disguise ($E = mc^2$). Thousands of years earlier, this scientific truth revealed a timeless insight found in the Principle of Vibration, which states that everything we see, touch, or feel is simply energy that is alive and in motion.

In human biology, the Principle of Vibration manifests at the microscopic level. Our bodies are composed of **cells**, **tissues**, and **molecules**. Molecules are made of **atoms**, **subatomic particles**, and **energy**. Subatomic particles, such as **quarks**, **leptons**, and **muons**, vibrate and rotate energetically within the nucleus.

Our bodies are complex molecular structures containing approximately 37 trillion cells. Brain cells, or neurons, form a network that communicates through electrical impulses, activating specific brain cells when we think, feel, believe, or move. Raising the quality of our **electric thoughts** will evoke our **magnetic emotions**, impacting the electromagnetic world around and within us. Each thought has a vibrational frequency. Neurons produce tiny electrical signals called brainwaves—like alpha, beta, and theta—that shift with our thoughts, moods, and focus. These waves can be measured using EEG machines, showing that thought and emotion are, at their core, patterns of rhythm and energy. Positive thoughts, feelings, beliefs, and actions vibrate at high frequencies, and negative thoughts, feelings, beliefs, and actions vibrate at lower frequencies. One can achieve a high-quality state of being by programming the mind to vibrate at higher frequencies consistently. Conversely, if what we desire does not have the same frequency as us, we will never be able to align with it or obtain it. Thus, when one changes their mind, they change their reality.

Each human vibrates at a baseline rate that is unique to them, but this rate can fluctuate based on spiritual, mental, emotional, or physical experiences. For instance, passionate and exciting emotions can increase one's vibrational intensity, while calm and soothing activities can decrease it. Environmental and internal forces also influence our vibrational rate.

Engaging in various daily activities can positively influence vibration rates and even our DNA. Physical activities like exercising and spending time in nature are beneficial. Listening to the Quran, with its harmonious rhythm, can alter our vibrational state by affecting our consciousness and serving as an effective memory aid. Consuming nutrient-rich foods such as organic fruits and vegetables, which have absorbed sunlight, raises our vibrations more effectively than highly processed or genetically modified (GMO) foods. People can find ways to vibrate at higher levels by living consciously and wisely.

VIBRATIONS & PSYCHOLOGY

Emotions

Understanding the body's electromagnetic field can help people better regulate their emotional and physical states. The heart produces the strongest electromagnetic field in the body and plays a key role in influencing physiological responses. The heart's magnetic field is approximately 100 times stronger than the brain's and can be detected several feet away from the body. The rhythms of the heart reflect and can impact our emotional states and feelings.

Emotions are energy in motion, flowing through the body and shaping its experiences. For example, worry is a natural emotion that helps with focus and solve problems. But if the individual dwells on it for too long, it can spiral into confusion or even anxiety, creating a loop of overthinking. Anger, on the other hand, is like fire, it can fuel one to take bold action, but if left unchecked or bottled up, it can burn out of control, leading to destructive outbursts.

Emotions are deeply connected to the heart's rhythm, which acts like a mirror for one's inner state. When emotions are balanced, the heart beats in harmony, creating a sense of calm and focus. But when an individual is overwhelmed or out of sync, the heart reflects that chaos, influencing how the body reacts. Learning to recognize and regulate these emotional energies is key to aligning mind, body, and spirit for a healthier, more empowered life.

Those who can control their mental states can choose to think positively when anger arises. They might also make physical changes to alter their emotional state; for example, if standing, they might sit, or if sitting, they might lie down (Abi Dawud). Washing with cold water can also help calm internal heat.[117] Physiological changes are the quickest ways to change the mind and emotional state.

---

117 'Atiyyah reported: The Messenger of Allah ﷺ said, "Verily, anger comes from Satan and Satan was created from fire. Fire is extinguished with water, so if you become angry then perform ablution with water" (Abi Dawud).

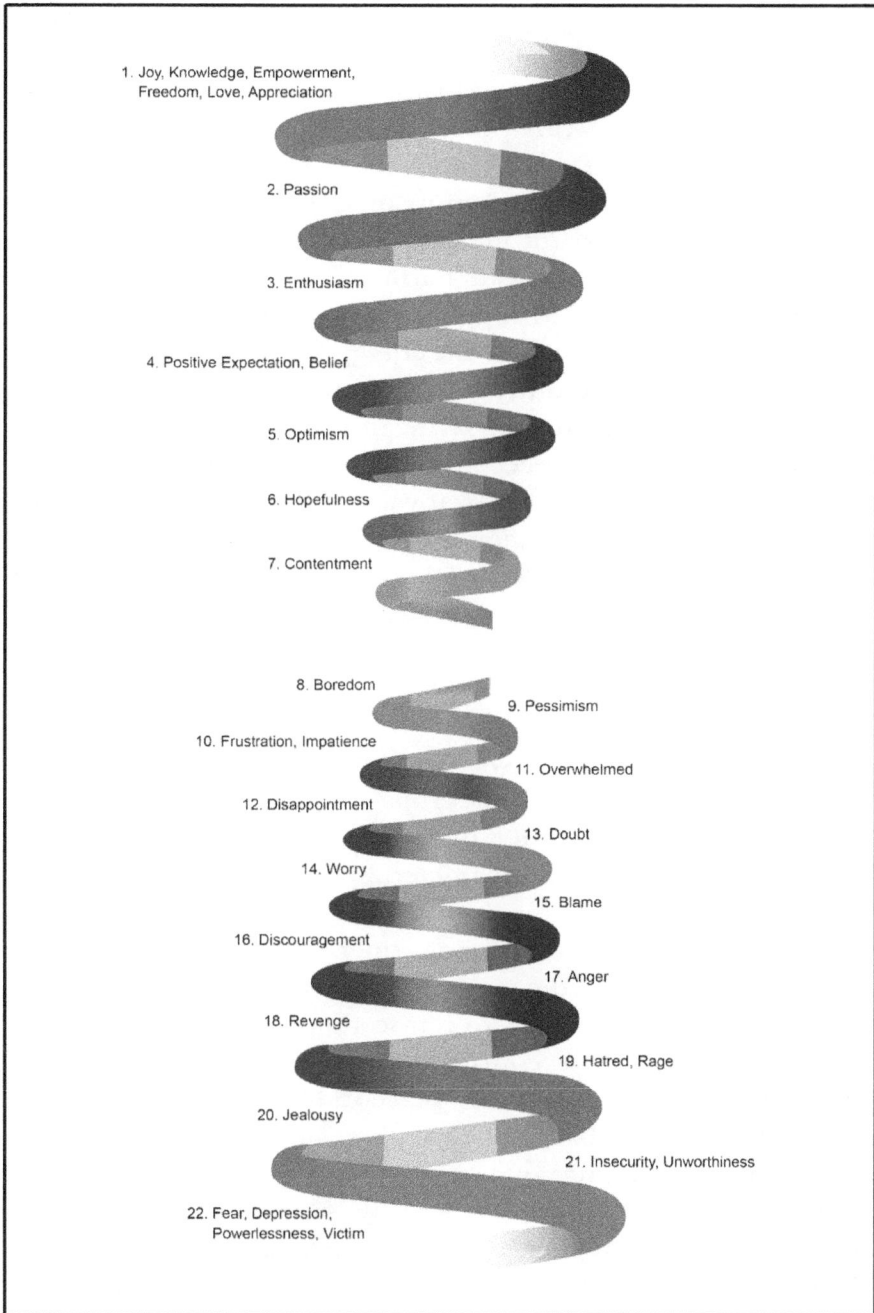

1. Joy, Knowledge, Empowerment, Freedom, Love, Appreciation
2. Passion
3. Enthusiasm
4. Positive Expectation, Belief
5. Optimism
6. Hopefulness
7. Contentment
8. Boredom
9. Pessimism
10. Frustration, Impatience
11. Overwhelmed
12. Disappointment
13. Doubt
14. Worry
15. Blame
16. Discouragement
17. Anger
18. Revenge
19. Hatred, Rage
20. Jealousy
21. Insecurity, Unworthiness
22. Fear, Depression, Powerlessness, Victim

Fig. 38 - The Emotional Guidance Scale, depicting both the Upward and Downward Spiral

When someone recognizes that they are experiencing lower emotions such as fear, anger, sadness, shame, or greed, they can consciously choose to transform these negative emotions into positive states. This process can be seen as a synergy of reason and emotion, with the heart playing a central role in this transformation. The rhythm of the heart connects us to the universal "Breath" of life, a concept representing the flow of energy that sustains and harmonizes our emotional and physical well-being. Through imagination, intention, and meditation, one can harness the energy from intense emotions, like rage, experienced during difficult events and channel these emotions toward achieving a meaningful goal. This process allows reason to take precedence over emotion, guiding actions consistently and intelligently toward higher emotional states like courage, reason, love, joy, and enlightenment.

Emotions serve as guides, helping to shift us into higher states of being fueled by the rhythms of the heart.

Perceptions

True happiness begins when we take charge of our thoughts, feelings, beliefs, and actions. This is when our energies shift and we begin to vibrate at a higher frequency. This shift fosters a positive mental state, characterized by joy, gratitude, and love, that grants greater control over perspectives, moods, and experiences. By mastering their mental state, we can consciously choose the frequency at which they vibrate, demonstrating their ability to transcend perceived limits.

The first step to controlling one's mental state is to understand the principle of "perception is projection." This concept suggests that our thoughts and beliefs shape our experiences, meaning that rather than passively perceiving the external world, we are actively projecting our internal landscape, our thoughts, feelings, beliefs, and values onto it. In this way, the world becomes a mirror, reflecting what lies within us. By understanding oneself and the inner aspects that shape one's outlook, knowledge can be effectively applied to achieve praiseworthy desires.

Our mental and emotional states produce vibrations that resonate within the universe, shaping our experiences and attracting corresponding energies. Like an organic antenna, each individual projects and receives vibrational energy, amplifying what we project and influencing the energies we attract. For example, if one wishes to explore a specific spiritual phenomenon or attain a material goal, one must first attune one's inner vibration to be receptive and open to the experiences one seeks. By cultivating awareness of these subtle vibrations through practices like mindfulness and meditation, we can enhance our ability to attract and realize our goals, ultimately aligning our lives, individually and collectively, with our true intentions and aspirations.

Desires

Have you seen the one who takes their **desires** as their **god**? Allah has left them to stray knowingly, sealed their hearing and their heart, and placed a cover on their sight. Who then can guide them after Allah?

Will you all not then be mindful? (45:23)

Of all human desires, sexual energy vibrates at one of the highest frequencies. It activates the aura like few other forces, producing a powerful energetic output. This elevated vibration is not only a channel for creating new life but also a powerful source of creative potential, which can significantly enhance imagination, courage, willpower, persistence, and creativity when consciously channeled upwards.

Human desires emit a unique vibrational frequency, with the desire for sex being among the most powerful. Sexual energy is a potent creative force that the financially wise choose to redirect to fuel **ambition**, **imagination**, and **productivity**. In Taoist teachings, sexual energy is described as a vital life force (*chi*) which, when conserved and refined, can be transmuted into higher forms of energy, which will nurture both the body and spirit.

In Islam, this energy finds its highest expression when aligned with divine intent, reflecting the Quranic affirmation that all creation vibrates in glorification of Allah (17:44).

289

Sexual energy impacts physical, emotional, and spiritual dimensions. Whether through procreation or the channeling of energy toward higher aspirations, this energy must be directed with mindfulness. The phenomenon of transmutation, recognized in various spiritual traditions, involves channeling this energy up the spine toward spiritual growth. Practical methods, such as controlled breathing and mindfulness, allow individuals to manage and recycle sexual energy effectively. These practices prevent energy from dissipating and instead channel it toward physical vitality and spiritual refinement, aligning with the principles of balance and discipline emphasized in Islamic teachings.

Islam emphasizes a balanced and purposeful view of sexual energy by encouraging believers to direct this powerful force towards procreation as opposed to manifestation.[118] Islam encourages moderation of desires, for extremes in either direction of sexual promiscuity or sexual chastity can lead to physical and emotional imbalance. Redirecting this energy with mindfulness not only aligns with divine purpose but also enhances overall health and well-being.

Without spiritual guidance and intentional redirection, however, this powerful energy can become destructive and may manifest as addiction, emotional instability, or feelings of emptiness. Suppressing sexual energy without cultivating spiritual discipline may lead to internal conflict and misaligned desires. Islam recognizes this potential and therefore provides structured avenues, such as marriage, fasting, and worship to channel, elevate, and harmonize this force in ways that benefit both the soul and society.

This sacred exchange of energy, often referred to as *Sacred Energy eXchange* (S.E.X.), is spiritually enriching and an expression of divine connection. In Islam, the ideal use of sexual energy is within the sacred institution of marriage, where fulfilling one's desires is not only permissible but also regarded as an act of worship and charity. This perspective elevates sexual union from a mere physical act to a profound

118 "Marry those who are loving and fertile, for I will boast of your great numbers before the other nations on the Day of Judgment." (Ibn Majah).

spiritual exchange that strengthens the marital bond and aligns with divine intent. When approached with proper intention, mutual respect, and love, this sacred union amplifies personal growth, fosters mutual respect, and deepens emotional and spiritual bonds. By fulfilling their desires within the boundaries of marriage, couples not only honor Allah's guidance but also contribute to the enlargement of the Ummah and ensure that their actions resonate with the divine purpose of life.

Recognizing and honoring the sacredness of sexual energy allows individuals to engage in a balanced and mindful exchange. This fosters harmony between worldly aspirations and spiritual elevation, ensuring that the powerful vibrational force inherent in sexual energy serves as a means to glorify Allah and achieve holistic well-being.

Raising one's Frequency to Return to Allah

The Principle of Vibration reveals that everything in creation is in constant motion, whether in the physical, emotional, mental, or spiritual realms. All matter, from the smallest particles to the largest celestial bodies, vibrates, forming an interconnected living field of energy. This truth is affirmed in the Quran where Allah says, "The seven heavens, the earth, and all those in them glorify Him. There is not a single thing that does not glorify His praises—but you simply cannot comprehend their glorification" (17:44). Recognizing this cosmic vibrational harmony helps us understand that every aspect of creation is infused with divine energy, glorifying Allah in ways beyond human comprehension.

An individual's vibration is raised or lowered due to their **words, thoughts**, and **actions**. In Islam, this is reflected in the concept of Iman (faith), which fluctuates with good deeds and sins. Acts like regular prayer (salah), remembrance of Allah (dhikr), and fasting are not only spiritual obligations but also practices that align the soul with divine frequencies. These actions elevate one's vibration, purify the heart, and draw the believer closer to Allah. The pursuit of Ihsan—living with the awareness that Allah sees everything—represents the highest vibrational state. When an individual acts with this consciousness, every moment becomes an act of worship, and their entire being resonates with divine light.

When adversity arises, individuals with high vibrations respond with patience and resilience, placing their trust in Allah's divine decree (Qadr). Instead of succumbing to stress or worry, they consciously elevate their mindset, counteracting lower vibrations with hope, confidence, and peace. This virtuous approach allows them to transform challenges into growth opportunities.

Islam teaches that our vibrations not only affect ourselves but also influence others. As Prophet Muhammad ﷺ illustrated in his parable of the seller of musk, being in the company of virtuous individuals uplifts and inspires, just as bad company can diminish spiritual energy. Those who consistently vibrate at higher frequencies become beacons of truth and compassion, guiding others toward paths of virtue and clarity. This responsibility calls for a conscious effort to lead with forgiveness, understanding, and love, aligning with the Quranic principle of spreading goodness and light in the world.

When we consciously live in harmony with these divine principles, we will fulfill our purpose as stewards of creation. High-frequency energy flowing through us brings vitality, love, and clarity, stimulating emotions like gratitude, generosity, and happiness. It inspires motivations like forgiveness, creativity, and service, transforming every aspect of life into a journey of spiritual fulfillment. By purifying our hearts and bodies through conscious living, we align ourselves with Allah's light, becoming seekers of truth and guardians of divine wisdom.

By aligning with these divine principles, we fulfill our role as leaders in sync with a universe that continuously glorifies its Creator. The Principle of Vibration invites us to live with purpose and heightened awareness, attuning ourselves to the divine energy that sustains all existence. This journey leads to a life of profound clarity and purpose, fostering an eternal connection with Allah, who is the ultimate source of light and energy.

SECTION 4
THE PRINCIPLE OF POLARITY

﴿ وَهُوَ ٱلَّذِى مَدَّ ٱلْأَرْضَ وَجَعَلَ فِيهَا رَوَٰسِىَ وَأَنْهَٰرًا وَمِن كُلِّ ٱلثَّمَرَٰتِ جَعَلَ فِيهَا زَوْجَيْنِ ٱثْنَيْنِ يُغْشِى ٱلَّيْلَ ٱلنَّهَارَ إِنَّ فِى ذَٰلِكَ لَأَٰيَٰتٍ لِّقَوْمٍ يَتَفَكَّرُونَ ﴾

"And He is the One Who spread out the earth and placed firm mountains and rivers upon it, and created fruits of every kind in pairs. He covers the day with night. Surely in this are signs for those who reflect (13:3)."

﴿ وَمِن كُلِّ شَىْءٍ خَلَقْنَا زَوْجَيْنِ لَعَلَّكُمْ تَذَكَّرُونَ ﴾

"And We created pairs of all things so perhaps you would be mindful (51:49)."

293

"Everything is dual; everything has poles; everything has its pair of opposites like and unlike are the same; opposites are identical in nature, but different in degree; extremes meet; all truths are but half-truths; all paradoxes may be reconciled."
~ The Kybalion

THE PRINCIPLE

Polarity teaches that everything comes in opposites, yet those opposites are not truly separate. They are the same in essence, differing only in degree. This duality appears in all natural phenomena, human experience, and metaphysical thought. Hot and cold are not distinct substances, but varying degrees of temperature. North and South are ends of the same axis. Liberal and conservative represent opposite poles of a political spectrum. Love and hate are both intense emotions; masculine and feminine express complementary forms of the same vital energy. Even spirit and matter are connected as different vibratory layers within the same reality. In truth, polarity reveals that opposites are simply two extremes of one reality, proving that all creation emerges from a single, unified source.

Nature holds many secrets, but polarity is its loudest whisper.

Unlike the first three principles, which remain fixed, the Principle of Polarity is mutable. *A student of these laws can consciously shift their internal state from one pole to another*, such as fear to courage or anger to calm, by recognizing that each emotion exists on a continuum. This practice is known as **mental transmutation**: the deliberate act of changing one's inner state by applying will and aligning with higher truths.

Because all polarities are essentially the same, transformation is possible by raising one's vibrational frequency and redirecting thought, emotion, and energy toward a more elevated plane of being.

In Islam, the inner work of mental transmutation is called the science of **Tazkiyyah**, the purification of the soul. Tazkiyyah is the intentional process of cleansing the heart from destructive traits like envy, pride, and anger, while cultivating virtues such as sincerity (*ikhlas*), humility (*tawadu*), patience (*sabr*), and God-consciousness (*taqwa*).

It is not a passive state, but a conscious journey of inner refinement. Through remembrance of Allah (dhikr), self-evaluation (*muhasabah*), repentance (*tawbah*), and sustained moral effort (*mujahadah*), the believer gradually elevates the soul, drawing it closer to Allah.

Mastery over polarity is not simply about emotional balance; it is about gaining control over one's character and choosing how to respond to life's inevitable trials. While one may not control external events, they can command their inner reactions to those events. The individual who practices mental transmutation learns to rise from sadness into gratitude, or from doubt into reliance upon Allah. They refuse to be enslaved by instinct or impulse. Instead, they become active participants in shaping their destiny by choosing responses based on clarity, virtue, and trust in Allah.

Conversely, those who lack awareness of this principle often spiral into blame, bitterness, and helplessness. Emotional experience itself is governed by polarity. Joy is known through sorrow, and peace is appreciated only after turmoil. Recognizing this duality allows the believer to reframe adversity as a necessary part of growth. Rather than resist discomfort, they learn to extract wisdom from it, through transforming pain into purpose, and loss into gratitude. This spiritual shift empowers the believer to live a more balanced and aware life, one in which even suffering becomes a means to get closer to Allah.

When we attempt to view circumstances from the Divine Lens, we can see the wisdom behind adverse situations. Life challenges help differentiate between true servants of Allah and those who are slaves to their whims and desires. Trials and calamities can purify believers of their sins. If a person is patient with the difficulties they face, they will attain spiritual rewards and be elevated in status in this life and the next. From the believer's perspective, trials are not random accidents, but are divine calibrations. Allah explains that adversity tests the depth of one's sincerity and separates the patient from the impulsive (22:11). For the believer who attempts to understand the world through the Divine Lens, they will know that hardship is a necessary part of life which can be a tool for purification and elevation in this world and the next.[119] Additionally, calamities can act as a means to purge hypocrites from within the ranks of believers and allow disbelievers to overstep their bounds, leading to their downfall (3:141). Ultimately, the true nature of people is revealed after a calamity; the righteous consciously respond with sabr and iman, knowing that every challenge carries with it a hidden mercy, while the hypocrites reveal their true nature, resorting to despair, blame and selfishness. In this way, trials are spiritual mirrors that reveal the unseen state of the heart.

At the center of every trial lies a choice: to draw closer to *Tawhid* or to descend into *Shirk*.

---

119 al-Tirmidhi narrated that Abu Hurayrah (may Allah be pleased with him) said: The Prophet ﷺ said: "Trials will continue to befall the believing man or woman in himself, his child and his wealth until he meets Allah with no sin on him."

THE POLARITY OF TAWHID & SHIRK

Allah mentions in the Quran that He created all things in pairs (51:49). Everything, animate and inanimate, has a pair of opposites, from the proton and electron pair at the atomic level to the sun and the moon at the cosmic level. Even organisms that reproduce asexually form a pair with those that reproduce sexually. Allah is beyond all opposites, and all opposites depend on Him. To understand the true purpose behind these pairs, we must grasp the most significant polarity: **Tawhid** and **Shirk**.

Tawhid is the affirmation that Allah is One, the source of all truth, and all goodness. Tawhid is not just a belief. It is a lens to view reality, a mirror to view the self, and a shield for protection. Shirk is its opposite. It is the association of partners with Allah. Unlike other pairs, there is no balance between them. Tawhid is truth, while Shirk is a negation of reality. Tawhid is the foundation of a Muslim's faith, reconciling and uniting all apparent contradictions through the understanding that Allah is One, Unique, and the only deity worthy of worship. Shirk, conversely, divides and misguides, leading to moral and spiritual ruin.

The polarity of Tawhid is not only theological but also shapes civilizations, influencing language, education, governance, and societal structures. At its core, Tawhid integrates all aspects of life under the umbrella of a singular divine truth, providing clarity, moral cohesion, and unified purpose. In contrast, Shirk separates truth, creating a culture of secular reasoning, moral relativism, and societal fragmentation.

This divide begins with how their languages are structured. Right-to-left language cultures, such as Arabic and Hebrew, are inherently holistic and inductive, prioritizing intuitive reasoning deeply rooted in divine revelation and submission to a Creator. These cultures have historically formed governments around a centralized, unified authority figure, reflecting their alignment with the spiritual and cognitive framework of Tawhid. Conversely, left-to-right language cultures like

297

English and French favor analytical, linear, deductive, and dialectical reasoning. Their epistemological foundations encourage questioning, individual critique, and secular logic, intentionally separating moral and social truths from divine revelation, leading to constantly changing laws and fragmented knowledge.

Education systems further illustrate this polarity. Arab-Islamic societies emphasize rote memorization of sacred texts (Quran and Sunnah) and transmission of established truths through scholarly authoritative figures (*ulemah*), maintaining unity and coherence of knowledge across generations. Western educational paradigms prioritize critical thinking, personal analysis, and debate, encouraging innovation but also producing a culture of moral ambiguity and multiple competing "truths".

In governance, this polarity translates into theocratic centralization versus secular democracy. Islamic nations tend toward governance systems explicitly based on divine law (*Shariah*), often at the expense of individual autonomy and public opinion. Western societies adopt democratic pluralism, valuing individual autonomy, debate, and decentralized authority, but often losing a unifying moral and spiritual anchor.

Ultimately, this distinction is not merely political or cultural; rather, it is epistemological and spiritual, shaping fundamentally different understandings of reality. Tawhid-based cultures seek unity, clarity, and spiritual coherence, while cultures rooted in Shirk or secular pluralism experience social fragmentation, moral uncertainty, and spiritual disconnection. Thus, the divide between East and West can be viewed fundamentally as a contrast between unity and division—between Tawhid and Shirk.

DEMOCRACY
AROUND THE WORLD

Countries are rated on a scale from 0 to 10, with the global average declining slightly to **5.2** in 2024.

GLOBAL DEMOCRACY INDEX SCORE 2024

1	2	3	4	5	6	7	8	9

AUTHORITARIAN | HYBRID REGIME | FLAWED DEMOCRACY | FULL DEMOCRACY

SHARE OF WORLD POPULATION

60 countries worldwide operate under authoritarian rule.

AUTHORITARIAN **39.2%**

FLAWED DEMOCRACY **38.4%**

HYBRID REGIME **15.7%** 6.6%

FULL DEMOCRACY

Iceland 9.4 | Norway 9.8 | Finland 9.3
UK 8.3 | SWE 9.4 | Denmark 9.3
Ireland 9.2 | GER 8.7 8.1 | Poland 7.4 | BLR 2.0 | Ukraine 4.9
France 8.0 | 8.3 6.5 | ROM 6.0
Portugal 8.1 | Spain 8.1 | Italy 7.4 | Georgia 4.7
MAR 5.0 | Türkiye 4.3
Canada 8.7 | Russia 2.0
United States 7.9 | Kazakhstan 3.1 | Mongolia 6.5 | PRK 1.1 | Japan 8.5
Tunisia 4.7 | Greece 8.1 | S.Korea
Cuba 2.6 | Haiti 2.7 | Algeria 3.6 | Libya 2.3 | Egypt 2.8 | Saudi Arabia 2.8 | Iran 2.0 | China 2.1 | Taiwan 8.8
Mexico 5.3 | JAM 6.7 | Dominican Rep. 6.6 | Oman 3.1 | India 7.3
Guatemala 4.6 | Nicaragua 2.1 | MRT 4.0 | Mali 2.4 | Niger 2.3 | Chad 1.8 | Sudan 1.5 | Yemen 2.0 | Myanmar 1.0 | VNM 2.6 | Philippines 6.6
Costa Rica 8.3 | Venezuela 2.3 | Senegal 5.9 | Algeria 4.2 | ETH 3.2 | Sri Lanka 6.2 | Malaysia 7.1 | Papua New Guinea 6.0
Colombie 6.4 | Suriname 6.8 | Liberia 5.6 | Ghana 6.2 | D.R.C 1.9 | 5.1 | Kenya | Indonesia 6.4
Ecuador 6.2 | Gabon 2.2 | 5.2 | Tanzania
Peru 5.7 | Brazil 6.5 | Angola 4.1 | 5.7 | 5.3 | Mauritius 8.2 | F 8.
Bolivia 4.3 | Namibia 6.5 | BW 3.0 | 7.6 | Madagascar | Australia 8.9
Chile 7.8 | Uruguay 8.7 | 7.2 | Lesotho 6.1 | South Africa | New Zealand 9.6
Argentina 6.5

Source: Economist Intelligence Unit Democracy Index 2024

Scores have been rounded. France is a flawed regime, Romania and Papua New Guinea are hybrid regimes, and Mauritania is authoritarian.

Fig. 39 - An illustrative map depicting a scale of democracies around the world, from what are considered "successful democracies" to what are regarded as "failed regimes." Note the use of the term "regime" often attributed to those governments that do not agree with the concept of western democracy.

The universality of Tawhid is exemplified by the Quran, which both confirms and unites all the truthful teachings of previous scriptures and guides Muslims toward a single point of devotion, symbolized by the Ka'aba.[120] The Ka'aba serves as both a physical and spiritual representation of Tawhid, uniting Muslims worldwide in worship and purpose. Similarly, Shariah (Islamic law), derived from the Quran and Sunnah, harmonizes diverse societies under divine principles, promoting unity and justice across all lands.

Without a strong grasp of Tawhid, individuals may be swayed by doubts and confusion, particularly in secular academic settings where dialectical thinking often challenges belief in Allah. Dialectical thinking seeks to reconcile opposites by analyzing issues from multiple perspectives, often leading to fragmented understanding and moral ambiguity when disconnected from divine guidance. Over 70% of English-speaking philosophy professors identify as atheists, creating environments that challenge belief in Allah. Such environments frequently present questions like, "Can God create a rock that He cannot lift?"—designed to instill doubt. For a Muslim rooted in Tawhid, these questions are dismissed as logical contradictions, as Allah's power is absolute and incomparable. Tawhid equips believers with intellectual tools, serving as both sword and armor in navigating the challenges posed by specious arguments, ultimately reaffirming that no creation can rival the Creator.

Tawhid affirms that Allah is One, transcending all pairs and opposites (2:163). As the Creator and Sustainer of all existence (6:164; 13:16), He alone has the power to harm or benefit (5:76). Therefore, believers are called to trust and fear Him alone (3:175; 5:44). It clarifies that we cannot benefit or harm ourselves except by Allah's will (7:188) and increases trust in Allah as the sole provider (34:24) and controller of all that affects us (48:11). Tawhid reminds us that Allah is our only protector (33:3; 64:13). In essence, Tawhid should be the focal point of our physical, mental, and spiritual energy, as it

---

120 "...confirmation of previous Scriptures..." 5:48; "...confirmation of what came before it..." 10:37.

is the purpose of our lives. By placing Tawhid at the forefront, Muslims can transcend evil and shift towards positivity by returning to Allah in thoughts, speech, and actions.

Conversely, all evil and injustice are united under Shirk, the act most warned against in Islam. Shirk involves ascribing partners to Allah, attributing divine qualities to others, or believing that power, harm, or blessings can come from anyone besides Allah. Shirk is an unforgivable sin (4:48), and those who die committing it are forbidden from entering paradise (5:72). Any good action performed by someone engaging in Shirk is not accepted (39:65).

Major Shirk is categorized into four types: First, **Shirk in worship**, where a person supplicates to other than Allah (29:65), and worshiping entities like monks, rabbis, or Jesus (9:31), and loving creation as much as Allah (2:165); second, **Shirk in intentions and actions**, where one's desires and purpose are directed toward others instead of Allah (98:5); third, Shirk in **knowledge**, by attributing divine knowledge or power to others (6:59); and fourth, **Shirk in love**, where one loves something or someone as much as they should love Allah (2:165). Ultimately, all such deeds are in vain (11:15).

Minor Shirk does not make one a disbeliever but is a major sin. It includes actions for praise, fame, or worldly purposes rather than for Allah. To avoid the desire to show off, good deeds like teaching the Quran, fighting in jihad should be done with pure intentions and giving charity should be done privately when possible.[121] Swearing by anything other than Allah and believing in superstitions or omens are also examples of minor Shirk, which can lead to major Shirk if habitual. This includes swearing on one's mother/ father or upon others, dead or alive, or upon friends, family members, or saints. Minor Shirk also includes the belief in evil omens or superstitions. All minor Shirk can lead to major Shirk if it becomes habitual.

Tawhid and Shirk are the most important polarities about which one must have knowledge. The Quran and all that it contains is about Tawhid, its rights, and warnings against the

---

121 Note: See hadith regarding the first three men thrown into Hell: https://sunnah.com/riyadussalihin:1617

seriousness of Shirk. It defines the people of Tawhid and the people of Shirk and describes the rewards and punishments for its people. Tawhid is the core teaching that all Messengers were sent with and has been the foremost topic of contention throughout time (16:36). It is opposed by the disbeliever because it is the greatest truth, and shayateen know that it pulls people away from the extreme polarity of Hell. Knowledge and practice of Tawhid compel believers to stay on the positive polarity of halal (permissible) and avoid haram (impermissible). Engaging in halal deserves praise and reward, while haram deserves condemnation and repentance. Halal is exemplified by Habil (Abel), while haram is exemplified by Qabil (Cain).

Allah created all humans with Tawhid as part of their fitrah, but many deviate from this natural state by committing Shirk.[122] Initially, their fitrah inherently recognizes the truth and maintains a spiritual awareness of Allah. However, as individuals grow older, they often begin to heed external influences instead of following their inner fitrah. This shift can lead to a calcification of the pineal gland, diminishing their spiritual awareness. Though well-intentioned, the teachings from parents, educators, religious leaders, and community figures often stray from the truth. They may discuss the spiritual and worldly realms, explaining what exists above and below, yet their knowledge is frequently based on traditions passed down without true understanding. Over time, they may lose the experiential truth they once knew. As the next generation absorbs these teachings, they gradually drift away from the natural alignment of their fitrah.

In the first 10 generations of human history, all humans were united by the same religion prior to them losing faith. Allah sent Prophets to promise future rewards for obedience and warn others of future punishments (16:36). They came

---

122 The Prophet ﷺ reported that Allah said, "I created my servants in the right religion but devils made them go astray". The Prophet ﷺ also said, "Each child is born in a state of "Fitrah", then his parents make him a Jew, Christian or a Zoroastrian, the way an animal gives birth to a normal offspring. Have you noticed any that were born mutilated?" (Bukhari and Muslim).

with textual knowledge from above which was proposed to judge between the people to resolve their disagreements. Only the arrogant and the jealous rejected the clear proof. And those who believed in the truth were guided further (2:213). Over time, the rejectors of truth imposed their wills on the rest of humanity and caused us to drift away from our fitrah.

Today, humanity stands at the brink of its own destruction. Rejectors of truth are drawn toward Shirk, symbolized in this text as **Sun-consciousness**: an egocentric orientation that seeks power and control through illusion. In contrast, **Moon-consciousness** reflects the spirit of Tawhid, guiding believers to harmonize with divine truth and vibrate at frequencies which lead directly toward Allah. This inner alignment defines one's spiritual trajectory. One path leads to *wilayah*, a state of divine friendship with Allah and a life of sacred mission. The other drifts down the path toward sorcery, illusion, and allegiance to Shaytan.

THE WALI VS. THE SAAHIR

These opposing archetypes represent two spiritual directions. The *Wali* walks in surrender and divine trust, advancing truth and mercy on earth. The *Saahir*, by contrast, manipulates perception and reality, aligning with deception and ego. One moves toward the **light** and **right-hand path** of **Jannah**. The other moves toward **darkness** and the **left-hand path** of **Jahannam**.

A wali lives in constant obedience to Allah, transforming lower desires into actions that align with divine pleasure. For instance, they eat to strengthen their bodies and to increase their ability to worship. They marry to fulfill their desires in a permissible way and produce offspring that will be raised upon the worship of Allah.

In contrast, a saahir uses the power of **imagination** and **willpower** to contact and control shayateen. These skills are acquired after many years of intense study regarding nature and the correct timings for ceremonies and rituals. The occult methods used in magic include using tools like stones, charms, talismans, chants, spells, prayers, dancing, herbs, and drugs to alter consciousness. *Alsahara* (magicians) practice magic to have shayateen help them find lost objects, attack enemies, astral travel, predict the future, heal sickness, manipulate emotions, or harm others. Although there are different types of magicians, they all commit Shirk by contacting shayateen for aid and support.

RITUAL & NUMEROLOGY

Additionally, alsahara use numerology as a tool to determine the exact timings to execute potent rituals, which are linked to specific numbers, planetary alignments, deities, or forces in nature. The most common method is gematria, a Kabbalistic system where letters are assigned numerical values, allowing the saahir to uncover hidden meanings in words and names. They believe they can unlock hidden energies and tap into unseen realms by calculating the numerical value of certain names, words, or dates. These numerical vibrations, aligned with planetary forces, are believed to amplify the saahir's magical operations, creating more powerful talismans, sigils, and incantations. This manipulation of numbers attracts specific jinn to assist them in their goals, ensuring their magic resonates with the desired cosmic or spiritual forces.

On the other hand, awliyah use numerical patterns established through the Sunnah of Prophet Muhammad ﷺ to combat shayateen and their legions of seen and unseen followers. For example, Muslims are encouraged to recite *Subhan-Allah*, *Alhamdulillah*, and *Allahu Akbar* 33 times each after the five daily prayers, which total 17 *rakats* per day (Bukhari and Muslim). These praises equal 99, corresponding to Allah's 99 names and attributes. These aren't just numbers. They're spiritual codes or keys to putting the soul in-sync with the divine rhythm.

Additionally, Muslims are recommended to eat 7 dates from Madinah each morning to repel the effects of sihr and witchcraft (Bukhari). The number 7 often appears in Islamic practice, symbolizing spiritual completeness and divine protection. For instance, there are 7 locations of the body that are covered with water during *wudu* (ablution) (hands, mouth, nose, face, arms, head, feet). There are 7 prostration (*sajdah*) parts of the body (forehead and nose, right hand, left hand, right knee, left knee, and the ends of both feet). During the Hajj pilgrimage, Muslims symbolically reject Shaytan by stoning the *Jamarat* 7 times, as well as performing tawaf around the

Ka'aba 7 times, completing a sacred cycle of devotion (Nasai and Bukhari). This ritual involves stoning a pillar, which was originally an obelisk. An obelisk is a structure that originated in ancient Egypt and was associated with the worship of the sun god Ra.[123] In 2004, the Saudi government changed this idol to a flat wall for safety reasons, although even more people have died in stampedes in that area since this change. Suspiciously, a new obelisk was erected at Arafat, where Prophet Muhammad gave his last speech, making it the highest monument in that area.

Awliyah constantly balance back and forth, performing **righteous actions** and expressing **truthful speech**. The righteous follow the path of the **Prophets,** and the truthful follow the path of the **Messengers**. Awliyah live a life similar to that of the Prophets and the Messengers when they **deliver good news** and **warn against evil**.[124] They know that the most righteous actions are those that are aligned with the **sunnah** of Prophet Muhammad ﷺ and the most truthful speech is that which is contained in the **Quran**.[125] The **scholars** and their **students** are the ones who understand and apply the Book and the sunnah the best.[126]

In contrast, alsahara are in a state of constant flux between being an evil person in actions or an evil person in speech. Their evil may emanate from the depths of their **souls** or externally via the support of shayateen. Like shayateen, their main goal is to cause harm to people, property, and relationships. They do this by reciting certain incantations and using special tools. But

---

123 Note: Phonetically, the word 'Obelisk' bears a resemblance to the invocation 'Oh Iblis.'

124 See Verses: 2:213; 2:119; 6:48; 4:165; 7:188; 11:2; 17:105; 18:56; 25-56; 33:45; 34:28; 48:8.

125 See Khutbah al-Hajah:
https://www.abuaminaelias.com/dailyhadithonline/2011/12/26/khutbah-al-hajah-how-to-begin-a-khutbah-sermon-in-arabic-and-english/

126 Abu Huraira reported: The Messenger of Allah, peace and blessings be upon him, said, "Is not the world cursed and everything in it? Except for the remembrance of Allah and what facilitates it, the scholar or the student." Sunan al-Tirmidhi.

most of it is some type of trick or sham that can be likened to a type of simulation for one's imagination. Their only true ability is deception.

HISTORICAL & SCRIPTURAL EXAMPLES

Some of the awliyah and their karamat are mentioned in the Quran, such as Maryam, the mother of Isa (ﷺ), who would have winter fruit during the summer and summer fruit during the winter (19:24-26). Asif, one of the righteous Ministers of Suleiman (ﷺ), had knowledge of the Book and used it to bring the throne of Bilquis to Suleiman (27:38-40). And Khidr (ﷺ), the one who had knowledge of the unseen and knew about the events before they occurred (18:65-82). In the above examples, these supernatural wonders broke the natural order of things only by Allah's will, and the awliyah had no power in themselves.

The Quran also mentions some alsahara and their forms of deception, such as the story of Harut and Marut, the two angels that were sent as a test to the people of Babylon, who were taught about the true nature of magic (2:102). The knowledge of the Divine Names was used to cause separation between the **man** and his **wife**. Those inclined to evil (shayateen), made use of sihr, by the selling of their souls (*sharaw bihi anfusahum*). From that knowledge came the Talmud, Kabbalah, and astrology. The branches of that knowledge include sleight-of-hand deceptions and the summoning of shayateen.

An example of illusory sleight-of-hand magic is the public challenge between Fir'awn's magicians and Musa.[127] During the contest, the magicians threw their sticks to the ground, making them appear to transform into snakes. One possible explanation for this illusion is that the magicians used mercury within the cords and staffs. When exposed to the heat of a fire lit on the appointed day, the mercury expanded and moved, causing the sticks and ropes to seem to crawl like snakes. This method required meticulous preparation and skill, using

---

127 Taha 60-70; al-A'raf: 116 - 117; 10:77.

mercury's property of rapid expansion when heated to create the convincing illusion of lifelike motion, highlighting the magicians' ability to manipulate natural phenomena for magical effect.

Another example is Samiri, the hypocrite who followed Musa and used physical alchemy (manipulation) and mental alchemy (deception) to create a golden calf and mislead the Israelites into worshipping it. This occurred during the Exodus of the Children of Israel from Egypt to Canaan. While Musa was on Mount Sinai speaking to Allah and receiving the Ten Commandments, Samiri convinced the Israelites to melt their gold and silver jewelry, which they had taken from the Egyptians, and form it into a golden calf statue. He placed holes in the statue so that when the wind blew, it would produce a mooing sound, creating the illusion of a living idol. Alternatively, the sound might have been made due to the handful of dust from Jibra'il's horse that Samiri used. He then persuaded the Israelites to worship the calf until Musa returned.[128]

The Israelites were influenced by the Egyptians, who worshipped living bulls. The golden calf symbolized the 'sacred' bull Apis, whom the Egyptians considered the god Ptah incarnate. Upon death, the bull's soul was believed to have transmigrated into Osiris, whom the Egyptians worshipped as God's son (see Uzayr: 9:30). In both examples, alsahara relied on deceiving the intellect through visual or auditory illusions, thus creating sihr.

Over time, awliyah draw closer to Allah by consistently increasing their Iman and taqwa (piety) (10:62-64). Iman comes about after a person's faith is true and realized in their heart, while taqwa is when that faith aligns with their speech and actions. This is a balance of both **theory** and **action**. The path towards becoming a wali is outlined in the following hadith:

The Messenger of Allah ( ) said, "Verily Allah ta'ala has said: 'Whosoever shows enmity to a wali of Mine, then I have declared war against him. And My servant does not

---

128 Taha: 83-97; al-A'raf: 148

draw near to Me with anything more loved to Me than the religious duties I have obligated upon him. And My servant continues to draw near to me with nafil (supererogatory) deeds until I Love him. When I Love him, I am his hearing with which he hears, and his sight with which he sees, and his hand with which he strikes, and his foot with which he walks. Were he to ask [something] of Me, I would surely give it to him; and were he to seek refuge with Me, I would surely grant him refuge." (Bukhari)

Enmity to a wali = Allah's enemy
Wajib + nafil = Allah's Love

The awliyah listen to Allah's guidance with their ears, observe the beauty of Allah's creation with their eyes, perform actions with their hands that remind others of Allah, and walk a path with their feet that leads towards Allah.

The awliyah embody the concept of Tawhid, using it as a paradigm through which reality is viewed. This enables them to distinguish between communication from Allah, the mala'ika (angels), and the jinn. [129] Conversely, alsahara draw closer to Shaytan by committing Shirk, engaging in blasphemous rituals, and waging war against the Awliyah. They form a personal relationship with Shaytan through intense training combining **theory** and **practice**.

The **theoretical** study of magic involves delving into occult texts and teachings from experienced practitioners, focusing on the relationship between physical existence and the four elements that govern the natural world. These elements correspond to various aspects of human anatomy, reflecting a microcosm of the universe within us. Understanding these relationships can unlock hidden potential. Additionally, magical theory explores the interactions between the physical, astral, and mental/spiritual planes. The physical plane is the tangible world of matter that is governed by the four elements and is perceived by the five senses. The astral plane is the one

---

129 Note: a paradigm is a mind program; a program within your subconscious mind with which you can control your behavior.

that is explored during dreams of astral travel. It is the realm in which angels and demons exist. Finally, there is the spiritual/mental plane, which is where the universal mind of the Creator exists. This realm of thought is formless, and it is the ultimate cause of all effects. Practitioners use their imagination, incantations, and rituals to set their mind toward a certain frequency in the astral plane to manifest an astral entity (jinn) on the physical plane, thus influencing themselves and the world around them.

The saahir develops their magical abilities through rigorous mental, psychic, and physical training exercises. These **practices** involve strategies for controlling thoughts, introspection, and mindful eating and breathing. They work on mastering the elements internally and externally through meditation and yoga, cultivating the ability to travel mentally, transform character and temperament, and project the astral body. Additionally, they learn to imbue talismans, sigils, amulets, and gems with power and elevate the spirit to higher planes, aiming for conscious communion with what they perceive as a divine entity. However, in their pursuit, the "**God**" they ultimately serve is **Shaytan**.

Alsahara acquires their tricks in two ways. Traditionally, they are initiated into secret societies that grant exclusive secrets as they progress, providing knowledge designed to impart wisdom and the ability to pursue and recognize truth. Alternatively, those without access to such resources may pursue self-initiation through books and videos teaching the art of deception, following Shaytan's path. Shaytan, the antithesis of goodness and purity, rebelled against Allah's authority and has been granted permission to influence humans who likewise desire to oppose Allah's command.

MODERN DECEPTIONS: ORDO AB CHAO

On the path towards being a saahir, they must learn to master all opposites: good and evil, positive and negative, magnetic and electrical, spiritual and material, freedom and necessity, reason and passion, laughter, and tears. In sihr, as in the political model of the Hegelian dialectic, progress comes through the reconciliation of opposites, thesis, and antithesis in a synthesis that transcends them.

High-level magicians form a shadow government, which employs that model to cause **problems**, influence people's **reactions**, and mandate **solutions**.[130] The solutions that they offer were the reason they introduced the problem in the first place. This is what is referred to in Latin as *Ordo Ab Chao*, order out of chaos. This is the motto of the 33rd degree of Scottish Rite Freemasonry and is the practical philosophy of many shadow agencies throughout the world, such as the CIA, who apply it with the goal of creating chaos domestically and internationally for the purpose of bringing about a new order.

Fig. 40 - Symbol of the Scottish Rite of the Freemason Order [131]

130 I.e., the 2019 - 2023 Coronavirus vaccination campaign.

131 Note: The Scottish Rite adopted the double-headed eagle, originally the symbol of the Habsburg Holy Roman Emperors, after Frederick the Great, the First Sovereign Grand Commander, conferred its use to the Rite in 1786. The emblem was introduced in France in the 1760s as part of the Kadosh degree and represented the dual realms of the Council of Emperors of the East and West. Masonic tradition holds that the Knights of the East represented Freemasons who stayed in the East after the construction of the First Temple, while the Knights of the East and West were those who spread the Order across Europe and returned during the Crusades. The symbol's significance, linked to the Templars and alchemical traditions, was further explored by Albert Pike, who associated the eagle with the Philosopher's Stone.

THE DIVINE TRUTH BEYOND DUALITY

Tawhid stands as the ultimate unifier, transcending all contradictions and aligning humanity with divine justice. It is the foundation of spiritual beliefs, societal structures, and intellectual frameworks, harmonizing areas where fragmentation might otherwise prevail. Through Tawhid, Muslims are called to fulfill their moral duty: to enjoin good, forbid evil, and embody a paradigm of unity that counters the divisive nature of Shirk.

In contrast, Shirk fragments truth, leading to spiritual, moral, and societal decay. It symbolizes humanity's departure from their innate fitrah and alignment with Allah's will. Tawhid, as the antidote to this fragmentation, offers a path of clarity, purpose, and harmony, guiding individuals and communities toward the ultimate goal of divine unity. By grounding their lives in Tawhid, Muslims transcend the polarities of this world and draw closer to Allah's justice and mercy.

Muslims must fulfill their moral duty to **call people to good** and **forbid people from evil** (*al-amr bi-l-maʿrūf wa-n-nahy ʿani-l-munkar*) as emphasized in the Quran (3:104).[132] Past nations were destroyed because they allowed evil to manifest until it became the norm of their culture. Allah declares the Ummah of Muhammad ﷺ as the best model for all nations because they enjoin what is right and forbid what is wrong. In some verses, the duty is linked to believers who engage in *jihad* (striving) until they are established in the land.[133] This obligation is also personal and was performed by the unlettered Prophet (*al-rasul al-nabi al-ummi*) to his followers (7:157) and advised by Prophet Luqman to his son (31:17).

In the Quran, enjoining good (*amr bil-maʿruf*) appears in diverse contexts: it begins with **belief and obedience**, calling people to affirm the oneness of Allah and obey Him and His Messenger (9:112); it extends to **worship and charity**,

---

132 This dual command appears in 7 other verses (3:110, 3:114, 7:157, 9:71, 9:112, 22:41, 31:17).

133 3:110, 3:114, 9:71.

commanding the establishment of prayer (2:43) and the giving of alms (2:110); it encompasses **invitation and striving**, urging believers to invite others to righteousness (3:104) and to compete in good works (5:48); and it includes reflection and **patience**, encouraging the recitation of Allah's signs (3:191) and steadfastness in adversity (31:17). Thus, commanding right covers every act prescribed by Allah and His Prophet, while forbidding wrong embraces all that they have prohibited.[134]

The obligation to enjoin good and forbid evil varies based on the believer's authority or level of knowledge.[135]

Allah's deputy on earth, *khalifat Allah fil-ard*, along with the custodians of His book and Prophet, can enforce *Shari'ah* to prevent wrongdoing and uphold justice. Scholars (*ulemah*) and teachers (*muealimun*) can speak out against evil with knowledge and understanding. The regular believer has the ability to hate evil within their heart. Regardless of status, the most pious and zealous in performing their duty and most loyal to their people are those who consistently command what is right and forbid what is wrong.

In contrast, the people of Shirk promote evil and discourage good. They view themselves as divine, with Dajjal as their model of self-elevated power and wisdom, using magic for self-evolution. They advocate for the one-eye symbolism of Dajjal, perceiving him as a leader capable of improving the world without the constraints of religion that turns people into "sheep." Dajjal embodies the liberated Luciferian Spirit, representing the self-illuminated one who achieves spiritual and material power through lawlessness and rebellion, ultimately seeking to awaken the god within.

They are worshippers of Shaytan and his ego-driven, transformative process. They develop their strength of will, spiritual independence, and knowledge of Black Arts to achieve their desires by force. They become initiates on a path that

---

134 See also 2:43; 2:110; 3:110; 3:114; 9:71; 22:41 for further examples of enjoining good and supporting communal righteousness.

135 Abu Sa'eed Al-Khudri narrated that Allāh's Messenger ﷺ said, "Whoever among you sees an evil (munkar), let him change it with his hand (*an yughayyirahu biyadihi*). If he is unable, then with his tongue (*bi-lisanihi*). If he is unable, then with his heart (*bi-qalbihi*)" (Muslim).

enables them to gain in this world. Many initiates have adopted professional roles wherein they can influence many, such as judges, lawyers, police officers, teachers, politicians, or Masons. They may outwardly claim to be Muslim, Christian, or Jew, but their real religion is self-worship, as embodied through the internal merger of both darkness and light, good and evil, animalistic and human. They believe man can be raised to the level of infinity when they combine and reconcile all opposites into a proper balance. From the two, they make 1, and then 1 becomes a part of the divine whole.

AFTERWORD

All praise is due to Allah, who granted the first Prophet, Adam (عَلَيْهِ ٱلسَّلَامُ), the gift of speech and the authority to name creation, and who then taught the first Messenger, Idris (عَلَيْهِ ٱلسَّلَامُ), to inscribe divine revelation on clay tablets and temple walls. From those earliest educators to our modern digital classrooms, the quest to know oneself, to understand the Creator, and to transform the world with wisdom has driven every age—from hieroglyphs to hyperlinks.

A Holistic Framework

This volume guides readers through a holistic framework from the unseen to the seen, illuminating the **Spirit** at the heart of reality.

- **Metaphysics:** We began by defining Metaphysics as the study of what lies beyond our senses, demonstrating that philosophers and mystics alike depend on divine revelation for complete answers. The Quran states that Allah alone unifies all creation—by His command, the heavens and earth came into being (2:117), and by that same decree, He sustains every particle. We choose either to affirm this truth with mind and heart or to place all our trust in our limited perspectives.

- **Physics:** Next, we surveyed the laws of energy, matter, space, and time. Each fundamental force—electromagnetism, the strong and weak nuclear forces, gravity—is upheld by angels appointed to sustain creation. From Jibra'il transmitting revelations like waves of light to Mika'il and Izra'il regulating unseen transformations and Israfil preserving cosmic order, we observed perfect harmony between visible and hidden dimensions.

- **Chemistry:** We traced Chemistry's roots in ancient alchemy, where seekers combined and transformed elements. Here, the realm of the jinn whispers through vibrational currents that modulate neural chemistry—shaping thought, speech, and action. If unchecked, these forces can draw the metaphysical soul and biological body into the chemical fire, reminding us that every molecular shift reflects a greater reality.

- **Biology:** Finally, we marveled at living beings: from single-celled organisms shaped from water (24:45) to the diversity of multicellular life, each unfolding by divine pattern (29:19). Instinct-driven creatures and self-aware humans inhabit ecosystems ordained by Allah. At the summit stands humankind—morally responsible and richly varied in languages, colors, cultures, and temperaments.

An Inner Journey

Having surveyed creation's foundations, we turned inward in Chapter 2, examining three essential tools to sharpen the mind, tongue, and spirit. As mentioned in the Preface, genuine insight grows through a dialogue between knowledge, lived experiences, and sincere contemplation:

- **Knowledge ('ilm)** charts reality through the systematic gathering of facts, observations, and data. Yet knowledge alone is a map without direction. As I reflected in the Preface, my early encounters with misinterpretations of history highlighted how knowledge, devoid of humility, can lead astray—much like Iblis, whose reasoning, lacking humility, led him to pride instead of submission.

- **Understanding (fahm)** synthesizes knowledge into coherent patterns and relationships, yielding deeper insights into reality. Understanding is the compass revealing the lay of the land. The angels embody this principle perfectly, submitting to Allah even without fully grasping the wisdom behind His decrees. Similarly, as highlighted earlier, my engagement with scholars, seekers, and rigorous reflection deepened my own understanding, showing how sincere contemplation guides us to greater truths.

- **Wisdom (hikmah)** seamlessly integrates understanding into lived practice, choosing actions conforming to the natural order and Divine Will. Wisdom is both the path and the destination. Adam embodied wisdom by transforming knowledge into genuine growth, learning from errors, and consciously committing to righteous choices. As emphasized previously, wisdom became most evident when theory met personal trials and disciplined practice, transforming intellectual insights into lived experiences and spiritual growth.

Hermetic Foundations

Chapter 3, Sections 0–4, provide the cornerstone of the Hermetic system, beginning with the Father of Esoteric Wisdom—Idris, also known as Enoch, Thoth, and Hermes Trismegistus, the sage whose voice echoes across ages, uniting prophetic revelation, philosophical inquiry, and alchemical transformation. Just as a provocative question from a coworker, described in the Preface, ignited my deep exploration into Idris' legacy, these insights invite readers to similarly pursue profound questions about reality.

From this legacy flow four Hermetic Laws:

- **Mentalism (Primacy of Divine Will):** All existence originates from Allah's command *"Kun"* ("Be!") (36:82), with every event recorded in the *Lawh al-Mahfudh* (Preserved Tablet, 85:22). As reflected in my personal journey described earlier, we do not know Allah's specific decree beforehand, yet we are called to sincerely align our intentions and efforts with divine guidance, trusting in His wisdom every step of the way.

- **Correspondence (Interconnection):** Reality reflects itself at every level, from cosmic motions to inner life. As revealed in my exploration of Islamic teachings, scientific discoveries, and esoteric insights, recognizing these cosmic connections enriches our perception and deepens our sense of unity.

- **Vibration (Divine Movement):** Creation thrives on ceaseless motion. *"There is not a single thing that does not glorify His praises"* (17:44); each vibration is a hidden hymn. As earlier discussions highlighted, aligning ourselves with the divine rhythms through Quranic recitation, dhikr, ṣalah, and mindful stillness enables profound spiritual transformation.

- **Polarity (Balanced Duality):** All things exist in pairs (51:49), revealing opposites on a single spectrum. True mastery lies in walking the middle path (*ummatan wasata*, 2:143), transforming life's trials into pathways of spiritual growth and inner balance.

From ancient monuments to AI-driven platforms, education shapes both character and intellect. Today's technology requires empathy, critical thinking, and ethical judgment—reminding us that technological brilliance needs timeless wisdom.

Practical Convictions

This book is not merely for reflection—it is a call to action. To truly benefit from the knowledge and wisdom explored here, the reader must integrate learning with lived experience. Let these three convictions guide your thinking, choices, and growth:

- **Unite Knowledge and Spirit**: Fuse empirical rigor with spiritual revelation. Each lesson becomes revelatory, opening gateways to the unseen.

- **Correspondence-Based Thinking**: Embrace cosmic connections. Observing universal patterns reveals the unified design woven into all reality.

- **Breath–Depth–Application Framework**: Encourage broad exploration, deep reflection, and practical application. Transform abstract understanding into lasting action, humility, and compassion, guiding souls toward wisdom.

By turning these convictions into daily habits—grounding ideas in context and moving quickly from information to insight to action—you embody the holistic framework explored here and inspire others to do the same.

May this history of education be your canvas for tomorrow's curricula. Debate it, adapt it, and continue the story of human learning with the wonder that inspired the first teachers. Learn deeply, live humbly, teach faithfully.

This marks the end of Book I:
Spirit

Return often to these pages.
Let each reflection renew your awe and sharpen your purpose.

WORKS CITED

Introduction

- Harari, Yuval Noah. *Sapiens: A Brief History of Humankind.* Harper, 2015.
- Harari, Yuval Noah. *Homo Deus: A Brief History of Tomorrow.* Harper, 2017.
- Note: All Quranic quotations in this book are taken from *The Clear Quran: A Thematic English Translation of the Message of the Final Revelation*, translated by Dr. Mustafa Khattab.

Chapter 1: The Divine Quadrivium
Section 1: Metaphysics

- Greer, John Michael. Elementary Treatise of Occult Science. Llewellyn, 2018, p. 118.
- Greene, Brian. *The Elegant Universe: Superstrings, Hidden Dimensions, and the Quest for the Ultimate Theory.* W. W. Norton, 1999, pp. 44-46.

- Dispenza, Joe. *Becoming Supernatural: How Common People Are Doing the Uncommon.* Hay House, 2017. Chapter 11.
- Cavendish, Richard. *Black Arts - An Absorbing Account Of Witchcraft, Demonology, Astrology And.* 1st ed., Tarcherperigee, 1967, pp. 68-69

Section 2: Physics
- Landauer, Rolf. "The Physical Nature of Information." *Physics Letters A*, vol. 217, no. 3-4, 1996, pp. 188–193.
- Al-Hajj Ahmad, Yusuf. *Scientific Wonders On Earth & In Space.* 1st ed., Darussalam, 2010, p. 303.
- Fazl-ur-Rahman Ansari, Muhammad. *The Quranic Foundations And Structure Of Muslim Society Volume Two.* 4th ed., Elite Publishers LTD, 2008, pp. 23-24.
- Martineau, John et al. *Sciencia.* Walker & Co., 2011, pp. 168-169.

Section 3: Chemistry
- Means, Casey, and Calley Means. *Good Energy: The Surprising Connection Between Metabolism and Limitless Health.* Penguin Publishing Group, 2024, pp. 14–17, 34-35, 165, 171-172, 176–177, 223–227, 232–233.
- Ibn Qayyim al-Jawziyah, M. (2004). *al-Fawā'id a Collection of Wise Sayings.* Al-Mansura, Egypt: Umm Al-Qura, p.95.
- Harari, Yuval N. *Sapiens.* Library And Archives Canada Cataloguing In Publication, 2014, p. 8.
- http://www.dajjaal.com/liar/articles/bgxjt-the-whispering-of-Iblis-satan-to-adam-with-four-matters.cfm

Section 4: Biology
- Miller, K. and Levine, J. (2008). *Biology.* Saddle River, New Jersey: Pearson Prentice Hall, p.15.

- Zaheer, Syed Iqbal. *The Inimitable And Physical Sciences*. Dar Us Salam, 2014, pp. 206-207.
- Munir, M., 1992. *God, Universe And Life (Spiritual Interpretation Of The Universe)*. 1st ed. New Delhi: Adam Publishers & Distributors, pp.42-66.
- Bardon, F. (1956). *Initiation into Hermetics*. Wuppertal, West Germany: Dieter Ruggeberg, p.28.
- Regardie, Israel et al. *The Tree Of Life*. 3rd ed., Llewellyn Publications, 2001, p. 60.
- Les Six Livres de la République v, i p. 686
- Ahmad DhahabiMuhammad ibn. *Al-Tibb Al-Nabawi*, translated by Cyril Elgood, 1962, p. 4.
- Wille, Staffan Müller. "Linnaeus and the Four Corners of the World."
- See Linnaeus, C. von. "Systema naturae, vol. 1." *Systema naturae, Vol. 1* (1758); Jean Bodin's *Methodus ad facilem historiarum cognitionem* (Method for the Easy Comprehension of History) (1596); H.P. Blavatsky's writings on the "root races"; Thomas Burgoyne's *The Light of Egypt*, and Max Heindel's *The Rosicrucian Cosmo-Conception*.
- Ibn Khaldūn, and Franz Rosenthal. *The Muqaddimah*. 5th ed., First Princeton, 1981, p. 63.
- Moll, Kirsten, et al. "The ABO Blood Group System and Plasmodium." *Blood*, vol. 110, no. 7, 2007, pp. 2250-2258, ashpublications.org.
- Greer, John Michael. Elementary Treatise of Occult Science. Llewellyn, 2018, p. 128, 143, 181-204.
- James, King. "Questions and Answers." Holy Bible, Heirloom Bible Publishers, Wichita, KS, 1988, p. 27.
- Science. Llewellyn, 2018, p. 128, 143, 181-204.
- Genesis 10:6-20; 10:2-5; 10:15-20
- Langum, Virginia. "Cold characters: Northern temperament in the premodern; *Visions of north in premodern Europe*. 2018. 123-144; Hippocrates, *Airs, Waters, Places*, part 16:115; part 23:131, 133.
- World Population Review. "Blood Type by Country

2024." *World Population Review*, 2024, https://worldpopulationreview.com/country-rankings/blood-type-by-country. Accessed 15 July 2024.

- Brickell, John. "The Natural History of North Carolina." Dublin: James Carson, 1737.
- "Genetic History of the Indigenous Peoples of the Americas." *Wikipedia*, 25 May 2023, en.wikipedia.org/wiki/Genetic_history_of_the_Indigenous_peoples_of_the_Americas. Accessed 15 July 2024.
- Langum, Virginia. "Cold characters: Northern temperament in the premodern imaginary." *Visions of north in premodern Europe*. 2018. 123-144.
- "Blood Type by Country 2024." *World Population Review*, 2024, https://worldpopulationreview.com/country-rankings/blood-type-by-country. Accessed 15 July 2024.
- Heath, Richard. *Sacred Geometry*, Inner Traditions, Rochester, VT, 2021, p. 196.
- Booth, M. (2018). *The illustrated secret history of the world*. New York, NY: The Overlook Press, Peter Mayer Publishers, Inc, p.50.

Chapter 2: The Divine Trivium
Section 1: Iblis's Knowledge

- Ibn Qayyim al-Jawziyah, M. (2004). *al-Fawā'id a Collection of Wise Sayings.* Al-Mansura, Egypt: Umm Al-Qura, p.101.
- Zaheer, Syed Iqbal. *An Educational Encyclopedia Of Islam.* Iqra Welfare Trust, 2010, p. 170.
- Islamqa.info. (2019). *Life on Earth Before Adam - Islam Question & Answer.* [online] Available at: https://islamqa.info/en/answers/72470/life-on-earth-before-adam [Accessed 18 April 2019].
- Baly, Waheed Abdusslaam. *How To Protect Yourself From Jinn And Shaytan.* 2nd ed., Al-Firdous Ltd, 2009, p. 65.
- Ibn Qayyim al-Jawzīyah, M. and Mabrouk, L. (1990). *The soul's journey after death: an abridgement of Ibn Al-Qayyim's Kitab ar-Ru'h.* 2nd ed. Indiana University: Dar al-Taqwa, p.12.
- Passions of the Soul (*Les Passions de l'âme*), published in 1649.
- Booth, M. (2018). *The illustrated secret history of the world.* New York, NY: The Overlook Press, Peter Mayer Publishers, Inc, p.50-78.
- Nichols, D.E. N,N-dimethyltryptamine and the pineal gland: Separating fact from myth. J. Psychopharmacol. 2017, 32, 30–36. [CrossRef] [PubMed]
- Tan DX et al. *Pineal gland aging and melatonin loss: A review. Mol.* 2018; 23(2):301. Link.
- Kunz D et al. *Decreased melatonin and pineal gland calcification. Neuropsychopharm.* 1999; 21(6):765-72. PubMed.
- Sandyk R, Kay SR. *Abnormal EEG and calcification of the pineal gland in schizophrenia. Int J Neurosci.* 1992; 62:107–111.
- Belay DG, Worku MG. *Prevalence of pineal gland calcification: A systematic review and meta-analysis. Syst Rev.* 2023; 12(1):32. doi:10.1186/s13643-023-02205-5. PMC.

- Adeloye, Adelola, and Benjamin Felson. "Incidence of normal pineal gland calcification in skull roentgenograms of black and white Americans." *American Journal of Roentgenology* 122.3 (1974): 503-507.
- Luke, Jennifer Anne. *The effect of fluoride on the physiology of the pineal gland.* Diss. University of Surrey, 1997.
- Bryson, Christopher. *The Fluoride Deception.* Seven Stories Press, 2006.
- Baly, Waheed Abdusslaam. *How To Protect Yourself From Jinn And Shaytan.* 2nd ed., Al-Firdous Ltd, 2009, p. 28.
- Cavendish, Richard. *Black Arts - An Absorbing Account Of Witchcraft, Demonology, Astrology And.* 1st ed., Tarcherperigee, 1967, p. 6-7.
- Pappas, Stephanie. "Facts About Phosphorus". *Live Science*, 2019, https://www.livescience.com/28932-phosphorus.html. Accessed 6 Apr 2019.
- *Blitzed: Drugs in the Third Reich.* Translated by Shaun Whiteside, Houghton Mifflin Harcourt, 2017.
- Ibn Qayyim al-Jawziyah, M. (2004). *al-Fawā'id a Collection of Wise Sayings.* Al-Mansura, Egypt: Umm Al-Qura, p.102.

Section 2: The Angels' Understanding

- al-Munajjid, Saalih. "Life On Earth Before Adam - Islam Question & Answer". *Islamqa.Info*, 2019, https://islamqa.info/en/answers/72470/life-on-earth-before-adam. Accessed 22 Apr 2019.
- Zaheer, Syed Iqbal. *An Educational Encyclopedia Of Islam.* Iqra Welfare Trust, 2010, p. 172
- Chittick, William C. "Reason, Intellect, and Consciousness in Islamic Thought." *Reason, Spirit and the Sacral in the New Enlightenment: Islamic Metaphysics Revived and Recent Phenomenology of Life*, edited by Anna-Teresa Tymieniecka, Springer, 2011, pp. 20-22.

- Al-Shabrāwi, Abd al-Khaliq. *The Degrees Of The Soul*. Quilliam Press, 1997, p. 2.
- *Izālatus-Sitār ʿan Al-Jawāb Al-Mukhtār li-Hidāyatil-Muhtār* of Ibn ʿUthaymeen, p. 10.
- Mackey, *Encyclopedia of Freemasonry*, 33.
- Nomani, *Lughat — al-Quran*
- Dorsey, E. Ray, et al. "Funding of US biomedical research, 2003-2008." *Jama* 143-137 :(2010) 303.2.
- Beggelman, M. (2019). *Why Do We Doctors So Often Fail To See Symptoms Are Drug Side Effects?*.
- Nix, Elizabeth. "Where Did The Rx Symbol Come From?". *HISTORY*, 2019, https://www.history.com/news/where-did-the-rx-symbol-come-from. Accessed 26 Apr 2019.
- https://www.ethnologue.com/insights/how-many-languages/
- Martineau, John. *Trivium*. Bloomsbury, 2016.
- Kamili, M., Bakar, O., Batchelor, D. and Hashim, R. (2016). *Islamic perspectives on science and technology*. 1st ed. Singapore: Springer, pp.23-24.

Section 3: Adam's Wisdom

- "Our Three Brains - The Reptilian Brain". *The Interaction Design Foundation*, 2019, https://www.interaction-design.org/literature/article/our-three-brains-the-reptilian-brain. Accessed 25 May 2019.
- Greene, Robert. *Mastery*. Penguin Books, 2013, pp. 175-176.
- "What Is The Limbic System In The Brain? - Definition, Functions & Parts - Video & Lesson Transcript | Study.Com". *Study.Com*, 2019, https://study.com/academy/lesson/what-is-the-limbic-system-in-the-brain-definition-functions-parts.html. Accessed 25 May 2019.
- "The Concept Of The "Triune Brain"". *The Interaction Design Foundation*, 2019, https://www.interaction-design.org/literature/article/the-concept-of-the-triune-brain. Accessed 25 May 2019.

- Arif, Sarosh. *Ghazali's Personality Theory: A Study on the Importance of Humility in Early Childhood.* MS thesis, Ibn Khaldun University, Alliance of Civilization Institute, 2018, pp. 35-38.
- Kahneman, Daniel. *Thinking, Fast and Slow.* Farrar, Straus and Giroux, 2011.
- Ibn Kathir, A. (2013). *Stories of the Prophets.* Riyadh: Darussalam, pp 8-9, 10-11.
- Laitman, Michael. *Awakening To Kabbalah: The Guiding Light Of Spiritual Fulfillment.* Jewish Lights Publishing, 2006, p. 27.
- Booth, M. (2013). *The Sacred History.* New York, NY: Atria Books, pp.14-15.
- Srour, Marissa K., et al. "Natural large-scale regeneration of rib cartilage in a mouse model." *Journal of Bone and Mineral Research* 308-297 :(2015) 30.2.
- Malabari, Ibrahim H. "From Heaven to Earth – Where did Adam First Land?" *About Islam,* 23 Oct. 2023, aboutislam.net/understanding-islam/adam-first-land.
- Zaheer, Syed Iqbal. *An Educational Encyclopedia Of Islam.* Iqra Welfare Trust, 2010, pp. 172, 467.
- *Mishkaat al-Masaabeeh,* 3/122. *Saheeh* according to Shaykh Naasirudeen al-Albaani.

Chapter 3: The 7 Divine Laws
Section 0: The Father of Occult Wisdom

- Ibn Kathir, A. (2013). *Stories of the Prophets*. Riyadh: Darussalam, pp 19-20.
- Muhammad, M. and Seoharvi, H. (2004). *Stories From the Quran*. 1st ed. Karachi: Darul-Ishaat, pp.82-83, 85.
- Karagözoğlu, Bahattin. *Science and Technology from Global and Historical Perspectives*. Springer International Publishing, 2017.
- Gros de Beler, Aude. *Egyptian Mythology*. Molière, 1999.
- VanderKam, James C. 1 Enoch: A New Translation. Fortress Press, 2001.
- Hermes Trismegistus and Arab Science," *Studia Islamica*, ii, 1954, pp. 45-59; and idem, article "Hirmis" in *Encyclopaedia of Islam*, new ed., iii, Leiden, 1971, pp. 463-65.
- *A Dictionary of Islam*, T.P. Hughes, Ashraf Printing Press, repr. 1989, pg. 192
- Ghayb.com. 2022. *The Prophet Idris (as) In History Pt.1 - Ghayb.com*. [online] Available at: <https://ghayb.com/2019/01/the-Prophet-idris-as-in-history-pt-1/?fbclid=IwAR3bkKbjFfPVjOMDem92nG0WWYrcK-TACtnXKFawMbKXbuy2_m0WaIBlcQA> [Accessed 12 January 2022]
- Lachman, Gary. *The Quest For Hermes Trismegistus*. Floris Books, 2011, p. 17.
- Tafsir al-Qurtubi19:56
- Nasr, Seyyed Hossein, et al. "The Study Quran." A new Translation and Commentary. New York (2015), pp 1357.
- Lachman, Gary. *The Quest For Hermes Trismegistus*. Floris Books, 2011, pp. 16-17.
- Pinch, Geraldine. *Magic In Ancient Egypt*. University of Texas Press, 2006, pp. 61-63.
- Neil Powell. *Alchemy, the Ancient Science* (Aldus Books Ltd., 1976) p. 127.

- Schuchard. *Restoring the Temple of Vision*, p. 236; "GEN 140 - The Evolution of Writing". *Youtube*, 2019,
- https://www.youtube.com/watch?v=DpXAjekdQNM. Accessed 31 Oct 2019.
- Chourry, Josselyne. *The Tarot in the Light of Kabbalah.* Grand Lodge of the English Language Jurisdiction, AMORC, Inc., 2024, pp. 12-13, 22-23, 115-117.
- Mark, Joshua J. "Thoth." *World History Encyclopedia*, 16 Feb. 2017, www.worldhistory.org/Thoth/. Accessed 21 Nov. 2024.
- Booth, M. (2018). *The illustrated secret history of the world*. New York, NY: The Overlook Press, Peter Mayer Publishers, Inc, p. 143.
- Mackey, Albert G. "Name." *An Encyclopedia of Freemasonry and Its Kindred Sciences*, edited by Charles T. Mcclenachan, L. H. Everts & Co., Philadelphia, PA, 1886, p. 256.
- *The History of the World* (New YorK: B. Franklin, 1829) Chap. XI, p. 385
- Salfuĕre, Rubaphilos, and Paul Hardacre. *The Hermes Paradigm*. Salamander And Sons, 2009, p. 23, 57.
- Note: Classical literature has many references to Atlantis, such as the works of Prochus, Diodorus, Pliny, Strabo, Plutarch and Posidinus.(Booth, Mark. *The Illustrated Secret History Of The World*. The Overlook Press, 2018, p. 160.)
- Walbridge, John. *The Wisdom of the Mystic East: Suhrawardi and Platonic Orientalism*. SUNY Press, 2001, pp 43-44.
- Translation: Ghayb. "The Prophet Idris (as) in History Pt. 1." *Ghayb*, 14 Jan. 2019, ghayb.com/2019/01/the-Prophet-idris-as-in-history-pt-1/. Accessed 18 Aug. 2024.
- Pico della Mirandola, Giovanni. *Oration on the Dignity of Man*. Gateway Editions, 1956, p. 3. Internet Archive, https://archive.org/details/orationondignity0000unse/page/2/mode/2up.
- *The Secret History of Hermes Trismegistus: Hermeticism*

from Ancient to Modern Times, by Florian Ebeling et al., Cornell University Press, 2011, p. 90, 93–97, 112.

Section 1: The Principle of Mentalism
- Zaheer, Syed Iqbal. *An Educational Encyclopedia of Islam.* Vol. 1, Iqra Welfare Trust, 2010, p. 5, pp. 427-428.
- Ibn al-Qayyim al-Jawziyya. *Kitab Ar-Ruh: Soul's Journey After Death.* Translated by Muhammad Husnain, Islamic Book Service, 2001, pp. 15–19, 45–50.
- Ibn Mandhur, M. (n.d). Lisna al-Arab al-Muhit. Beirut: Darr al-Lisan al-Arab.
- Extracted by Ibn 'Abdul-Barr in Tamhid. (Sharah Sudur page 216.)
- Rashid, Asrar. "Understanding Our Body - The Ruh & Nafs". *Youtube. Com,* 2013, https://www.youtube.com/watch?v=flx0zUN_ox0.
- Mujib, A. (1999). Fitrah dan Kepribadian Islam; Sebuah Pendekatan Psikologis (1st ed.). Jakarta: Darul Falah.
- al-Faraj Ba'd ash-Shiddah

Section 2: The Principle of Correspondence
- Mubārakfūri, Safial-Rahmān. *The Sealed Nectar.* Darussalam, 2011, pp. 208-212.
- Joseph, Harry B. *The Book of Wisdom.* Vol. 2, 2024, p. 135.
- Nasr Husain, 2015. In *The study Quran: A new translation with notes and commentary.* New York, NY: HarperOne, an imprint of HarperCollins Publishers, p. 1513.
- Al-Shabrāwi, Abd al-Khaliq. *The Degrees Of The Soul.* Quilliam Press, 1997.
- Fadiman, James, and Robert Frager. *Essential Sufism.* HarperSanFrancisco, 2000, pp. 20-23.
- Sunan Abu Dawood, Hadith 4753;
- Cavendish, Richard. *Black Arts - An Absorbing Account Of Witchcraft, Demonology, Astrology And.* 1st ed.,

Tarcherperigee, 1967, p. 80; 83, 176-196.

- Bauval, Robert, and Adrian Gilbert. *The Orion Mystery: Unlocking the Secrets of the Pyramids*. Crown Publishers, 1994, p. 107.
- Lehner, Mark. *The Complete Pyramids: Solving the Ancient Mysteries*. p. 147.
- Diop, Cheikh Anta. *The African Origin of Civilization: Myth or Reality*. Translated by Mercer Cook, Lawrence Hill Books, 1974.
- Vail, C. H. *Ancient Mysteries And Modern Masonry*. 2nd ed., Global Grey, 1909, p. 159.
- Clark, J. (2008). Did the ancient Greeks get their ideas from the Africans? Retrieved April 25, 2008, from http://history.howstuffworks.com/history-vs-myth/greek-philosophers-african-tribes.htm
- Palmer, R.R., and Joel Colton. *A History of the Modern World*. 9th ed., McGraw-Hill, 2002.
- Aristotle. *Metaphysics*. Translated by W.D. Ross, The Internet Classics Archive, Massachusetts Institute of Technology, classics.mit.edu/Aristotle/metaphysics.html.
- Jackson, John G. *African-Origin-of-the-Myths-Legend-of-the-Garden-of-Eden*. Black Classic Press, 1990.
- Ashby, Muata. *The Kemetic Tree of Life: Ancient Egyptian Metaphysics and Cosmology for Higher Consciousness*. Sema Institute, 2007.
- Saussy, F.T. (2002) "Chapter 4," in Rulers of evil useful knowledge about governing bodies. Reno, NV: Ospray Bookmakers, p. 23
- Gershom Scholem, *Major Trends in Jewish Mysticism*, Schocken Books, 1941.
- Scholem, Gershom. *The Origins of the Kabbalah*. Princeton University Press, 1987.
- Scholem, Gershom. *Sabbatai Sevi: The Mystical Messiah*. Princeton University Press, 1973.
- Bernstein, Henrietta. "Basic Ideas." *Calabah Primer: Introduction to English/Hebrew Calabah*, Devorss, Marina Del Rey, CA, 1984, p. 21.

- Mullins, Eustace. *Curse of Canaan*. Omnia Veritas Ltd, 2016, p. 49.
- Livingstone, David. "Ibn Taymiyya, and the Occult Origins of the Salafi Movement." *Ordo Ab Chao*, 1 Feb. 2021, ordoabchao.ca/articles/ibn-taymiyya-occult-origins-of-the-salafi.
- Livingstone, David. *The Dying God*. 2002, pp. 3-4; 8-9.
- Muhammad, M. and Seoharvi, H. (2004). *Stories From the Quran*. 1st ed. Karachi: Darul-Ishaat, pp. 504-505
- Loper, D., 2019. *Kabbalah Secrets Christians Need to Know: An In Depth Study of the Kosher Pig and the Gods of Jewish Mysticism*. Independently published, p.35.
- Kurzweil, Arthur. *Kabbalah For Dummies*. Wiley Pub., 2007, pp. 55-73.
- Hall, Manly P. *The Secret Teachings of All Ages: An Encyclopedic Outline of Masonic, Hermetic, Qabbalistic, and Rosicrucian Symbolical Philosophy Being an Interpretation of the Secret Teachings Concealed Within the Rituals, Allegories, and Mysteries of the Ages*. Jeremy P. Tarcher/Penguin, 2003, p. 366.
- Mookerjee, Ajit. *Kundalini: The Arousal of the Inner Energy*. Destiny Books, 1982, p. 10.
- Khanna, Madhu. *Yantra: The Tantric Symbol of Cosmic Unity*. Thames & Hudson, 2003.
- Joseph, Harry B. *The Book of Wisdom*. Vol. 1, 2024, p. 18; 60.
- Dispenza, Joe. *Becoming Supernatural: How Common People Are Doing the Uncommon*. Hay House, 2017, pp. 159-160
- Judith, Anodea. *Wheels of Life: A User's Guide to the Chakra System*. Llewellyn Publications, 1999.
- Clark, David. *On Earth As In Heaven: The Lord's Prayer From Jewish Prayer To Christian Ritual*. Fortress Press, 2017, pp. 195-196.
- Feuerstein, G., Kak, S. and Frawley, D., 2008. *In search of the cradle of civilization*. Delhi: Motilal Banarsidass,

p.180.

- Atallah, Hashem, translator. *Picatrix: Ghayat Al-Hakim.* Edited by William Kiesel, Ouroboros Press, 2002, pp. 123-142.
- Booth, Mark. *The Illustrated Secret History of The World.* The Overlook Press, 2018, p. 71.
- Ijma' (consensus of opinion of the Ummah) Ulama, M. *Sihr (Magic, Sorcery, and Witchcraft)* (p. 14). Mujlisul Ulama of South Africa.

Section 3: The Principle of Vibration

- Spevack, Aaron. "Chapter 2/ Al-Bajuri's View of Religion and Method in the Egyptian Milieu." *The Archetypal Sunni Scholar: Law, Theology, and Mysticism in the Synthesis of Al-Bajuri*, State University of New York Press, Albany, NY, 2015, pp. 46–47.
- Al-Abbaad, Shaykh Abdur-Razzaak. *Causes Behind The Increase And Decrease Of Eemaan.* Al-Hidaayah Publishing, 1999, p. 8; 12.
- Dispenza, Joe. *Becoming Supernatural: How Common People Are Doing the Uncommon.* Hay House, 2017, p. 48
- Khateeb Al-Baghdaadee, 'Iqtidaa-ul-'Ilm al-'Amal' (Knowledge Mandates Action)
- Juslin, P. N., & Sloboda, J. A. (2010). *Handbook of Music and Emotion: Theory, Research, Applications.* Oxford University Press; Emoto, Masaru. *The Hidden Messages in Water.* Beyond Words Publishing, 2004.
- HeartMath Institute. "Energetic Communication." *HeartMath Institute*, https://www.heartmath. org/research/science-of-the-heart/energetic-communication/. Accessed 2 Oct. 2024.
- Hill, Napoleon. "The Mystery of Sex Transmutation." Think and Grow Rich, The Ralston Society, 1937, pp. 259-289.
- Chia, Mantak. The Alchemy of Sexual Energy: Connecting to the Universe from Within. Destiny Books, 2009.

- Peirce, Penney. *Frequency*. Atria Books, 2011, pp. 26-43.

Section 4: The Principle of Polarity
- Acemoglu, D., & Robinson, J. A. (2012). *Why Nations Fail: The Origins of Power, Prosperity, and Poverty.* Crown Business.
- Bourget, D. and Chalmers, D., 2014, 'What Do Philosophers Believe?', *Philosophical Studies*, 170: 465-500.
- Abdul Wahhab, Muhammad ibn. *The Four Foundations of Shirk*. Translated by Abu Maryam Isma'eel Alarcon, Al-Basheer Company for Publications and Translations, 1997.
- *Sharh at-Tahaawiyyah*, p. 88, 1st Edition. 1392 *al-Maktabul-Islaamee*
- Cavendish, Richard. *Black Arts - An Absorbing Account Of Witchcraft, Demonology, Astrology And.* 1st ed., Tarcherperigee, 1967, p. 110-114.
- The Freemasons' Repository, p. 220
- Hajj: Saudi Arabia Replace Jamarat 'Devil Obelisk' with Pretty Wall, Put Obelisk at Mt Arafat." *NewsRescue*, https://newsrescue.com/hajj-saudi-arabia-replace-jamarat-devil-obelisk-pretty-wall-put-obelisk-mt-arafat/. Accessed 11 Dec. 2024.
- Hikamah As-Shadhali number 41
- Ameen, Abu'l-Mundhir Khaleel ibn Ibraaheem. *The Jinn And Human Sickness*. Darussalam, 2005, pp. 177-179.
- Bardon, Franz, and Gerhard Hanswille and Franca Gallo. *Initiation Into Hermetics*. Merkur Publishing, 2014.
- Livingstone, David. *Zionism: A History of a Jewish Heresy*. Sabililah Publications, 2024, p. 131.